McDowell's MILL FORT
in Markes, Pennsylvania, 1753-1840

French and Indian War to the Establishment of a New Nation

PAMELA A. BAKKER

Mechanicsburg, PA USA

Published by Sunbury Press, Inc.
Mechanicsburg, Pennsylvania

www.sunburypress.com

Copyright © 2020 by Pamela A. Bakker.
Cover Copyright © 2020 by Sunbury Press, Inc.

Sunbury Press supports copyright. Copyright fuels creativity, encourages diverse voices, promotes free speech, and creates a vibrant culture. Thank you for buying an authorized edition of this book and for complying with copyright laws by not reproducing, scanning, or distributing any part of it in any form without permission. You are supporting writers and allowing Sunbury Press to continue to publish books for every reader. For information contact Sunbury Press, Inc., Subsidiary Rights Dept., PO Box 548, Boiling Springs, PA 17007 USA or legal@sunburypress.com.

For information about special discounts for bulk purchases, please contact Sunbury Press Orders Dept. at (855) 338-8359 or orders@sunburypress.com.

To request one of our authors for speaking engagements or book signings, please contact Sunbury Press Publicity Dept. at publicity@sunburypress.com.

FIRST SUNBURY PRESS EDITION: June 2020

Set in Adobe Garamond | Interior design by Crystal Devine | Cover design by Lawrence Knorr | Edited by Lawrence Knorr.

Publisher's Cataloging-in-Publication Data
Names: Bakker, Pamela A., author.
Title: McDowell's mill fort in markes, pennsylvania, 1753–1840 : french and indian war to the establishment of a new nation / Pamela A. Bakker.
Description: First trade paperback edition. | Mechanicsburg, PA : Sunbury Press, 2020.
Summary: The history of the McDowell family and their frontier fort in Franklin County, Pennsylvania, are detailed, from their arrival from Ireland in the early 1700s through antebellum times.
Identifiers: ISBN: 978-1-620064-11-5 (softcover).
Subjects: HISTORY / United States / State & Local / Middle Atlantic | HISTORY / United States / Colonial Period (1600-1775) | HISTORY / United States / Revolutionary Period (1775-1800).

Product of the United States of America
0 1 1 2 3 5 8 13 21 34 55

Continue the Enlightenment!

Dedicated to
my children, Alissa and David;
granddaughter, Payton;
siblings, Diane, Kitti, and Robert;
mother, Ruth;
and all the McDowell descendants
spread around the world.

Contents

List of Illustrations, Photos, and Maps   vii
Preface   ix
Acknowledgments   xiii

CHAPTERS

1. 1682–1716: Distress in Northern Ireland   1
2. 1717–1729: The Family Arrives in Penn's Woods   12
3. 1730–1749: Building a Mill in the Cumberland Valley   28
4. 1750–1755: Becoming a Chief Fort in Gen. Braddock's Campaign   59
5. 1755–1756: McDowell's Mill Fort in Defense of the Frontier   90
6. 1757–1759: McDowell's Mill Fort during Gen. Forbes' Campaign   144
7. 1760–1764: McDowell's Mill Fort during Pontiac's Rebellion   159
8. 1765–1769: McDowell Interaction with the Black Boys   185
9. 1770–1784: McDowell's Mill Fort during the Revolution   195
10. 1785–1840: The Fort is Dismantled   234

APPENDICES

A. A Partial Genealogy of the McDowell Family   249
B. Monarch of England and Governors of Pennsylvania   268

Notes   272
Bibliography   297
Index   306
About the Author   312

List of Illustrations, Photos, and Maps used by permission

1.1	Photo of McDowell's Mill Fort Monument.	2
1.2	Photo of McDowell's Mill Fort historical marker.	3
2.1	Photo of Appalachian mountain boundary in southern Pennsylvania	13
2.2	Map by author of the New London, Pennsylvania, area.	20
2.3	Old Donegal Presbyterian Church.	22
2.4	Little Chicquesalunga "Chiques" Creek.	23
2.5	A typical Pennsylvania cabin, stock photo.	24
3.1	Map of the Indian purchases from William H. Engle.	29
3.2	Photo of Falling Springs, Chambersburg.	31
3.3	Photo of the West Conococheague Creek by Markes.	32
3.4	Photo of Mt. Parnell in the snow.	33
3.5	Photo of view of Mt. Parnell from McDowell property.	34
3.6	Photo of Mt. Parnell from McDowell Road.	35
3.7	Photo of the valley from Mt. Parnell.	36
3.8	Photo of French uniforms at Fort Niagara.	45
3.9	Photo of a typical grain bin and mill wheel from this period.	48
4.1	Map of the area by McDowell's Mill Fort.	62
4.2	Photo of Spring Grove Cemetery.	73
4.3	Illustration of the fort by Charles J. Stoner.	88
5.1	Seventeen sixty-nine survey of an allowance granted to John McDowell.	91
5.2	Illustration of the fort.	92
5.3	Photo of an aerial view of the existing fort location.	93
5.4	Map of the Frontier forts.	103

5.5	Illustration of the Indian depredations.	110
5.6	Photo of a simple militia tent.	121
5.7	Photo of Fort Loudon.	136
6.1	Photo by author of a British soldier.	149
6.2	Photo of Scottish Highlanders.	153
7.1	Photo of the Mason and Dixon line.	164
7.2	Photo of the Mason and Dixon line.	164
7.3	Photo of the Enoch Brown Memorial.	181
7.4	Photo of the Enoch Brown grave.	181
7.5	Photo of settlers and Indians.	184
8.1	Photo of Justice William McDowell's home.	190
9.1	Photo of a Pennsylvania frontier rifleman.	199
9.2	Photo of a colonial soldier.	209
9.3	Photo of a militia campfire.	210
9.4	Photo of the exterior of a cabin at Valley Forge.	218
9.5	Photo of the interior of a cabin at Valley Forge.	219
9.6	Photo of a canon at Valley Forge.	219
9.7	Photo of 6th Pennsylvania camp at the Battle of Monmouth.	221
10.1	Photo of John McDowell's grave.	239
10.2	Photo at Markes.	244
10.3	Photo of Falls at Markes.	245
10.4	Photo of McDowell colonial secretary.	246
10.5	Photo of Elizabeth Robinson McDowell Rankin.	247
10.6	Drawing of fort location based on 1700s survey.	248

Preface

McDowell's Mill Fort stood in what is now Markes, Franklin County, Pennsylvania, from about 1753–1840. It began with John McDowell's log one-and-a-half-story mill and two-story log home, constructed about 1740. The mill became a private fort protecting area settlers following George Washington's loss of Fort Necessity at the outbreak of the French and Indian War. It may have had a simple enclosure around it by 1754 when it was listed in a plan for the defense of the Cumberland Valley written most likely by John Armstrong. The valley suffered multiple Indian raids with much loss of life and many abductions of settlers of all ages.

McDowell's Mill Fort was formally stockaded in 1755, by the governor of Pennsylvania, becoming a chief fort to hold Pennsylvania's supplies for General Braddock's campaign against the French at Fort Duquesne in the Pittsburgh area. A provincial road was cut by Col. Burd from McDowell's to meet Braddock's road near the forks of the Youghiogheny River, which was only completed a few miles west of Raystown/Bedford but then halted due to Braddock's loss. Settlers by the fort were then assaulted by traveling bands of Indians under French leadership using that same road. The fort held volunteer militia until the Assembly finally released money to pay them.

A few years later, General Forbes led another campaign against the French at Fort Duquesne. He chose to use part of Colonel Burd's Road instead of Braddock's Road in Virginia and constructed several forts along it. Fort Loudon, two miles north of McDowell's, replaced McDowell's Mill Fort as a Chief Fort. McDowell's then returned to private fort status but still housed troops and rangers, and an element of the Black Watch

Highlanders regiment. Forbes was successful in his venture, and the area had a few years of peace, but then the American Indian Chief Pontiac formed an alliance of tribes to fight the British in hopes of removing settlers and encouraging the French to return. Many settlers were again attacked and abducted by Indian bands. The fort was a place of refuge with troops on active duty as area homes were once more burned to the ground.

The Black Boys incident was the first assault of British forts by colonial forces, and the first time colonials actively took possession of a fort, long before the Revolutionary War. It centered on settlers blocking the re-supplying of Western Indians with war goods. The McDowell family was swept into the events as peacemakers due to their marital ties to the leader of the Black Boys.

After the struggle was resolved, the valley had a few years of peace, but then events in Boston changed things. Men from the area around the mill formed "Associator" troops based mainly on those who had served during the French and Indian War. They marched off to assist fellow colonists at the Siege of Boston. Many of the Associator troops were then adopted into the formal Continental Army, and many men who had served at McDowell's Mill Fort became military leaders in General Anthony Wayne's Pennsylvania Line, fighting the entire length of the Revolutionary War under challenging conditions through many colonies. The miller, John McDowell, was Lieutenant-Captain and surgeon during the War. His family members and neighbors also served as officers and in regimental formations.

The mill within the stockade continued processing wheat for flour, which helped the community. Some of it most likely went on to help the troops, but there is no formal record of that. There were no standing troops stationed there, but the barracks were still in place for regional use. American Indians in uncomfortable treaties with the British began attacks once again on the western settlements in Pennsylvania, and people sought safety in places like the fort.

My draw to the story of this fort within this community came from listening to family stories about the McDowells. I am a descendant of

Preface

Justice William McDowell, son of patriarch William McDowell, and his son Nathan who served during the Revolutionary War and later in Harmar's regiment fighting Western Indians under orders from new President George Washington. I became curious as I walked through the Spring Grove Cemetery in Lemasters, with its rows of relatives' tombstones. I read the local historical markers and wondered about the events which effected so many settlers living there.

Looking at the area where the fort once existed along a peaceful farm road nestled under the careful watch of Mt. Parnell, I tried to envision an active McDowell's Mill Fort with American Indian bands under French officers assaulting and scalping settlers. I tried to picture militia troops dashing out to rescue those in distress, but it all looked too quiet for such dramatic bloodshed. The happy fields of crops by the West Branch of the Conococheaque (pronounced Conoco-chic) Creek were hiding the dark story.

As I began my research, many questions began to surface. Why were the Ulster-Scots intentionally directed by the Pennsylvania government to settle in this valley? What happened in the British dealings with the American Indian tribes, which resulted in such violence? Why did the French government in New France want the Pennsylvania frontier? Why did sister British colonies struggle to take parts of Pennsylvania for themselves? What would be the ultimate result of settlers placed within a troubled area who were forced repeatedly to provide for their self-defense under a seemingly disinterested crown and inactive colonial Assembly? These questions sent me on a search.

When looking at material on McDowell's Mill Fort, I found only fragmented material. A small pamphlet titled *Fort McDowell* had been published in 1916 by Cyrus Cort when the historical stone marker was placed in Markes. The record of the instillation service had small sections on the fort. Local county histories by Samuel Bates, Eugene Etter, Frederic Godcharles, I. H. McCauley, Israel Daniel Rupp, Jay Gilfillan Weiser, the Woman's Club of Mercersburg, William A. Hunter and others also held small sections with mini-biographies on certain people and small references to the fort. The Pennsylvania Historical and Museum

Commission had a short history on the fort, but it was focused on early correspondence without any pictures. There was no large book focused on just this fort and no new information tying things to global events.

In the end, I found the best way to see the period was through the many volumes of letters and petitions sent to and from the Pennsylvania provincial government during that period, now housed within the state archives. While reading volume upon volume, the real voices of people came to life with their inflections with odd spellings. I tried to include some of those without corrections to add to the flavor of the events. Text about the fort flowed with passion and horror, and I began to see it functioning with real people living in the valley, people who were often related to each other through marriage. Ulster-Scots often had ten or eleven children. The lists of militia in the archives helped me to see some of those who were housed within the fort at a given time. Knowing that a mill was functioning in it brought to mind the necessity of the simple processing of flour for both settlers and militia.

This book is the result of a process of carefully collecting pieces of the story which others have preserved and re-assembling them with family and local history to try to give a clearer picture of the fort during a time of great struggle in Colonial American and European history which effected governments, colonists, Americans Indians, and African Americans. I hope that the sacrifice made by those people will be remembered as they contributed to the formation of the United States of America.

Acknowledgments

The Pennsylvania Historical and Museum Commission's brief section on the fort and the Colonial Records held within the Pennsylvania State Archives were of great help in the research of this book. The volumes of early letters held pieces of information which, when combined, gave a clearer picture of the fort's function, particularly during the French and Indian War. Thank you to James M. Vaughan, Executive Director of the Pennsylvania Historical and Museum Commission, and Jonathan R. Stayer, Supervisor of Reference Services, for the searches done for items related to the book. Karen Galle, Historical Marker Program Coordinator, provided photos of the *Fort McDowell, Markes, Pennsylvania,* marker, and the *Fort McDowell plaque, Markes, Pennsylvania,* with permission to use them. I was pleased to learn of their interest in this project. The land records in the Pennsylvania State Archives were also used to establish the McDowell presence in the Pennsylvania colony and to search for a possible site for the fort. The discovery of one tract of land, in particular, led to some real possibility. Archivist Aaron McWilliams was one of those making the surveys available for public use.

Marty Curfman of Curfman and Zullinger Surveying, Inc., in Chambersburg, Pennsylvania, kindly helped me understand the dimensions found on a survey from the 1700s. John McDowell had purchased additional land which had angular shapes and an unusual man-made rectangle found on it. Mr. Curfman converted the perches on the survey to feet for me, and this helped me see how vast the tract of land had been, which housed the fort.

I'm grateful to several historical societies in the Franklin County, Pennsylvania, area: The Franklin County Historical Society-Kittochtinny in Chambersburg; the Mercersburg Historical Society; the Fort Loudon Historical Society; and the Conococheague Institute of Mercersburg which each do continual work in maintaining records on this period of history and sponsor on-going educational programs. Robin Houtz, Secretary of the Fort Loudon Historical Society, permitted me to use photographs of the stockade fort, which helped in picturing what McDowell's Mill Fort must have looked like. Fort Loudon/Loudoun replaced McDowell's Mill Fort as a Chief Fort. The stores of British General Braddock's material at McDowell's were moved to Fort Loudon during General Forbes campaign against the French at which time McDowell's returned to a private fort status but still housed militia and an element of the Black Watch Scottish Highlanders.

Dan Guzy, author and volunteering at the Conococheague Institute, wrote a terrific book on the Black Boys, which helped establish the McDowell family's relationship to that event. Each of the county groups faithfully checked their records for possible information on the fort. Ingrid Winckler, Administrative Assistant of the Franklin County Historical Society-Kittochtinny in Chambersburg, sent me a map. I also visited their facility and read through the material. Cheryl Custer Librarian at the Fendrick Library of Mercersburg provided photos of the 1848 mill and the bridge at Markes, which were close to John's mill. That mill was converted to produce electricity. This helped me to visualize the location after the structure of the fort was removed. Thank you also to the people at history@pa.net for searching their photos of the Markes area.

I am very appreciative of Dr. Paula Stoner Reed, Ph.D.'s permission to use the pen and ink drawing by Charles J. Stoner, her father. His recreation of the fort was fascinating as he attempted to set it within the area by Mount Parnell. It was also used on the cover of the book *History of Lemasters, Pennsylvania: Centennial Celebration: June 22-25, 1972* edited by Eugene Etter with Mary M. Etter and Janet W. Ray.

It was a pleasure to correspond with Joseph McDowell of Parnell Springs Retreat house. He provided me with his family's genealogy, which

Acknowledgments

was added to many other genealogies, some from my family records, church and burial records, and some from county historical collections. Obtaining a definitive lineage for the early family is a little challenging with many conflicting reports, but a humble attempt is made in Appendix 1, which was reviewed by a historian at the Franklin County Historical Society. Joseph was in conversation with other McDowell family members still present within the valley, which made the project touch living people. William S. McDowell has a website on the graves at Spring Grove Cemetery, and he searched his memory in response to my questions. The descendants of the McDowells are now spread across several states, but they have regular reunions.

Thank you to Portia Brian, chair of the Donegal Presbyterian Church Historian Team in Lancaster County, for photos of the patriarch William McDowell's 1759 grave, the spring and the original church building which helped in understanding how the family related to that community before and after their trip to Franklin County. The Ulster-Scots in the Cumberland Valley were deeply tied back to that church through their Synod. The original sanctuary is still in use, and the beautiful spring bares testimony to the events which took place next to the Conestoga Indians.

The 6th Pennsylvania Regiment's reenactments of military engagements during the colonial period and their participation in educational programs helped me see regimental life during the Revolutionary War. Bob Bendesky, President of the Regiment at the time of the book's beginnings, pointed me to the Valley Forge Muster rolls, which contained McDowell names. A trip to Valley Forge made that encampment come to life. The miller John McDowell served as a 1st Lieutenant, Captain and surgeon at that encampment and during the War. Two of his nephews were also there. Thank you to David S.K. Rosehill, Valley Forge National Historic Park Visual Information Specialist, for assistance in identifying the canon used in one of the photos.

Michele Buckley, Supervisor in the Office of Communications and Visitor Services of the New Jersey Division of Parks and Forestry, permitted to use photos taken by me of the Battle of Monmouth reenactment at Monmouth Battlefield State Park in Monmouth County, New Jersey. I am grateful to those groups doing educational reenactments of this period in the state parks.

John McDowell, LL.D., the nephew of the miller John, was housed within the fort as a child while his father, Justice William McDowell, served in the militia. John McDowell, LL.D., became the first principle of St. John's College and the third provost of the University of Pennsylvania. Catherine Dixon and Cara Sabolcik from the Greenfield Library, St. John's College, Annapolis, Maryland, gave me access to the *McDowell/Maynadier Correspondence Archives*. Elizabeth A. Novara, Curator of Historical Manuscripts in the Special Collections in Hornbake Library at the University of Maryland, was very helpful in providing copies of letters sent to John McDowell, LL.D., in the *John McDowell Papers* (1751–1820). I was able to help them identify some of those referenced within the letters. Nancy R. Miller from the University of Pennsylvania sent me a digital portrait of John.

Lastly, I'm grateful to John N. Lovett, Jr., Ph.D., owner of Falls Mill & Museum, Belvidere, Tennessee, for his estimates on the length of time it might have taken colonial settlers to construct a mill in the 1740s. His explanations made it possible for me to visualize the mill in its original state and to appreciate how difficult it would have been on the frontier to get supplies, with only packhorse-wide Indian trails that could not support wagons. Construction by hand in the wilderness with limited workers must have been daunting.

CHAPTER ONE

1682—1716

Distress in Northern Ireland

On October 5, 1916, citizens gathered on the lawn of Seth Lemaster's home to unveil a new granite monument on the corner of Lemar Road and Mercersburg Road in Markes, Pennsylvania which was dedicated to the memory of McDowells Mill Fort. McDowell heirs, the Enoch Brown Association, the Pennsylvania Historical Commission, and the Fort McDowell Memorial Association of Markes had all worked hard for that day. The seven foot tall marker weighed 7½ tons and had been erected by the Forbes Granite Company in Chambersburg. Amid the Mercersburg band playing and Greencastle Glee Club singing, the dignitaries told the story of the fort and pointed to the inscription printed in Philadelphia on a bronze keystone shape.

At the top of the tablet was the Penn coat of arms and below it were the following words: "This stone marks the site of the Fort at McDowell Mills, erected by John McDowell before 1754. It was used as a base of supplies and as a magazine until the erection of Fort Loudon in 1756. The military road from Pennsylvania connecting with the Braddock road at Turkey foot was built from this point in 1755 under the supervision of Colonel James Burd. During the period of Indian hostilities the Fort at McDowell's Mill was the scene of many thrilling events. Erected by the

McDOWELL'S MILL FORT

The seven foot tall, seven and one-half ton granite Fort McDowell monument stands at the corner of Mercersburg and Lemar Roads in the village of Markes, Franklin County, Pennsylvania. It was dedicated on October 5, 1916, by the McDowell heirs, the Enoch Brown Association, the Pennsylvania Historical Commission, and the Fort McDowell Memorial Association of Markes. It commemorates the period of time the fort stood in that area during the French and Indian War, Pontiac Rebellion, Revolutionary War and the War of 1812. The historical marker is a trademark of the Pennsylvania Historical and Museum Commission and the marker text is copyright protected. Used with Permission.

The Pennsylvania Historical and Museum Commission erected this blue state historical marker by the Fort McDowell Monument at the corner of Mercersburg and Lemar Roads in the village of Markes, Franklin County, Pennsylvania, in 1947. The historical marker is a trademark of the Pennsylvania Historical and Museum Commission and the marker text is copyright protected. Used with Permission.

Pennsylvania Historical Commission, The Enoch Brown Association, The Kinsfolk of John McDowell and the citizens of this region 1916."[1]

In 1947 the Pennsylvania Historical and Museum Commission erected a blue sign perpendicular to the granite monument. At the top of the sign was the Pennsylvania coat of arms and the words in gold: "Fort McDowell. John McDowell's mill, stockade in 1755 by local settlers. Used by Provincial authorities until building of Fort Loudon, 1756. Starting point of Col. Burd's road to the west, 1755."[2]

The two signs, which do not rest on the actual site of the fort, do little to explain the transition which happened among the settlers in this region who arrived with a strong sense of independence and a desire to prosper through farming. They were quickly swept into battles with the French and Western Indians, and slowly developed a system of military self-defense while their pacifistic Quaker government argued over the Christian issue of not providing for war. Years later, colonial men in this region were the first to fire on a garrisoned British Fort, ten years before Lexington and Concord, and became key figures in General George Washington's Continental Army during the Revolutionary War, beginning with the Siege of Boston. To get a clear view of what happened within this community one needs to first look back at Europe during the end of the 17th and beginning of the 18th century. The state of political and religious flux drove many to the shores of America, searching for economic, religious and political freedom. Pennsylvania welcomed many who did not find the same acceptance in other colonies.

John McDowell (1716–1794), who would build an American mill in the distant future, was born an Ulster-Scot[3] in Antrim County, Northern Ireland. He was the son of pioneer William McDowell (1682–1759),[4] also born in Antrim County. Some family genealogists list William's father as Thomas McDowell (1631–1682) who had married Anne Locke (1640–1682). Those genealogists trace William all the way back as a descendant of Lord Fergus (1090–May 12, 1161) of Galloway and the Isle of Man, and his wife Elizabeth, bastard daughter of English King Henry I. Fergus was referred to as possibly being Norse-Gaelic in origin but Mc/Mac means son of and Dowal/Dowell/Dool/Douall/Dougal/Dughall, etc. means "the dark stranger," a term which usually referred to Danes. "Fair strangers" would be Norse. There are about forty variations on the spelling of the name McDowell, some with the prefix and some without it. Even in the colonial records we see it spelled various ways for the same men. This family, however, usually spelled it McDowell. More work outside the scope of the book would need to be done to see if the connections to the Lords of Galloway are correct.

Scottish Highlanders and Lowlanders were different ethnic groups. The Highlanders were ethnic Celts, originating in Ireland and tended to be Roman Catholic at this time. Scottish Lowlanders were mostly Anglo-Saxon with Picts, Scoti, Vikings and Roman blood. The mixed groups in the Lowlands had been encouraged to settle that region by King David of Scotland (born 1084).[5] McDowells had been Lowlanders in Scotland.

One has to look at their move to Ulster in Northern Ireland to understand why they eventually found their way to the North American Continent. Scotland initially was a separate and independent country from England. The Scottish Presbyterian King James VI (1566–1625) had become joint ruler of Scotland, England and Ireland under the name King James I following the death of Queen Elizabeth in 1603. He is best known for beginning the succession of Stuart (Stewart) rulers in Britain, though his great-grandmother had been a Tutor. He is also noted for his translation of the Bible, the King James Version. He did not like Roman Catholics or Puritans.

In a move to suppress the Catholics in Ireland and to secure a Protestant British throne, loyal Lowlander Scots, British merchants and Anglican clergy were settled in Northern Ireland as a type of farming-military force. The Scots swore an oath of allegiance to the British Crown. Local Catholics were barred from holding public office and from joining the army. The McDowells were said to have originally moved from Galloway in southern Scotland to Northern Ireland in the 1590s.[6] The family name of McDowell was present in Antrim County records by 1595. McDowells were also listed in the 1607–1633 Muster Rolls and Estate Maps in County Down which means they were among the earliest settlers, and taxable under James I.

The Muster Rolls listed the weaponry each man possessed should they be needed for battle. This usually included armor, spears, bows, arrows, picks and axes. The McDowells appear to also have worked in mills and to have produced linen, both of which were strictly controlled by the government. All mills and kilns belonged to the king, clergy or a land owner and the tenant was expected to use their lord's services and pay whatever fee was demanded.[7] The miller's toll or wage for the grinding of their flour was set. Bread was a main stable of the people and the mill was necessary for survival. Flax, also necessary, was made into linen for cloth.

King James I reigned until 1625 and was succeeded by Charles I who ruled from 1625 to 1649. Charles was married to a Roman Catholic. Civil war in England followed. The migration of Scots to Ulster halted from 1630 to the 1640s because King Charles required the use of *The*

Book of Common Prayer (Anglican) during worship in all of his realm. Under the enforcement of that act, Presbyterian Ulster-Scots resisted and thousands upon thousands of them, all ages and genders, were slaughtered by English troops. The massacre on October 27, 1641, would never be forgotten by Presbyterians who formed a Covenant to remember. They would refer to themselves thereafter as Covenanters. The McDowell family name on registries witnesses the fact that members were in Ulster during the massacre. The McDowell family in Pennsylvania, along with their neighbors, would all be strong Covenanters, remembering English atrocities. Many Ulster-Scots returned to Scotland during this period in order to practice religious freedom. This left the protestant presence in Ireland in jeopardy.

With the lower number of Ulster-Scots, an Irish revolt happened in 1641 which moved even more Scots back to Scotland. The Irish Earls of Tyrone and Tyrconnell attempted to overthrow the King during this rebellion. Their plan was to place a Roman Catholic on the throne of England. To prevent this Cromwell (1649–1658), a Puritan, was placed in charge of a newly constructed Commonwealth in England as Charles I was executed. Cromwell re-conquered Ireland and deported many Irish to the West Indies. Estates amounting to about 500,000 acres were seized from the Irish Earls by the Crown and divided into settlement tracts. Once things settled down, the Ulster-Scots returned to the plantations and rural life in Ireland.[8]

In the first settlement stage, the eastern counties of Antrim and Down were populated. Antrim had Sir Randal MacDonald as Chief. Down had Hugh Montgomery and James Hamilton, Lairds of Northern Ayrshire and Ayrshire, Scotland, as Chiefs. A second insurrection by the Irish resulted in the confiscation of more property in six counties in Ulster by the British. Counties Antrim, Armagh, Cavan, Donegal, Down, Fermanagh, Londonderry and Tyrone were then settled with those loyal to the Crown. The second settlement was better planned then the first and land owners had tenants renting lots and sharing in the harvest. Both English and Lowland Scots moved back into the area to improve their lives.

Scottish Highlanders were denied access to Northern Ireland as they had been supporters of a Catholic monarchy. Lowlanders were not only to help "civilize" and farm Northern Ireland, but would again serve as a military force should their services be needed. The English who settled in Ulster were outnumbered by Scots 20 to 1, but they were given preferential treatment because they were Anglican. Most of the English came with London merchant companies and some served the established Church of Ireland (Anglican). Between 1605 and 1697 about 200,000 Lowland Scots crossed the North Channel to settle the new tracts of land. Lords owned the land and ruled as monarchs.

The freeholders or gentry were below the lords which included burghers (from towns) and lairds (squires from the countryside). The rest of the population served as joint tenants (too poor to own a single family farm, so they were assigned by a laird to work together in an area), and sub-tenants and their workers, who were renters given small tracks of land or gardens with a home in return for work. They all served a given nobleman in military service.[9]

The Scots in Northern Ireland developed a separate culture from those remaining in Scotland. Most of them had been Lowland Scots, a different ethnic mix from the Highlanders. They had suffered continual raids in their Scottish burghs and developed into a more aggressive and sober group living among different cultures. Pioneer William, father of John, settled down with his wife Mary Irvine McDowell in Ulster. The Irvines had settled in Northern Ireland at about the same time as the McDowells and often intermarried with them, as well as with Campbells. As a member of the middleclass, William would have cultivated his own land and served his own noble but the pastoral life would be punctuated with continual turbulence in Northern Ireland.

Meanwhile to the west in the American colonies, King Charles I of England had granted Cecilius Calvert, Lord Baltimore, a colony in Maryland during his reign. It comprised all of the land from the 38th degree of Northern Latitude "unto that part of Delaware Bay which lieth under the fortieth degree of north latitude, where New England terminates; and all that tract of land, from the aforesaid bay of Delaware, in a right line, by the degree aforesaid, to the true meridian of the first fountain of the river Potomac." This wording would become a large problem between the Maryland and Penn colonies in the future. It would set up a long border struggle between them with each claiming a different king's grant with conflicting understanding of North American geography. The Cumberland Valley in southern central Pennsylvania, where the McDowells would ultimately settle, would fall into the contested area.

When Oliver Cromwell (1599–1658) had come to power, he sought to establish a Puritan government in Britain, but failed. His son ruled from 1658–1659 and then the house of Stuart was restored under Charles II (1630–1685) who ascended to the throne. Ireland once again felt religious oppression. *The 1662 British Act of Uniformity* required all ministers to conform to the established Church of England which resulted in all others being called "non-conformists," particularly Roman Catholics, Presbyterians, Puritans and groups like the Quakers. Presbyterian clergy were deposed, excommunicated and driven from the country, however during this time Charles II had granted Quaker William Penn a land grant in North America in 1681, one year prior to the birth of the patriarch William McDowell.

When Charles II died in 1685, the Duke of York, James II, became King. James II created chaos by reverting to Catholism. This set off another round of conflicts within the realm. With a Roman Catholic in power, the fear of reprisals began to surface, but James II was forced to flee from the throne under what was called the "Glorious Revolution." William III, Prince of Orange (1689–1702) and his wife Mary Stuart II took the throne. King William III was heralded as the "Savior of Protestantism," supported by the Whig party. Parliament then passed legislation blocking Catholics access to the throne. *The Toleration Act of 1689* then gave all non-conformists to the established Church of England, except Roman Catholics, freedom of worship. It seemed an answer to prayer for Presbyterians.

Much of William's reign was embroiled in blocking the French ruler Louis XIV's expansionism. The English and Dutch joined forces with the Holy Roman Emperor Leopold I, King Charles II of Spain, Victor Amadeus II of Savoy and other princes of the Holy Roman Empire to fight the French in the Nine Years War, War of the Grand Alliance or The War of the League of Augsburg (1688–1697) as it is sometimes called. They tried to contain French King Louis XIV's aggressive behavior and some of the battles took place in Ireland and Scotland as well as in colonial America.

The Ulster-Scots became staunch defenders of Protestantism, and life revolved around the Kirk (Church) as they developed their own language which was a combination of Gaelic and English. Their daily lives were spent working on large plantations and smaller farms as they attempted to improve their standard of living while eating oat cakes, oatmeal, greens, ale, fish or mutton. Tenants paid their rents in relationship to their crops. The tenant's wife had to deliver chickens and eggs to the landowner. Sheep were tended, wool was made into cloth, and flax was fashioned into linen. It was a hard life because there were many oppressive economic laws enforced by the British.

Yeoman William McDowell would have been seen as below nobility and above a nave. A yeoman usually served a nobleman and sometimes were in the legal profession as constables. In America, the McDowells served in the legal profession as Justices of the Peace, constables, judges and military leaders as well as physicians. They were well educated and often placed in leadership positions. The Presbyterian faith also strongly supported education so that the common man could read the Bible for themselves. Presbyterianism was a Scottish-ethnic version of French John Calvin's Reformed faith developed in Switzerland during the reformation. The elected representation within an assembly structure appealed to the Scottish sense of fairness, and Calvinism was embraced with great passion. Ruling elders were ordained to their service of church governance and in Calvinism that meant they were to serve as community leaders as well. It was not simply a faith of private piety but of public piety, much like the Puritans in Massachusetts Bay Colony or the Dutch in New Netherlands. In America, many McDowells would serve as ordained ruling elders overseeing their communities.

Life in Ireland was tied to the land, producing goods for market. Irish goods were well made and of good quality but they began to compete with English merchants, and restrictions were quickly established. The *1660 Navigation Act* had allowed Irish ships to trade with the colonies. The *1663 Staple Act* prohibited direct exportation from Ireland to the colonies except for cargo of indentured servants, horses and provisions. The 1671 law limited importation to Ireland of colonial goods. The measures were meant to especially suppress the wool and linen trades. The *1699 Woollens Act* formally prohibited exportation of Irish wool and woolen cloth to any place but England and Wales.[10] In addition, landlord's raised rents as leases expired. A common lease term had been for 31 years. In some cases the rents were doubled or tripled. Farmers who did not pay the higher fees were then dispossessed. Coupled with this was a drought in Ireland from 1714 to 1719. Crops were ruined, food prices soared and the sheep contracted rot in 1716. Northern Europe also endured a severe frost, and later in the spring and summer of 1718 small pox broke out in Ulster.[11]

Another war also loomed in Europe, as well as more religious persecution. English King William and his wife Mary had no children and so the throne went to Queen Anne (1665–1714), daughter of James II and sister-in-law of William. She was an Anglican with heavy Tory support. Her husband was Prince George of Denmark. Anne's reign was also steeped in the struggle to contain French expansion during the War of Spanish Succession which had begun in 1702. When Charles II of Spain died, there were two contenders for his throne: Philip of Bourbon and Charles of Austria, a Habsburg. England, Austria, and Holland, with the support of the Holy Roman Empire, fought against France to keep the Bourbons from becoming too powerful.

In 1703 Queen Anne also enacted a law requiring those holding office in Ireland, either military, civil service, or governmental seats, to take their sacraments according to the established Church of England. Presbyterian ministers again were turned out from their pulpits by the hundreds for not complying. The people in Ireland could not legally marry outside the established church and children born to parents married outside the

Anglican faith were considered bastards. Their parents were then called fornicators.[12] One could not even bury the dead without the proper clergy. Children also were to be taught only according to the established church. They could not be tutored by other religious educators. This caused great concern among the Ulster-Scots and many considered crossing back to Scotland but in 1707, through the *Act of Union*, England and Scotland were joined under a single monarch. Ultimately, Queen Anne was dismissed from the throne when the Whig party gained power. She was the last of the Stuarts.

King George I (1660–1727) succeeded to the British throne in 1714, a few years prior to the McDowell's departure from Ireland. He was Anne's cousin. George was the Ruler of Duchy and Electorate of Brunswick-Luneburg (Hanover, now Germany) in the Holy Roman Empire. He was a German protestant. Jacobite Catholics tried to replace him with Queen Anne's half-brother James Francis Edward Stuart, but they failed. George I was married to Sophia of the Palatinate, granddaughter of King James I of England. Sophia became a naturalized English subject to make the transition more acceptable.

The shifting political scene and assorted acts repressing religious expression often threatened the faith of people like the patriarch William McDowell. The economic restrictions and natural climatic changes threatened his livelihood. The increase in rental fees made it harder to live affordably. Any one of these triggers could have been the motivation to move. Combined, they seemed to leave little choice. William prepared to leave for the American colonies with his brothers and their families.

CHAPTER TWO

1717–1729

The Family Arrives in Penn's Woods

Quaker William Penn (1644–1718) had suffered greatly under the religious persecution instituted by James II. James had converted from Presbyterianism to Roman Catholicism. Penn and fourteen hundred Quakers had spent time in prison labeled non-conformist, however, his father Sir William Penn had been an admiral in the royal navy. Admiral Penn served in the West Indies during Cromwell's rule. He also had commanded the English fleet against the Dutch Coast for which he had been knighted. When the Admiral died, the Crown owed his estate sixteen thousand pounds for funds he had fronted in military campaigns. Charles II decided to pay William Penn, the heir, with a colonial land-grant he called Penn's Woods in honor of the admiral. The land grant was made March 4, 1681. Penn's Woods would later be known as Pennsylvania. The new colony initially served to empty the English prisons of unwanted Quakers.[1]

William Penn offered colonists freedom of religious expression, though only Protestants would be allowed to vote. He offered them self-government but it was tightly controlled by Quakers, even so it appealed to those dispossessed in Europe. The early Provincial Quaker Assembly in Penn's Woods was composed of pacifists who chose not to establish a military presence in the colony with forts or to provide funds for militia. This would result in a series of future problems. When Penn took possession of the commonwealth, Swedish, Finnish and Dutch settlers were already well established along the Delaware River. The American Indians had been trading with them for a considerable period of time.

Penn declared American Indians equal under God and stated that they were to be treated with great respect. He did not foresee a problem with them because he intended to purchase Indian lands "fairly" with trade goods[2] and to establish treaties which would be honored by both sides. It would be a great experiment in brotherly love (the Greek word for brotherly love, philos, was used in the naming of Philadelphia). Penn slowly purchased tracts of land from natives and settled small groups of colonists in them. Most of the initial settlements in the colony were

The Appalachian Mountains formed the western boundary for the British colonies in America. Beyond them were the Western Indians and some French explorers. This photo taken by the author in Franklin County, Pennsylvania, demonstrates how formidable the chain would have been, rising like a great wall.

along the Delaware River and in the southern part of the state. The rest was wilderness. The Appalachian Mountains were a natural western barrier with Indians beyond them and the French making inroads along the Mississippi River. Trade with western tribes in Pennsylvania occurred along the breaks in the mountain chain and by water ways and trails.

There was little understanding of the geography of the American Colonies in Europe and there were no accurate maps when the Penn's Woods Colony was formed. Things which seemed simple in court in England would become difficult when actualized on the ground far away. This was particularly true of the southern and western borders of the state. A succession of English monarchs had given land rights to differing colonies which were in conflict with each other. The colonies also had been established with differing religious and political structures resulting in competition for trade and power. Nothing was unified on the new continent.

The southern border of Penn's colony would be a continual problem for Lord Baltimore in Maryland. Penn's grant to the south was to be the 40th degree parallel, north of the equator. A parallel is a line of latitude running north or south, parallel to the equator. It is usually recorded in degrees, minutes and seconds. Longitude runs from pole to pole east and west of the prime meridian also using degrees, minutes and seconds. The use of both Longitude and Latitude gives a general large area on a map. Without degrees, minutes and seconds, a specific point is vague because there are about 69 miles between parallels, varying with the earth's ellipsoid shape. The exact border line within the 69 mile area without minutes and seconds grew to be a problem. The grant of the Commonwealth muddied it still further by stating that the border would intersect a twelve mile circle around New Castle (first in Pennsylvania and later placed in the newly formed Delaware), but the parallel actually fell north of Philadelphia. If the line was to be the most northern section of parallel, then Maryland would obtain Philadelphia. If it was the most southern point, Pennsylvania would have Baltimore and Virginia, all of which confused the matter. Added to the initial grant to Penn by the Duke of York were three counties as satellites of Pennsylvania which later became part of Delaware. Penn needed those satellites in order to have a route to the Atlantic Ocean via the Delaware River which would be free of tolls charged by Lord Baltimore. Delaware would be separated from Pennsylvania in the early 1700s.

Maryland claimed Pennsylvania was legally their land from a prior grant from another royal. Lord Baltimore was aggressive in trying to establish his Catholic settlement into the southern portion of Pennsylvania in order to support his claim to the territory. This resulted in serious struggles. Maryland settlers became squatters on Pennsylvania land. The Pennsylvania sheriff with posse was sent to drive squatters out and to burn their dwellings. The sheriff from Maryland responded in kind, set on collecting taxes in what he saw as Maryland domain. Continual petitions were sent to the King for clarification. A temporary line would eventually be established in May of 1738 at 39 degrees, 43 minutes and 18 seconds Latitude but the boundary line issue between the two colonies would not be resolved permanently until the establishment of the Mason and Dixon Line, 1763–1767. That line would finally clarify the border between Maryland, Virginia (later to become West Virginia) and Pennsylvania. The final western border of the state would be clarified much later due to struggles with American Indians.

Connecticut later also tried to establish settlements in Pennsylvania, claiming rights given through the Massachusetts Bay Charter. The charter granted land reaching south all the way to Lord Baltimore's border in Maryland, and west to the Pacific Ocean. Connecticut colonists avoided disputes with New York because it was the possession of the King's brother, the Duke of York. They were sent, instead, into Pennsylvania to try to establish homesteads so that Connecticut could lay claims to land at court.

Virginia also tried later to stake a claim in the Ohio territory of Pennsylvania by Pittsburg and sent settlers into the area with the same intent. The competition for land in Pennsylvania would include English colonies fighting each other, French and English governments striving for dominance particularly in the western part of the state, settlers frustrated with their colonial governors and parliament, settlers seeking land and aggressively pushing American Indians farther west, and power struggles between individual American Indian tribes against the two main Indian confederacies.

Pennsylvania had a number of Indian tribes dwelling within the colony, some peaceful and some very violent. Looking at the present size of the state of Pennsylvania, which did not exist at this point, the northwest portion by Lake Erie was inhabited by the Erie Indians. Below them, filling the Ohio Valley, were the Shawnee and Ohio Valley tribes. In the central northern area the Iroquois (mainly Seneca and Oneida) lived. To their east, in the north, were the Munsee Delaware. The Lenape Delaware were along the Delaware River, and the Susquehannok (called Conestoga) were along the Susquehanna River. Each tribe spoke a different dialect, for example the words man, woman and water are distinct in the following languages: Lenape use the words lënu, xkwe and mpi for each; the Susquehannock used Itae'aetsin, Achonhaeffti and Oneega; and the Shawnee used Hileni, Kweewa and Nepi. The need for interpreters between them was great. The Lenape used the word Hè (pronounced hay) for hello. This is still widely used as a greeting in American culture today.[3]

Lenni Lenape, Lenapé or Unami Delaware, were called the original people or grandfathers by other tribes. They had traveled to the area from the west before the arrival of the Dutch and English, and settled with their distinctive huts along the Hudson River area down to the Potomac River.[4] The English named them Delawares.[5] The Monseys/Munsee, or Wolf clan of the Lenape, lived on the Susquehanna River and were considered fierce by both settlers and more passive tribes.

A confederacy of different tribes had formed northeast of the Penn colony known first as the Five Nations. It was based in upstate New York, west of the Hudson River and through the Finger Lakes region. Within the first confederation, prior to 1712, were the tribes of the Senacas, Mohawks, Oneidas, Cayugas and Onondagas. Some called themselves Mingoes, the Dutch called them Maguas, other tribes called them Mengwe and the French called them Iroquois. They called themselves Haudenosaunee, Hodenoeshonee or Ganonsyoni which means "people building a long house." Each tribe had its own organization and leaders.

The Family Arrives in Penn's Woods

The Lenni Lenape or Delaware had lost to the confederacy in prior battles and were in an uncomfortable vassal state. As the Delaware were moved from the waterways of the Delaware River through land sales brokered between the Five Nations and the British, Delaware were initially given hunting rights in areas like the Kittitinny Valley by the confederation. With each land deal, however, they lost ground and were pushed farther west. The distance from the confederacy and the vassal status bread discontent in the Delaware.[6] Some bands of Delaware continued moving west towards the Ohio River country to obtain greater freedom and a large number of them settled on the Allegheny River at Kittanning around 1725.

The Tuscaroras, who had been expelled from North Carolina, were adopted by the Five Nations in 1712. This addition changed the confederation to Six Nations. William Penn signed treaties with the Six Nations and was intent that his colony value American Indians as represented through that one confederation, which was easier than dealing with individual tribes, and local tribes were also given gifts. Penn tried to settle small tracts with colonists after formal purchases of land were made, but encroachments were inevitable and the terms of land sales brokered by his heirs were always slanted in favor of the British, using unclear language like that of the notorious Walking Purchase, in scripts the Indians could not read.

It was difficult for the American Indians to understand land possession and titles as viewed by Europeans. Within their cultures goods were given to use land which was more like a rental with no need for the original people to move out. The new "renters" would join them in fighting their common enemies and would occasionally renew the friendship with gifts. In their culture Chiefs were expected to give continual gifts to their people, so the British "chiefs" were just doing the same thing. Land deals were alliances for the protection of each party. The forests were full of game, so why tell the original people they could no longer hunt there? The rivers were full of fish. How could you own a river? The need to empty land of original people was perplexing.

The Walking Purchase of 1737 would create a great deal of strife. It was based on a supposed incomplete deed of 1680 from prior Lenape

Indians which gave the British ownership of land from the junction of the Delaware and Lehigh River by current Easton and extending west "as far as a man could walk in a day and a half." To confirm the old deed, it was to be walked out. The Indians expected this to be walked leisurely during the day, taking occasional rests, amounting to about 40 miles.

The Penn heirs' representatives, however, first cleared land and then hired three fast runners who were sent out on September 19, 1737, from Wrightstown running as fast as they could in a straight line west. Edward Marshall was the only one to finish, reaching current Jim Thorpe, Pennsylvania. The area gave Pennsylvania 1,200 square miles which was roughly the size of Rhode Island. The Delaware complained to the Six Nations about the process but their complaint was rejected. As vassals, they were forced to move from the area and harbored resentment thereafter. William Penn had intended to treat the Indians fairly, but after his death things were done differently.

The enemies of the Six Nations, Algonquians, were also in a confederation and tied by treaty and trade to the French in the Great lakes and Illinois region. Tribes working with the French included the Abenaki, Ottawa, Winnebago, Illinois Sioux, Mississauga, Huron, and Potawatomi. The natural rivalry between Indian confederacies and European nations combined with the dissatisfaction of colonists against their home governments, with ethnic and religious clashes, would result in turbulence within the colonies for many decades. Pennsylvania felt this early on.

William Penn had visualized a peaceful rural colony with thrifty farmers interacting in "fair" trade with American Indians. The colony was peaceful in its early stages. It seemed like his vision might take hold. Farms were established with persons of differing religious choice settling side by side. A thriving and licensed trade business was conducted with Indians for furs in exchange for iron goods and other manufactured materials which were welcomed by the tribes, but more aggressive groups looked upon the colony for easy conquest because the Quaker-led Assembly placed no value in things military.[7]

Penn's initial concept for his colony was attractive to Ulster-Scots who had suffered through repeated struggles in Ireland. A number of them had not been well received in either New England or New York. Most leaving Ulster were looking to prosper and escape economic and religious restrictions. Their culture tended to be more adventurous, as their ancestors had left their homes in Scotland for a better life in Ireland. In the colonies, the Ulster-Scots would be the groups which ventured farther and farther west as new territory was gained.

The Scotts exited Ireland in the tens of thousands in five waves: 1717–1718, 1725–1729, 1740–1741, 1754–1755, and 1771–1775.[8] They used five European ports: Belfast, Londonderry, Newry, Larne and Portrush.[9] William McDowell with some of his brothers and their wives were in the first wave exiting the emerald isle. The rest of the brothers came in the second wave. Most Ulster-Scots entered the colony through Philadelphia, Chester or New Castle (Delaware). They quickly set up the Philadelphia Presbytery in 1706. There were only seven Presbyterian churches in the colony in 1710: Philadelphia, Neshaminy, Welsh Tract, White Clay, Apoquinimy, Lewes and New Castle (the latter two are in area belonging to Delaware). A synod was formed in 1717 of four Presbyteries: Long Island, New York; Philadelphia, Pennsylvania; New Castle/Newcastle, Delaware; and Snow Hill on the Eastern shore of Maryland. Seventeen ministers were listed in the 1st synod.[10] This religious connectedness would later serve them in community building under elders and in military service, often led by clergy.

There was a parallel migration from the German states to Pennsylvania, mostly from the Rhineland Palatinate. Pennsylvania did not have an established church or compulsory tithing which appealed to many. The administration also seemed to be friendly and honest. The land was fertile with a promise of success if one worked hard, and most were willing to work hard.[11]

Most records report that William McDowell and his wife Mary arrived in the Penn colony in 1717. Some family records show him arriving as early as 1714, however their son John was born in Northern Ireland in 1716. The earlier date would not make much sense. It is possible that he visited the new world prior to that date, but that would have been expensive and a waste of money, something Ulster-Scots generally

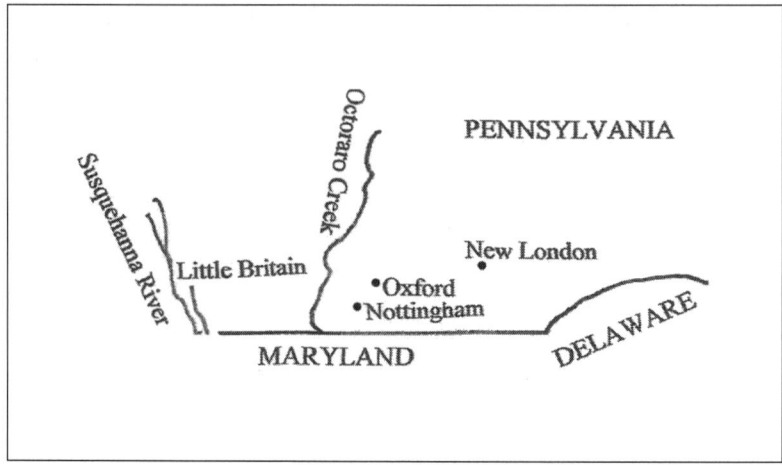

Patriarch William McDowell first moved with his family to New London in the extended Chester County, Pennsylvania, in 1717. The Penn Colony only had three large counties at the time. The brothers initially all lived within a few miles of each other just north of the Maryland border. Many of them purchased land along the Octoraro Creek. The area was in contention with Lord Baltimore.

did not do. Seventeen-seventeen was a strategic year in Northern Ireland because leases had just expired in Ulster. Landlords doubled and even tripled rents. Presbyterian pastors railed at the unjust nature of the increases from their pulpits and some brought their entire congregations to America. The educated Ulster Presbyterians were able to read the hand bills printed by those encouraging settlement in the new world and it would have been very appealing. The promise of religious freedom and land available for the taking would have given them hope.

William's three brothers, John, Ephraim and Alexander, also reportedly left Ireland with their families on different ships about the same time. Some family records speak of the crossing being very difficult for them with one of the ship captains being unscrupulous, extending the voyage and starving people for extra money and then taking the property of those who died of disease. Some of those McDowell family members are listed as dying during that crossing, though William and Mary apparently were successful in navigating the crossing in their ship.

The Family Arrives in Penn's Woods

The colony had Sir William Keith as Governor (1717–1726). It only had three very large counties: Bucks, Philadelphia and Chester. Chester County would later be broken down into many smaller ones. The entire western frontier of the province was within this extended Chester County. William McDowell settled first in New London. He applied for a survey of 96 acres in 1744 but another person's name is on the property at that point, perhaps he sold property that he held there. One of William's grandson would later be born in New London and there was taxable property owned by McDowells in that community in 1765.[12]

William's brothers also spent time in Pennsylvania in the larger Chester County where McDowell names are recorded on tax tables in Oxford Township/East Nottingham, New London Township, London Britain, Londonderry and in Little Britain. These rustic settlements in a line within the southeastern portion of the colony were formed along American Indian trails in the wilderness and not really formal towns. The brothers settled or camped largely along the Octoraro Creek by the border with Maryland. It was part of the problem area which fell into competition between the two colonies. That may have warranted a move further west for William. Some of the brothers then obtained land in New Jersey along the Raritan River, some in North Carolina and some in Virginia.

William Penn, founder of the colony, died May 30, 1718, shortly after the arrival of the McDowells. The cause was listed as apoplexy which was a term usually applied to a type of stroke. Penn had had children by both his first wife, Gulielma Maria Sringett Penn, and his second wife, Hannah Callowhill. His sons by his second wife would assume proprietary powers following the death of his older sons. John, Thomas and Richard would oversee the colony at this point.

A number of Ulster-Scots arriving during the early 1700s had settled on the Octorara Creek, and in Pequea, Donegal and Paxton. William McDowell seemed to have had strong ties to the Donegal settlement in Lancaster which functioned as an Ulster-Scot Presbyterian haven centered around the Presbyterian Kirk/Church which had been organized between 1714 and 1726.[13] McDowells are listed by Israel Rupp in his book in this new location before 1720.[14] Donegal was formally organized in 1722. The Chambers, founders of Chambersburg, are also listed at this place at this early time. The Old Donegal Presbyterian Church is currently located three miles west of Mount Joy within East Donegal Township, in the northwestern part of Lancaster County, Pennsylvania, but the county was called Chester at the time and the area simply called

Pioneer William McDowell moved his family to the Donegal settlement, now in Lancaster County, about the time that township was formed in 1722. This community was by the Conestoga Indians. He would leave this area to find his fortune to the west in 1730 but return east to Wrightsville during the Indian Wars in 1755. He would eventually be buried in the Old Donegal Presbyterian Church graveyard in 1759. The original building, used for twelve years, was a log meeting-house and the first pastor from 1727–1740 was Rev. James Anderson. The meeting-house was replaced by the structure above which is made of undressed field stones, covered in plaster. The floor was originally dirt and the interior unpainted at the time of William McDowell's death. The pastor performing services would most likely have been the second pastor, Rev. Joseph Tate who served from 1748–1774. The sanctuary, pictured to the left, is still in use. Photo courtesy of Portia Brian, Donegal Historical Team, Old Donegal Presbyterian Church, East Donegal Township, Pennsylvania.

The Family Arrives in Penn's Woods

The settlement at Donegal, located by the Susquehanna River, had a spring which fed into a stream called the Little Chicquesalunga Creek, or the Little Chicques Creek for short. The spring is still visible and used for fishing. Photo courtesy of Portia Brian, Donegal Historical Team, Old Donegal Presbyterian Church, Mount Joy, Pennsylvania.

Donegal. A larger Lancaster County would be formed in 1729 out of part of Chester County, and Lancaster would later be broken down still further into the current counties. The Donegal Presbyterian Classis would be the assembly overseeing congregations forming on the Pennsylvanian frontier.[15]

The Donegal settlement of the 1720s included farms on both sides of the creeks. William and Mary McDowell may have constructed a cabin because they began having other children that would ultimately number eleven, some born here and some born by Mount Parnell. Log homes were modeled after the local Scandinavian and German homes, which were widely adopted by Pennsylvanian Ulster-Scots. The Pennsylvanian log home was one and one-half stories high with a central chimney. The wealthy had a brick chimney. The poor had just an opening in the roof. The roof was made of shingles, thatched straw or bark. The downstairs of the cabin had two rooms: a hall/parlor, and an open hearth kitchen.

A typical Pennsylvania cabin from this early period.

A small staircase led to the upper story or loft. Parents often slept on the first floor with children in the loft. There was no cellar and the rafters rested on the top log.[17] Interior seating was provided by benches which were often rustic.

William McDowell was called a yeoman on land records which means he was middle class and owned land. Yeomen were able to pay for their trip to the colonies and did not serve as indentured servants. Usually they were able to afford at least 100 acres. Much of Pennsylvania's land had not been surveyed which made purchase impossible. The Donegal settlement was filled with squatters without an ability to buy land. Those by New London had initially been squatters as well. The Proprietary slowly and carefully purchased small tracts of land from the American Indians and then opened them for settlement of small European groups, stressing a pastoral colony. When the Indians would complain about a squatter on unpurchased land, the government carefully sent sheriffs to burn the squatter's cabin and to drive them out of that location, offering settlers another spot in an attempt to keep the trust with the local tribes.

Because of Penn's focus on planters, Pennsylvania would be known as the bread basket of the colonies but at this time it was largely forested. Groups like the Moravians, doing missionary work with Indians much like the Jesuits in Canada, recorded much information about local customs and language of the American Indians. There were many Christian converts among the Conestoga Indians, some were quite faithful and others were simply curious with no real interest in the new religion. The European Christians surrounding them, unfortunately, did not always treat them with brotherly affection and respect. Ulster-Scots tended to not be evangelical in seeking to convert tribes. They were merely interested in trade. Some of the rougher elements in the culture saw all Indians simply as pagans which would intensify with growing conflicts.

The area of Donegal came under strife in 1719. Violence broke out between various Indian tribes. To ward off the possibility of an Indian war involving the Confederacy, a meeting of the chiefs had been called by Governor Keith in 1721 at Conestoga, near the Donegal community. Ghesaont, Chief of the Senecas, spoke for the Five Nations. He conveyed fond memories of William Penn. The chain of friendship between the British and the Indians was "brightened" with gifts, but during the spring of 1722 an Indian was murdered at Conestoga which threatened some of the stability in the area. This was also carefully and calmly addressed.[18] A conference with Indians was called by all the Governors of the Colonies at Albany and temporary peace was restored.

While settlers were adapting to their Indian neighbors and discussing their plans for their farms, King George I died in England in June of 1727 and George II ascended to the throne. That year John, Richard and Thomas Penn formally took charge of the Penn Colony and Patrick Gordon was appointed the new governor (1727–1736). He called himself "a plain, blunt soldier" who would eventually die while serving in office.[19]

Back in Ulster, Northern Ireland, the farms had suffered three seasons of failed crops encouraging another exit of Ulster-Scots. It is estimated that in the 1700s about 200,000 Ulster-Scots left Ireland, most settling in Pennsylvania. In fact, the British feared Ulster was losing its Protestant element again which would make the country unstable, resulting in the Catholic elements gaining power. Immigration to American was then limited to slow their departure. Ulster born James Logan, Secretary to the Proprietaries in Pennsylvania, mentioned how glad he was that Parliament had limited the "too free emigration to this country" by Ulster-Scots in 1729. The Assembly had also "laid a restraining-tax of twenty shillings a head for every servant arriving" from there, but he commented that even with those measures it looked "as if Ireland is to send all her inhabitants hither, for last week, not less than six ships arrived, and every day two or three arive also. The common fear is, that if they continue to come, they will make themselves proprietors of the province."[20]

The balance of power had been Quaker, but with so many Ulster-Scots it could easily become Presbyterian. Those arriving by 1730 and settling in Conestoga were called "audacious and disorderly." Those in "Paxtang" were called squatters and viewed by the Indians as very rough. They were dispossessed by the Sheriff and thirty cabins were burned. This same group would later retaliate against Indians at that location.[21] The rough group arriving may have contributed to William McDowell's desire to move farther west.

With the influx of Irish to Pennsylvania came more Germans. 25,000 Germans arrived after 1725. Palatine Germans had fled to England between 1700 and 1720 for religious and political safety. Queen Anne sent many of them to America. In Pennsylvania, they settled largely in lower Montgomery, Bucks, Berks, and Lancaster Counties. Those arriving between 1720 and 1730 flooded Philadelphia and New York.

Germans who tried to settle in New York were treated badly by the Provisional government there. Between 1730 and 1740 a huge number of Germans arrived in Philadelphia in 65 vessels, and between 1740 and 1745 over 100 vessels came. Germans who did not become naturalized English subjects, could purchase land, but could not pass it down to their heirs. They were considered aliens in the colony.[22] They could become naturalized and swear allegiance to the crown. This, however, was a problem for a number of them.

First, many German settlers did not understand the language contained within the oaths. Second, some were prohibited altogether by their faith to take any oath, fearing it went against a prohibition of Christ (Matthew 5:34–37). British Kings George I, II, and III of the House of Hanover were originally Germans, in fact George I had spoken little

The Family Arrives in Penn's Woods

English. Each of these kings returned yearly to their home in the German province. George III would later employ units of Hessian soldiers to fight against the rebellious colonists. The crown had deep bonds with many of the independent German states, but allegiance to England was demanded in the colonies.

Penn's Woods now had a mass of German settlers, and some rough Ulster-Scots often in conflict with the Germans. Officials believed the Ulster-Scot character might well match the wild frontier better. They just might have the inner strength to keep the French and Western Indians away and form a line of defense along the Appalachian Mountains. James Logan commented, "At the time we were apprehensive from the Northern Indians . . . I therefore thought it prudent to plant a settlement of such men as those who formerly had so bravely defended Londonderry and Enniskillen as a frontier against any disturbance."[23] He later found them difficult to control in the wilderness, though the McDowells appeared to have been law abiding.

The upper area of Chester County was formerly broken off in 1729 to form a larger Lancaster County. This signaled another move west for the McDowells. Perhaps conversations had been occurring in the Donegal community. Members of the Chambers family in the same congregation of the Donegal Church also sought to establish settlements to the west. William McDowell would choose a spot west of Ben Chamber's Falling Spring settlement (Chambersburg), in the wilderness by Mount Parnell.

CHAPTER THREE

1730—1749

Building a Mill in the Cumberland Valley

The Cumberland Valley is situated with the Tuscarora Mountains along the western boundary and the Kittatinny Mountains along the eastern and northern boundary, called North Mountain. Kittochtinny or Kittatinny was an anglicized version of the Delaware name Kekachtannin meaning endless hills or great mountain.[1] The Kittatinny range is part of the Appalachian Mountains. The Appalachian Mountains are relatively level, between 700 and 1200 feet in height.

South Mountain also lays to the east, rising 600 to 700 feet above the valley. It was a narrow mountain range, part of the Blue Ridge Mountains running northeast to southwest and was rich in iron ore and material for making arrowheads. The valley between these western and eastern mountains, part of the great Appalachian valley, is about 600 feet above sea level. Mount Parnell or Parnell's Knob, in Peters Township to the north, stands out from the other mountains at about 2,021 feet. The mountains in this region provide the source water for the many springs, streams and creeks running through the valley, making it very desirable for settlement.

The Proprietary did not encourage settlement in this valley prior to 1736, when the land was formally purchased from American Indians.

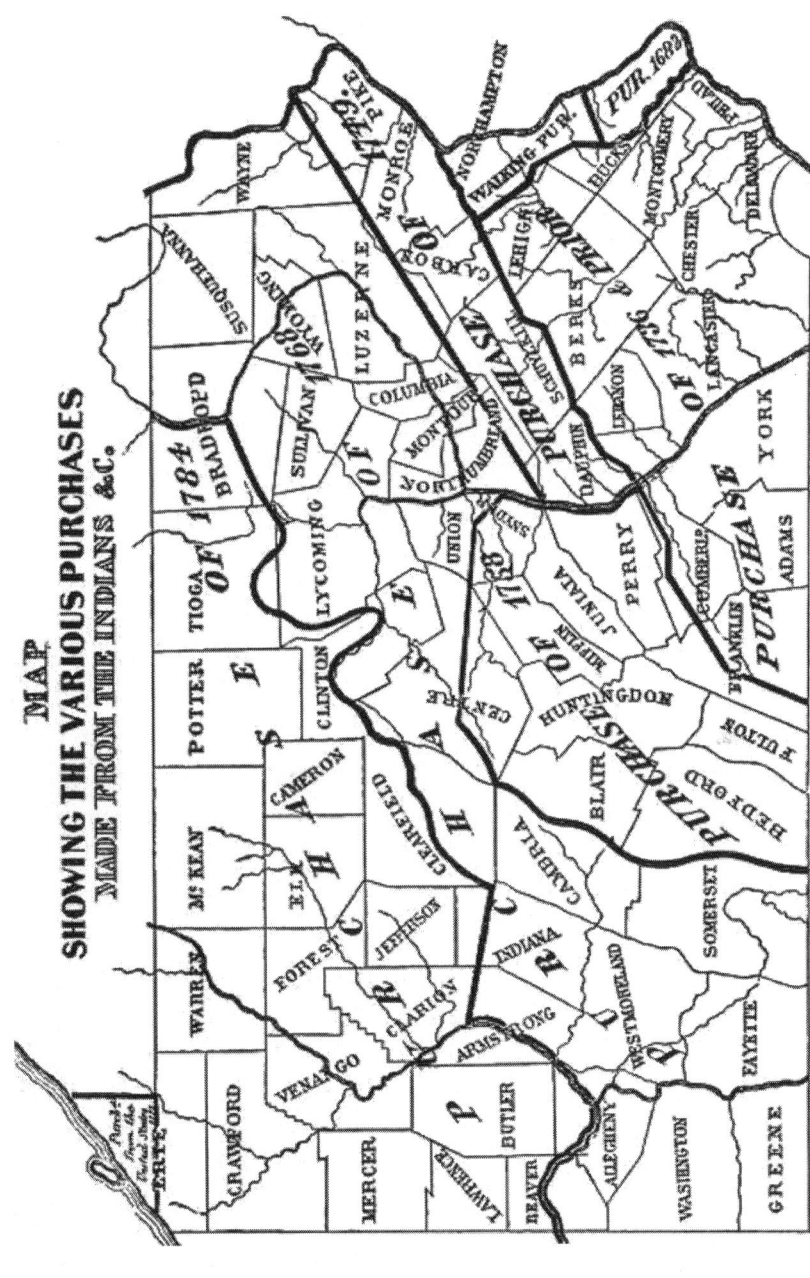

This map of Pennsylvania shows the dates of the Indian land purchases. It is from William H. Engle, *An Illustrated History of the Commonwealth of Pennsylvania, Civil, Political and Military, from its Earliest Settlement to the Present Time* (1876), 208.

That land deal would be brokered by the Six Nations and the name of the valley would be formally changed from Kittatinny to the Cumberland Valley, North. It had no permanent Indian settlements in it, but was used seasonally by tribes for its excellent hunting and fishing. The area was a wilderness filled with wild turkeys, beavers, geese, ducks, deer, elk, wolves, bear and streams filled with trout. The Iroquois Confederacy to the north had initially given their subjects, the Lenape/Delaware Indians, the rights to hunt in this valley as they were moved by land deals with the British ever farther west from the Delaware River waterways. In the new land exchange, the Delaware would be restricted again and they were not happy.

An ancient Indian burial ground was located in what would be known as Green Castle/Greencastle and one was south of the old Falling Spring Churchyard in Chambersburg, though these were long since abandoned by natives and most dated to pre-historic times.[2] The northern end of the valley by Parnell's Knob was the pathway to the western Indians of the Ohio country, current Pittsburgh. The path was only a rough trail at this time, wide enough for occasional pack-horses. There were a few adventurous traders who made their way along it carrying goods to trade for furs with the western Indians.

Meandering through the region are the East and West Branches of the Conococheague Creek, pronounced "Conica-jig." Conococheague in the American Indian dialect means "very long indeed." The creek travels through Pennsylvania and Maryland, emptying into the Potomac River.[3] The East Branch of the Conococheaque Creek was a trade highway used by American Indians. It rises in South Mountain and flows to Falling Springs in Chambersburg. Seneca Iroquois of Western New York, Maryland and Virginia used the west branch of the Susquehanna River to reach the mouth of the Conodoguinet Creek by Harrisburg. Traveling up that creek to the northwestern area by Shippensburg, the Indians then carried their goods across an eight mile area to the Conococheague Creek northeast of Chambersburg to avoid the rapids on the Susquehanna River below Harrisburg; the dangerous Susquehanna Indians controlling the lower Susquehanna and the stormy Chesapeake Bay. The Conococheague Creek enabled them a quick and safe way to reach Maryland

Falling Spring, East Conococheague (pronounced Conica-jig) Creek, Chambersburg, Pennsylvania, where Ben Chambers set up his settlement. Conococheague means "very long indeed" in the American Indian dialect. Photo by the author.

and Virginia to trade furs for items they needed. The natives often sank canoes in the creek when not in use.[4]

The Western Branch of the Conococheague Creek, less navigable, traveled from the northwest in the Tuscarora Mountains, tumbling over

The West Branch of the Conococheague Creek at Marks, Pennsylvania, where John McDowell's mill was constructed. Photo by the author.

rocks as it flowed southward through Amberson's and Path Valleys past Loudon to unite with the Eastern Branch of the creek three miles north of the Mason-Dixon line in Greencastle.[5] It covers most of the western side of what is now Franklin County.

William and Mary Irvine McDowell traveled west with their children to the valley in the larger Lancaster County around the time Benjamin Chambers began his settlement by the confluence of the Conococheague and Falling Spring, a few miles east of the McDowells. The Chester County deed book shows a William and John McDowell in New London selling land in the 1730s. Perhaps that was their deed transfer in preparation for the move.[6] The McDowells and Chambers were now each within a region that became known as the Conococheague Settlement, along the two branches of the Conococheague Creek.

The four Chambers brothers (James, Robert, Joseph and Benjamin) had come to the colonies between 1726 and 1730 from Antrim, Northern Ireland where they had encouraged Ulster-Scots to join them in a cross-Atlantic trip to paradise. Benjamin and Joseph Chambers purchased 400 acres from William Penn and established a settlement at the Falling Spring in 1734. Benjamin (1708/9–1788) built a dwelling and mills which were later stockaded during the French and Indian War and became the nucleus of what we know as Chambersburg, though the town

The McDowells traveled to Mount Parnell or Parnell's Knob in Peters Township about the time Benjamin Chambers established his settlement at the Falling Springs. Mount Parnell, in Peters Township, stands out of the Appalachian range at about 2,021 feet. The winter photo is courtesy of the Fort Loudon Historical Society.

A view of Mount Parnell from McDowell Property. William McDowell, patriarch, settled by Mt. Parnell in Peters Township in 1730 and obtained a license for the land after it was purchased from the American Indians. He had no neighbors when he established his plantation, only Indians traveling through the area who hunted and traded for British goods. This is some of the original acreage. The area was originally in Chester County, and then part of Hopewell Township in Lancaster County. The town name was later changed to Peters Township in a newly formed Franklin County. Photo by author.

was not formally laid out until 1764. Benjamin welcomed Ulster-Scots particularly from Antrim. James established a settlement at the head of the Great Spring near Newville. Robert established a settlement at the head of the Middle Spring near Shippensburg.[7]

The Harris Ferry Road, later called the Great Road or Big Road, at this time was merely a simple Indian path. It was the way to reach the

Building a Mill in the Cumberland Valley

A view of Mount Parnell from McDowell Road, Peters Township. Photo by author.

Cumberland Valley from the east. Everything in this pristine area needed for survival had to be carried on pack-horses or by hand, caught in the wilds, or constructed on the spot. Wagons could not negotiate the rough trails and pack-horses or mules could only carry about 200 pounds, so people were limited in what they could carry. Family members generally walked the far distance, camping along the way under fallen branches. It would have taken quite a while to walk with small children through dense forests filled with wild animals and passing Indian bands.

The McDowells settled within an area currently known as Peters Township, Franklin County, Pennsylvania, along the northwestern bank of the West Branch of the Conococheague Creek on the south/southeastern side of a mountain called Parnell's Knob with its spring. They

A view of the Cumberland valley looking south from Mount Parnell.
Photo by author.

would expand outward from there. The area was not known by that town or county name at the time of their arrival. It was first in the extended Chester County, and then in the larger Lancaster County. The town had no name at this point because it had not been formally purchased from the Indians. Their arrival here was estimated between 1730 and 1731.[8] They were squatters for their first six years.[9] The area would likely have had Indians passing through to reach the Western Indians or hunting in the area but not living in settlements. Unlike many others, William

McDowell had the money to purchase land and the purchase of property would consume him and his heirs.

Some documents on the family mention their ability to speak with American Indians and that they did not find the language difficult. No mention is made of which dialect they understood, though Lenape would seem likely. The family valued Latin-based education and would have understood language construction. A "McDowell," perhaps a cousin, would later serve the military as interpreter.[10]

Thomas Francis Gordon in his 1829 history of Pennsylvania commented on the Lenape language which was widely spoken in varied dialects through Canada, the Northern United States down to Roanoke, Virginia, and along the western Mississippi River region. "Their language is said to be rich, sonorous, plastic, and comprehensive in the highest degree. It varies from the European idioms chiefly in the conjugation of the verbs, with which not only the agent and patient may be compounded, in every possible case, but the adverbs are also blended; and one word is made to express the agent, the action, with its accidents of time, place, and quantity, and the object effected by them. And, though greatly pliant, it is subjected to rules, from which there are few exceptions. It has the power of expressing every idea, even the most abstract. The Old and New Testaments have been translated into it, and the Christian missionaries have no difficulty, as they assert, of making themselves understood on all subjects by the Indians."[11] Though the accent spoken in Pennsylvania became extinct, there is a current move to re-create the original one used there.[12]

William and Mary McDowell continued giving birth to children in the wilderness. William's son John (1716–6/6/1794) was about fourteen when they reached the base of Mount Parnell in 1730. He had lived in Pennsylvania for most of his life, having left Ulster as an infant. He would later marry Agnes Craig (1717–August 8, 1766) and begin his own family. His wife's family name had also been listed in the Donegal registry, perhaps they met there. Craigs would settle in the valley. The remaining McDowell children were nine year-old Elizabeth (1721–1814) who later married Lieutenant James Holliday; eight year-old William (1722–September 17, 1812) who later married Mary Maxwell (1727–April 9, 1805), daughter of Justice William Maxwell; seven or eight year-old Nathan (1722–6/2/1802), who may have been eight to nine months younger than William born the same year or a twin. He later married Mary's sister Catherine Maxwell. Five year old Thomas (born 1725–6/2/1806) was born next and later married a woman named Annabelle; and then two year-old James (2/5/1728–2/5/1811) who later married Jean "Jane" Smith (1743–8/28/1784), sister of Captain James Smith and sister-in-law of Justice William Smith. Sisters would also be born in following years while the family hacked out a homestead at the base of the mountain: Jean B. (4/19/1736–8/16/1814) who would later marry Archibald Irwin (1734–1799); Sarah (11/30/1738–9/5/1805) who would marry William Piper who served as a Captain in Colonel Clayton's Regiment in 1763; Margaret (?-1/1803) who would marry Robert Newell; Annabelle (1741–4/11/1800) who would marry Lieutenant-Colonel John Johnson (1747–10/21/1826), her cousin, and live by Fort Loudon; and Susan (born after 1747) who later married a man with the last name of Reynolds.[13]

Food was plentiful in the valley for a clever hunter, but ammunition would always be a problem, as would be gun repair. In England only the wealthy were allowed to hunt and own guns. That, out of necessity, was relaxed on the frontier for the colonists but getting an ample supply of lead and powder in remote areas would continually plague the settlers, with few able to afford long rifles or muskets, though the McDowells were considered wealthy. Because England sought to ever bolster her own economy, she tended to sell heavy obsolete weapons to the colonists. Colonists, however, could order weapons from Europe if they had the means and could wait for them to slowly sail across the ocean.

Repair of weapons required a trip to civilization. Chambersburg had a man named Mr. Shillito by about 1740 and Lancaster had a noted gunsmith used later by George Washington for the Virginia troops, and there were a number of gunsmiths within the German population, though they were separated from Ulster-Scots by the government.[14] Trapping animals or catching fish was more practical for obtaining food and saved on ammunition, both were abundant in the valley because of the many springs. The focus of the Ulster-Scots who would slowly fill the valley was upon establishing farms and becoming self-sufficient which meant growing crops and raising some livestock. Most settlers in the area seemed to be more focused on grains than animal husbandry as per tax records. Driving livestock west would have been very difficult through horse trails.

The Kittitinny Valley was formally purchased by the Proprietors of the province from the Iroquois Confederacy on October 11, 1736, and promptly renamed the Cumberland Valley, also called North Valley to distinguish it from Virginia. No regard was given to the Delawares' hunting ground. The Delawares, as vassals to the Indian Confederacy, had to obey the decision to sell their hunting ground.

Two townships were then created: Pennsborough (much of current Cumberland County), and Hopewell (much of current Franklin County). Many smaller townships were later formed out of those two large geographical regions. The McDowells were settled in Hopewell Township with smaller areas associated with settler's names. The area in which they lived had a section called Path Valley, or Tuscarora Path. It was named by the American Indians for the horse-path to the western Alleghany Mountains. Land warrants were issued with the desire on the part of administers to collect taxes with property later surveyed. This was Pennsylvania's frontier wilderness in the southern-central part of the province, the farthest extend of western civilization. It was considered the protection line from the west for the colony.[15] Ulster-Scots were then encouraged by the colonial government to move to this new settlement from Paxton, Swatara and Donegal Townships as were new arrivals at the ports. The Ulster-Scots were to guard the western line.

The process to acquire ownership of land took five steps:

1. The purchaser had to fill out an Application to Warrant

2. A Warrant was then issued with a survey ordered

3. An Official Survey was completed listing the property description

4. An Application for a Patent was then filled out

5. Once reviewed, the Patent granted the full title to the purchaser

William McDowell obtained a Blunston License for 800 acres on December 13, 1736, from Thomas and Richard Penn. It listed the property as "On the Northwest Branch of Conocochegue, the Mountain {Mount Parnell} and about 3 miles Northwest from Edward Parnells."[16] Edward Parnell had been issued a warrant for two hundred acres in 1730 with the understanding that he would pay one-half penny sterling tax per acre each year which he did not do and his warrant was vacated on November 12, 1742, and granted to one James Gardner.[17]

The Blunston License was named after Justice Samuel Bluntson, a Quaker living by Wrights Ferry at Columbia who served Lancaster County. He was the agent granting licenses west of the Susquehanna for the Proprietors.[18] He also co-owned a gristmill with ferryman James Wright which would later supply flour for General Braddock and General Forbes in their campaigns. A license usually began with the words "By order of the Honorable Proprietary" and granted the person named the right to settle and improve a tract of acreage with a property description, date and official signature. An official survey would follow the license. William most likely used Wrights Ferry to cross the Susquehanna River on his way to the Cumberland Valley. He would have had to travel back there to fill out his license, or a representative might have visited the new settlement.

William McDowell paid 69 pounds, 2 shillings, and 7 pence for his land.[19] The sons of William purchased their own land in 1737 with surveys ordered. William continued to purchase acreage in other communities, and at one point the McDowell sons owned almost 3,000 acres of land. Descendants are still farming on some of the original tracts. The McDowells initially had no direct neighbors. The family slowly cleared the land and planted crops. They were not dairy farmers, per se, though they did eventually have a small number of cows for their own personnel use. Crops were the main source of their livelihood. McDowells in Northern Ireland had been heavily involved in linen production. It would seem likely that that was one of their crops in America, and we do learn later that settlers in that region were growing flax. Their eventual construction of a gristmill also points towards grains. Corn, oats, wheat and rye were popular crops. There were plenty of McDowells to do the work on the farm with eleven children slowly growing.

Other settlers began to arrive. By 1737 The Reverent John Black and Samuel Harris obtained licenses, and in 1738 Andrew McCleary obtained one. Henry Johnston and John Taylor are recorded in 1742 followed by James Glenn, William Burney and James McClellan in 1743 and Robert McClellan in 1744,[20] but they were not settled into a village. They were widely separated from each other with miles of open land.

Pioneer William reportedly had a log home on his property, which was later burned by Indians. In 1877 Thomas Creigh described the cabins in the valley during this early period as being 20–25 feet by 28–30 feet is size. He stated that the windows usually had three or four panes of glass or oiled paper if one was too poor for glass. The chimney of some homes was simply plastered sticks of wood on a stone foundation. The fireplace was wide and could fit a 6–8 foot long log which burned for days. For furniture, most homes had split-log benches on four legs or three legged stools. There would have been a simple table. Some settlers had bed frames but many slept on simple mattresses filled with straw. Pegs on the walls held garments, and a rifle with its powder horn and pouch. The walls might also have had shelves constructed on them to hold items. The ocean voyage and long trip west without wagons would have made it impossible to transport very large pieces from the east at first. Fine furniture would take time to accumulate.

The clothing worn by the settlers was hand made mostly of wool, linen or silk with some leather and animal hides. Men wore a tri-corner felt hunting hat, hunting shirt of wool with wool breeches and long stockings when working in the fields. They gradually adopted the deer-skin moccasins of the Indians. Formal ware for men included a better quality felt three-corner hat, silk waistcoat with breeches with a knee buckle, a silk shirt, long stockings, and shoes with a buckle. Women wore a short gown and petticoat or skirt with a flared waistcoat and an apron during the week. They had a white kerchief carefully draped around their neck by their blouse to cover the upper portion of the breast. A white ruffled cap collected their hair, perhaps adding a straw bonnet when outside.

For finer occasions they donned silk dresses with lovely bonnets, and fine satin shoes with pointed toes and low heels.

Creigh mentions the books common to the settlers in this area at this time as being *The Bible*; *The Westminster Confessions of Faith*; a Psalm book; *The Pilgrim's Progress* by John Bunyan; Scottish Thomas Boston's *Human Nature in its Fourfold State* (innocence, sin, grace, eternal life); and Richard Baxter's *The Saint's Everlasting Rest*.[21] All of the books were practical for faith instruction. The valley became largely settled by strict Presbyterian Covenanter Ulster-Scots who had been directed there by the Pennsylvanian government. The Proprietaries of the Penn colony decided to keep the Ulster-Scots, called Irish, from York County which was given over to German settlement.

The Ulster-Scots quickly established Presbyterian congregations in the Cumberland Valley beginning in 1736. They were an organized culture overseen by ruling elders who gathered on Session. A log Presbyterian meeting-house was constructed on the Conodoguinett Creek two miles north of Carlisle and the Greencastle log meeting house, called the Old Red Church at Moss Spring, was constructed in 1738. The Presbyterian places of worship were connected to each other and to the Donegal Presbytery. Most, as Covenanters, remembered well British religious and economic persecution.

The Presbyterian log meeting-house at the West Conocochegue settlement was erected at Church Hill between 1738 and 1739. That area was chosen because it was centrally located. Members raised the church and it was initially led on an irregular basis by pulpit supply from Donegal. The elders would have done visitation and simple ministry with the congregants. Deacons would have tended to the sick and poor.

The Synod of Donegal in 1737 made it very clear that only college educated clergy who had been carefully examined by the Presbytery could serve as pastors. Europe was highly respected as the training place for clergy. Those maintaining this view were called "Old Lights" or "Old Side" as the Great Awakening later brought in a push to educate clergy in the colonies or in some cases to let uneducated clergy into pulpits. Princeton College (now University) became the center of the "New Side" in 1746, which had been influenced by persons like George Whitefield/ Whitfield (12/27/1714–9/30/1770). A breach would form between the New and Old Sides in the Cumberland Valley which would take many years to resolve.

The McDowells, as elders, would hold to the education and examination of their clergy to insure they had proper training and Biblical knowledge to teach others. The Presbyterian denomination had a keen interest in the education of all persons so that they could understand the Bible for themselves and Latin-based education was highly valued. Elders examined congregants on their understanding of the shorter catechism. A ruling elder was placed over each district to make sure the people had the proper understanding of their faith. Communion was served twice a year in the spring and fall.[22] British law prohibited Bibles being printed in colonial America without the permission of the Crown, though editions in Indian and German languages were permitted. All other sacred printing was done in England and transported to the colonies.

Log cabins slowly began to dot the valley with wide spaces between them as settlers cleared and planted their fields. Seeds were planted by hand after wooden plows broke the earth or sticks poked holes in the soil. In the fall sickles were used to reap bushels of grain which then needed to be bundled and processed. It took groups of people to reap a field and labor was often shared by neighbors or done by hired help. Settlers petitioned the court in Lancaster County for a road in 1735 to proceed from John Harris' Ferry (Harrisburg) towards the Potomac ending at the mouth of the Conococheague. The county appointed six viewers to review the request and a report was presented by them to the court in May of 1744. A narrow dirt road was ordered at that time. It was called the Harris Ferry Road, Great Road or Big Road and it followed the simple Indian path take by settlers which was then enlarged but would only have been large enough for simple wagons because the process of constructing a road was slow and difficult as trees were chopped by hand and boulders pulled out by oxen.[23]

Some Germans and Swiss settled in the southern section of the Cumberland Valley. Swiss Mennonites and Huguenots; German Baptists, called Dunkards after their form of baptism; Moravians; Seventh-day Baptists; Lutheran; and German Reformed groups chose an area in dispute between Maryland and Pennsylvania. The German Lutherans and Reformed were the largest of those groups. The German Reformed and Swiss Huguenots had the same basic Calvinistic faith in common with the Ulster-Scott Presbyterians. All were considered part of the "Reformed family of Protestantism" which included the Dutch Reformed, with each culture adopting their own ethnic version of French John Calvin's work. The Scots followed John Knox's version of Calvinism.

Palatine German Reformed, Palatine German Lutherans, and the Dutch Reformed held the 1563 Heidelberg Catechism as a common confession of faith which had been created as a peace measure between the Palatine Reformed and Lutheran groups. Its uniting material included instruction on *The Apostle's Creed*, Baptism and the Lord's Supper, *The 10 Commandments* and *The Lord's Prayer*. The German Lutheran and Reformed groups in the Cumberland Valley shared a log meeting-house with some Dutch, evidence of the uniting work of the Catechism.[24] For the most part, Germans and Ulster-Scots, called Irish, were kept separate by the Provisional Government because struggles had occurred between them near the Donegal settlement, especially by the more aggressive in each group. Germans were generally encouraged to settle in what is now York County. Later, when militia was called from the Cumberland Valley, Ulster-Scots did have German Reformed and Lutherans join them while the more pacifistic German faiths resisted self-protection, causing great frustration by those bearing all the burden for defense.

While the McDowells and others were carving out homesteads, the French in 1732 crept into the Ohio River area and the Upper Allegheny River area, building log forts. Toussaint LeCavelier, a French fur trader began visiting the Shawnees who originally came from the eastern section of Pennsylvania and had settled on the Kiskiminetas River, courting friendships with natives and instilling resentment towards the British for land lost.[25] This new move made by the French was a direct encroachment on the British colony which would begin a series of struggles for dominance on the frontier. The Western Indians were assured by the

The French colony of New France in Canada came under the authority of the French Ministry of Marine and was focused on the fur trade. The French would devise a plan to unite their northern colony with their holdings along the Mississippi River down to New Orleans. They would claim the water sources that drained into the Mississippi back to their sources on both the western and eastern side of the river to protect their transportation routes. The center of their new venture would be the area later now known as Pittsburg. This photo of French uniforms is of the French garrison at Fort Niagara, New York, taken by Alissa Bakker and used by permission.

French that they would not establish settlements. They were encouraged to push out British settlers and trades people in the area. The Indians, familiar with Europeans, gladly traded with the French for firearms, metal utensils and material.[26]

The French settlement of New France in Canada had been established for the fur trade, particularly beaver used in makingfelt for hats.[27] The settlement was formed under the Ministry of Marine ruled by the King of France with no self-government. The settlement was Roman Catholic with censorship of all other material. Two chief executives carried out the King's orders: the Governor, usually a naval officer who oversaw military operations and settled Indian disputes; and the Intendant with economic, executive and policing powers.[28] A council, presided over by the Governor who rarely attended meetings, was made of the Intendant, the Bishop and a dozen councilors appointed by the King who judged all civil and criminal matters in an arbitrary manner. Land was held by a few of the upper class or the church, and leased to colonists who were largely uneducated, except those entering the priesthood.

New France was conceived as a naval trade center with three types of soldiers: untrained Militia, Canadian regulars of La Marine Regiment and French soldiers of the regular army. Fur traders had the most freedom and were often placed over bands of loyal Indians, intermarrying with the daughters of prominent chiefs. They would prove to be the most deadly agents in conflicts against the British colonists.

The system of government in New France differed greatly from the British colonies which were more like independent states loyal to their king but left to their own administration. Pennsylvania had its own internal conflicts between many Governors and the Assembly, and it had land disputes with other colonies. Soon after the arrival from England of Thomas Penn in 1732 and John Penn in 1734, Lord Baltimore of Maryland applied to Parliament to have Penn's Woods transferred to his colony. This forced John Penn back to England to defend the proprietary rights at court and he never returned, dying in 1746.[29]

Pennsylvania Governor Patrick Gorden died in August of 1736 and James Logan, the Scottish President of the Council, served as a type of

Governor for two years (1736–1738). Logan was highly educated with extensive linguistic abilities. He was a scientific writer in Latin and translated several works of people like Cicero.

The issues with Maryland increased west of the Susquehanna River, then Lancaster County and now York County. Settlers were securing titles to land from Maryland and then trying to re-instate their rights to Pennsylvania to avoid taxes. The Sherriff of Maryland with 300 men came into Pennsylvanian territory to drive out the settlers for lack of payment of taxes. Samuel Smith, Sheriff of Lancaster County, Pennsylvania, then stepped in with a posse of citizens to drive the Maryland Sherriff out. A skirmish followed whereupon the Governor of Maryland sent a commission to Philadelphia to demand the release of prisoners from his colony. He was not successful. He then seized four Pennsylvanian settlers and incarcerated them in a Baltimore jail. A party from Maryland began warfare on settlers and the Sheriff of Lancaster County was called on again to drive them out. Finally, sixteen Maryland men led by Richard Lowden broke into the Lancaster jail and liberated Maryland prisoners. This forced the King of England to step in and order restraint. He adopted a plan of settlement and temporary boundary between the two colonies, but it was far from settled.[30] The Cumberland Valley remained in contested land.

During all the political wrangling over colonial grants at court, William McDowell's son John constructed a one and one-half story log gristmill on what is now Mercersburg Road in Markes, Pennsylvania, within Peters Township just north of the intersection of Lemar and Mercersburg Roads. Behind it was the eastern side of the West Branch of the Conococheague Creek. He did this, most likely with the help of his family and neighbors. The mill was located about four miles north of what would become Mercersburg, known at this time as Black's Town and later as Smith's Town. The area by the mill became known as McDowell's Mill and carried that name until 1825 as a small cluster of buildings developed around it.[31] Bringing heavy mill stones over horse trails without the help of wagons in that early period was no easy task. Mill stones were often made of volcanic rock called French Buhr Stone and would be a challenge for horses to either pull them or carry them for long distances.

This is a typical mill flour shoot and wheel from this period. Mill work was labor intensive with the miller doing much of the work by hand. John McDowell constructed a one and a half story log grist-mill about 1740 along a stream which was fed by the West Conococheague Creek. Photo by author.

Building a Mill in the Cumberland Valley

John N. Lovett, Jr., Ph.D., owner of Falls Mill & Museum in Belvidere, Tennessee, estimates that a simple log mill constructed in a frontier setting during this time period under perfect weather conditions with about five men could have taken about six months or more to accomplish depending upon the skill of the men. The weather, remoteness, lack of roads and wagons to carry supplies would have contributed to the difficulty. There were a number of men attempting to do the same thing within the area at the same time who were connected ethnically and religiously, so they may have worked together on each mill, speeding the process. Black had a mill as did the Chambers.

Lovett estimates that to complete the building by itself out of hewn logs might have taken five skilled men working daily a month, however many of the mills had masonry foundations which would have increased that time. He states that a mill "requires a dam, which was usually constructed of timbers in that time period (although it could have been stone), and that was typically accomplished in late summer when water was at its lowest level."[32] The millrace leading to the wheel from the dam, he continues, would have been dug by hand for part of the way. The waterwheel powering the millstones, shafts and gears and mill machinery would then follow, but at this date most of the hauling was done by hand. Lovett states that "The stones may have been placed on an upper level with a primitive hand operated bolter (sifter) underneath."[33]

Colonial mills were usually small and placed along waterways. A sluicegate allowed water to flow over the vertical waterwheel outside the building to make it turn. A larger gear-wheel or pit wheel was mounted on the same axle as the water wheel. It rotated the main drive shaft running vertically to the top of the building on the inside. Grain was hoisted to the sack floor at the top of the building and then emptied into bins above the millstones. A bottom millstone (bed stone) was fixed to the floor and a top millstone (runner stone) was mounted on a separate spindle driven by the main shaft. Grain was emptied into the center whole of the runner stone. The stones were cut, dressed with angled channels called furrows which cut open the grain. The space between the furrows, called lands, collected and channeled the flour which was then sent to the outside edge of the stone through centrifugal force and friction. Crushed flour was then collected from the grooves in the runner stone. Flour was fed down a chute to sifter screens and then placed in sacks on the bottom floor. It would have required a lot of manual labor.

John McDowell succeeded in the construction project and reportedly ran a store out of the mill, which was common for millers. They sold flour for bread which was a basic staple in the colonial diet. The miller's "toll" or wages were often paid in trade goods since coinage was sparse, tough the toll price was still fixed by law. Those trade items would have been available for resale. His extended family and neighbors would have frequented the mill as would have passing traders. Many of the colonies did not export flour because of the fear of starvation, but it seems the people within the Cumberland Valley did bring their extra flour to Baltimore, Maryland, where it was then sent on to the West Indies. John also constructed a two story log home thirty yards from the mill with "a liberal supply of port holes" for defense.[34] He farmed his own property by the mill with his own crops.

Samuel Bates and Richard Fraise, writing on Franklin County in 1887, list the construction of the original mill by John McDowell between 1730 and 1731, which would have been when the McDowell's first arrived in the valley. That early date would have been when John was 14. The McDowells in Northern Ireland ran mills. It would have been possible for a teen who had apprenticed in eastern Pennsylvania to run a small mill with family familiarity of the industry. Most of the colonial mills were one-man operations and the miller generally grew to become very strong from hoisting grain bags. Teens were considered adults at this time. Most of those living in the valley who had trades did them part-time while they farmed their land, so milling might have been a part-time job for him.

Eugene Etter in his *History of Lemasters, Pennsylvania*, however, lists the mill's construction in 1740 and that John later fortified it.[35] John would have been 24 at that date. That date seems more likely for his lead in undertaking the project, but little is known of the actual construction date of the first mill on this site. The family were squatters before the land was available for purchase. The land warrantees of Lancaster County list a John "McDowold" with 200 acres on November 1, 1736. This could have been one of the many spellings of the family name. John "McDowell," correct spelling, is listed purchasing 400 acres on December 7, 1737 and 200 acres on March 2, 1737. Later John added 50 acres on October 20, 1750; 150 on December 1, 1750; 117 on November 21, 1751; 40 on November 1, 1754; 100 on May 12, 1755; 150 on July 1, 1762; 400 on June 8, 1762; 200 on 16, 1766 and 300 on February 12, 1768. He kept adding land beyond the Revolutionary War in a variety of counties as the west was opened. He seemed to have been making a good living and he may have also sold one property to purchase another.

Two William McDowells are listed (father and son). One with 300 acres in March 2, 1737, and one with 200 acres December 7, 1737. William adds 160 acres on August 10, 1749 and 400 on June 8, 1762. Thomas McDowell purchases 400 acres on December 7, 1737. He adds 20 acres on May 5, 1752 and more beyond that. James later purchases 40 acres on March 23, 1752, and Nathan has 250 acres on June 8, 1762. They all continue purchasing land through the Revolutionary War like their brother. They also served on the Pennsylvania Line during that war and receive donated western land following that conflict.[36]

The land warrants show us that they were definitely in the county. Some historical documents merely list John McDowell's mill being constructed sometime prior to 1753/1754. What adds to the complex dating of the original mill is the fact that mills often caught on fire when fine dust was ignited by a spark, or they decayed over time as they were largely constructed from wood and were nestled by water in flood plain. We learn in 1846 that the mill standing near the original McDowell mill was the third one on that site.[37]

John married his wife, Agnes Craig (1717–8/8/1766), in 1737, when he was twenty-one and she twenty. Living on their new property they eventually had five daughters: Agnes (9/9/1740–6/9/1790), Mary "Molly" (1743–4/22/1833), Elizabeth "Betsy" (died 12/12/1822), Catherine (1753–2/10/1818), and Margaret "Peggy" (1758–1828).[38] Daughter Agnes later married Elias Davidson (1736–4/15/1806) on March 19, 1771. Elias was a large land owner who later served as a Captain in the Cumberland County Associators from 1777–1779 during the Revolutionary War.

He was a member of the Greencastle Old Red Church at Moss Spring where he served on Session. Mary later married Dr. Richard Brownson (5/3/1737–3/25/1790) in 1765. Richard became a surgeon for Colonel Samuel Culbertson's 6th Battalion during the Revolutionary War. Elizabeth later married the Rev. John King, pastor of the Upper West Conococheague Presbyterian Church, on April 2, 1771. Margaret later married George King, brother of the pastor, on June 6, 1786.[39] Catherine later married Hugh Davidson, brother of Elias, on November 21, 1774.[40]

While the agrarian life was progressing in the Cumberland Valley, on October 23, 1739, war was declared between Great Britain and Spain. It was called the Anglo-Spanish War of 1739–1748, The War of Jenkin's Ear, or Guerra del Asiento by the Spanish. Spain and Britain had had a rocky relationship as each tried to dominate the sea. As part of the Treaty of Utrecht, which ended the War of the Spanish Succession (1701–1714), Britain had been given a thirty year trade agreement or Asiento by Spain. In that Asiento, Britain could trade 500 tons of goods per year, and an unlimited number of slaves to Spanish Colonies. Following the Anglo-Spanish War of 1727–1729, Britain gave Spain the right to stop British ships to ensure the terms of the Asiento were being kept. The Spanish then claimed merchant ships were involved in smuggling which gave them the right to board and seize British ships and to torcher crew members. Both sides tried to avoid war, however mediation failed. The term "Jenkins' Ear" relates to the Spanish boarding of Captain Robert Jenkins' ship the *Rebecca* in 1731. Jenkins' ear was cut off by the Spanish and when he was called to speak at Parliament on the matter, he produced his severed ear. With the new declaration of war, the Governor of Pennsylvania tried to organize militia but the Quaker Assembly would not vote for funding. This would be a continual problem with a variety of governors trying to obey the crown and protect the colony while the Quaker dominated Assembly blocked the means to do it.

A new governor tried his talents with the Assembly. George Thomas, son of a West Indian planter, was appointed Governor from 1738–1747. He too was appalled by the Assembly's behavior. "The Demeanor of the People called Quakers may have merited the Protection of the crown and the esteem of mankind; and as I believe this is the first Instance of a Number of them having made use of Liberty of Conscience for typing up the Hands of His Majesty's Subjects for defending a valuable Part of His Dominions, situated almost in the Center of those in North America, I heartily wish that it may not be attended with any ill Effects, either on the Minds of our Fellow Subjects or on the Fortunes of the People of this Province . . ."[41] The Crown finally ordered a call be given for volunteers, and eight companies were formed in the colony to defend the coastal area. Most of them, however, were servants of land owners who in turn demanded payment.

Thomas tried to solve some of the border disorder in the Cumberland Valley between the colonies. Settlers were to give their allegiance to the Governor under whom they settled until a division line could be surveyed and marked to show the boundary between Pennsylvania and Maryland.[42] Pennsylvania would also have another colony begin to seek land in its grant. The Ohio Company, made of gentlemen from Virginia and Maryland, organized to set up trading posts at the forks of the Ohio River (current Pittsburg). They received permission from the Crown to settle one hundred families there within seven years, protected by a fort. The Governor of Virginia and George Washington's brother held shares in this company. The young George Washington had surveyed the area with his own interests in obtaining property. The settlement was to be on the south side of the Ohio River between the Monongalia and Kanawha Rivers and would serve as the basis for a claim to the area by Virginia.

While plans were being hatched to invade Pennsylvania's land to the west by her sister colony, Great Britain formally declared war on France in March of 1744. The war in Europe did not initially effect those on the frontiers, though a call was given for Pennsylvania volunteers and 10,000 men enlisted. Those who enlisted from Pennsylvania were expected to bring their own arms as funding was not provided for that. The focus of defense for Britain was on the Atlantic Ocean and not on the western part of their colonies which lay exposed. As the British Crown worried about conflicts on the European continent, the French established more trade with the western Indians on the American content and continued to breed dissatisfaction towards the British among native tribes.

As early at 1747 Indian trader Conrad Weiser, writing from Tulpehockin to Richard Peters in Philadelphia, warned about the inroads made by the French with the Indians. He commented,

> I shall be sick of Indian Affairs If no medium is found to do them Justice. I assure you, Sir, I find it very hard sometimes to Excuse the Government, and must hear words entirely disagreeable. I am satisfied the Indians have just reason to Complain at the behaviour of some of our people. As to the Treaty of Col. Johnson and Mr. Lydias, with the Mohawks, I dislike it, and the Six Nations are offended at the people of Albany because we pay their people with goods against the opinion of the Chief Counsel. If these two Gentlemen had as much Judgment as they have pride, they would never have over persuaded the Mohawks into the war in a privat way, for it may turn out that both their scalps may be taken and carried to Canada.[43]

He later repeated his views, "I for my part am fully satisfied the Indians Complaint is Just in the mean . . ."[44] Many of the men meeting with the Indians like Weiser had Indian trader licenses issued to them by the government. Traders tended to understand the Indian customs better than military personnel who expected natives to simply be obedient subjects of the crown. Traders developed friendships and often took the Indian's side in issues. George Croghan, John Potts, Adam Hoops (a whiskey keg maker), Samuel Chambers and John Armstrong were all licensed traders in Pennsylvania.[45]

Since no provision was given for military aid to settlers by the Assembly, inhabitants decided to form themselves into voluntary companies of associated regiments, Associators, for protection. Settlers of the West Conococheague area, as early as 1748, saw the potential danger and began organizing themselves for defense. They established a type of guard with a few small private block houses. Justice Major William Maxwell, Justice Lieutenant William Smith and John Winton of Peters Township guarded the west side of the valley. James and Joshua Patterson, the Irvins,

William Rankin, Matthew Shields Sr. and Jr., and Daniel Shields served in the early militia/rangers.[46] Justices Maxwell, Smith, and Irvine would become in-laws to the McDowells. Justice William McDowell, Jr., was already married to Mary Maxwell, Maxwell's daughter. Nathan McDowell would later marry Catherine Maxwell, her sister. James McDowell would later marry Jean "Jane" Smith, sister-in-law of William Smith. Jean McDowell would later marry Archibald Irwin. They all attended church together where the Justices served together as elders on session.

The formal Associated Regiments of the West End of Lancaster County on the Susquehanna River formed between 1747 and 1748 is as follows:

Officers of Associated Regiment of the West End of Lancaster County, on the Susquehanna, 1747–1748
Colonel Thomas Cookson with Lieut. Colonel James Galbraith. Major Robert Baker
Captain Hugh Patrick with Lieut. Thomas McDowell, Ensign Thomas Grubb
Captain James Gillespie–[to] Lieutenant Colonel John Harris, from Ensign, August 4, 1748 with Lieut.–James Gilchrist, Ensign–Samuel Jemison
Captain Gabriel Davis with Lieut. Robert Ellis, Ensign Edward Davis, Jr
Captain Samuel Crawford, Lieut. William Rowland, Ensign Richard McDonald
Captain Samuel Anderson, Lieut. John Woodside, Ensign John Barkley
Captain Jedediah Alexander, Lieut. Hugh Whiteford, Ensign James Smith
Captain Andrew Gregg, Lieut. William Crawford, Ensign Samuel Simpson
Captain James Snodgrass, Lieut. John Alexander, Ensign John Snodgrass
Captain James Galbraith, Lieut. James Sample, Ensign John Harris–to Captain August 4, 1748
Captain John Smith, Lieut. William Crum, Ensign Joseph C_____
Captain Adam Read, Lieut. John Crawford, Ensign John Young
Captain John McCuen, Lieut. James Anderson, Ensign James Finney
Captain John Galbraith, Lieut. William Allison, Ensign Nathaniel Little
Captain David McClure, Lieut. Thomas Foster, Ensign Andrew Boggs
Captain James Armstrong, Lieut. Alexander Armstrong, Ensign John Dougherty

Officers of Associated Regiment of the West End of Lancaster County, on the Susquehanna, 1747–1748

Captain Thomas McKee, Lieut. Robert Smith, Ensign William Baskins (Baskell)

Captain James Graham, Lieut. John Purrins, Ensign William McMullin

Captain Robert Baker, Lieut. William Mitchell, Ensign Henry Rennicks

Captain James Patterson, Lieut. James Smith, Ensign Thomas Mitchell

Captain Thomas Harris, Lieut. _____ , Ensign John Wilson

Officers of the Associated Regiment of Lancaster County, over the River, Sasquehanna, 1747–1748

Colonel Benjamin Chambers, Lieut.-Colonel Robert Dunning, Major William Maxwell

Captain Richard O'Kane (O'Cain), Lieut. William Smith, Ensign John Mitchell

Captain Robert Chambers, Lieut. Andrew Finley, Ensign John Cesna

Captain James Carnahan, Lieut. James Jack, Ensign John Thompson

Captain John Chambers, Lieut. Jonathan Holmes, Ensign Walter Davis

Captain James Silver, Lieut. Tobias Hendricks, Ensign Joseph Irwin (Irvine)

Captain Charles Morrow, Lieut. James Dyssart, Ensign John Anderson

Captain George Brown, Lieut. John Potter, Ensign John Randals (Reynolds)

Captain James Woods, Lieut. John McCormick, Ensign Samuel Fisher

Captain James McAteer, Lieut. William Trindle, Ensign Moses Starr

Captain Matthew Dill, Lieut Andrew Miller, Ensign George Brennan

Captain Benjamin Chambers, Lieut. Charles McGill, Ensign Robert Mull

Captain William Maxwell, Lieut. John Winton, Ensign James Wilkey

Captain Robert Dunning, Lieut. John Mitchell, Ensign– Adam Hayes

Indian attacks began on the frontier of Penn's Woods in 1748, but the Assembly felt that it was the Crown's job to protect the colony and to call for and pay volunteers. Pennsylvania was unique in this resistance to developing a militia which frustrated the other colonies, and the British Parliament. Queen Anne had established the law in 1702 regarding the mandatory conscription of all males ages sixteen to fifty in the provincial militia. If war was imminent, the age extended to 15 to 60.[47] Parliament felt the colonies owed their allegiance to the King and should shoulder their own expenses for protection. Because of this lack of preparedness, the Pennsylvania colony seemed to be unusually easy prey. Miller John McDowell was now thirty-two. He and his siblings all had young families nestled within the frontier valley with trouble brewing to their west.

The Treaty of Aix-la-Chapelle, signed on October 1, 1748, ended formal hostilities between Great Britain and France in Europe but did not end conflicts in the colonies. What is now known as the French and Indian War began with the European conflict in 1744 and lasted until 1756, with additional Indian conflicts continuing long after that. While talking peace in Europe, the French became more aggressive on the American continent, expanding control not only over their own colony of New France but encroaching upon British territory.

A month after the signing of the peace treaty, November 23, 1748, James Hamilton arrived from England to become the new Lieutenant-Governor of the Penn Colony. His first administration lasted from 1748 to 1754. He was American born, the son of the former speaker of the Provincial Assembly. He replaced President Anthony Palmer (1747–1748) who was the presiding officer after Governor Thomas resigned. Richard Peters served as the secretary of the colony through a number of governors, and his name would be honored in 1750 in the incorporation of Peters Township in an area which was often simply referred to by dominate land holders like the McDowells.

Conrad Weiser, Indian interpreter, was then sent to help resolve property disputes in the Cumberland Valley where settlers were encroaching on Indian land. White settlers were removed from unauthorized areas. He and Andrew Montour were highly esteemed by the Indians. Weiser's wisdom would be appreciated over time by the men in the Cumberland Valley and many would follow him in times of war.

With the promise of peace with France, gentlemen and merchants from Virginia who had organized The Ohio Company began surveying 400 acres on the Cacapon River. The Marquis de la Galissoniere,

Governor-General of Canada also began on June 15, 1749, placing plates of lead with inscriptions in the name of the French King from La Chine, along the southern shore of Lakes Ontario, and Lake Erie. A French expedition led by Pierre Joseph Céloron de Blainville (1693–1759) entered the Allegheny River from Lake Erie to lay claim to the land that was originally discovered by La Salle. Céloron descended by boat to the mouth of the Miami and claimed the entire area for France, warning off British traders.[48]

In response to the movement of the French and the Virginians in what is now the Pittsburgh area, proposals to construct forts or blockhouses to protect Pennsylvanian traders were sent to the Assembly from settlers but they were not acted on. The French continued penetrating deeper and deeper into the basin of the Alleghany Mountains, establishing trading posts along the Ohio and Allegheny Rivers.[49] A line of French military posts was then established to connect French Canada down through the Mississippi River basin to Louisiana. The Pennsylvania government was still focused pastoral farming. They were not prepared for what was about to happen.

CHAPTER FOUR

1750–1755

Becoming a Chief Fort in Gen. Braddock's Campaign

The area by the mill fell once more into a changing geographic region. It began in the enlarged Chester County which was broken off into an enlarged Lancaster County with two townships. In 1750 an enlarged Cumberland County was carved out of Lancaster County, placing the mill in Cumberland where it would remain for a number of years. The county seat was set at Carlisle.

Antrim Township, formed in 1741, was a large region which covered most of what is now Franklin County. Regions within this large township were given names based mostly on those dwelling there. Mercersburg, just south of McDowell's Mill was initially called "Black's Town" after James Black who built a mill in the area. Black later sold his property to Justice William Smith, Esq., and from about 1750 to 1764 the town was called "Smith's Town." The streets were not formally laid out at this early period. It was just a cluster of log cabins with a tavern. William Smith's son would later formally grid out streets.

Smith's Town was a place of trade with Western Indians and early settlers. Fifty to one hundred pack-horses in line would pass through there on their way to the Allegheny Mountains. William and brother-in-law James Smith would later issue vouchers for the traders which documented their goods and the integrity of the traders.[1] This process was intended to block unscrupulous traders from carrying war goods to Western Indians and to comply with colonial laws but would later be the center of controversy. The traders were to be licensed and regulated by colonial law.

The Smiths in Smith's Town frequently interacted with the McDowells. William McDowell, Jr., Esq. (1722–September 17, 1812), son of the pioneer, also served as a County Justice of the Peace in what would soon be called Peters Township. Justices ruled over county courts in those days and served as judges of the courts of common pleas and quarter sessions of the peace. Three of them made a quorum. There were usually four terms of county court each year. Justices were chosen based on their character and their knowledge of their duties. Many Justices like Smith and McDowell chose the role because they wanted to make sure justice was administered properly within their communities. In addition to this, Judges of the Supreme Court made two circuit runs into each county each year to hold court and the Governor presided over the Provincial Council as the highest court. [2] Their decisions were final.

The families of Justices Smith, McDowell, and Justice Maxwell attended church together where they also served as elders and in-laws. Constable James McDowell, Esq. (February 5, 1728–February 5, 1811), brother of John the miller and Justice William, would later married Jean "Jane" Smith (1743–August 28, 1784) on June 7, 1761, but that was still eleven years away. Jane was sister to James Smith. Justice William Smith, Sr. married Jane's sister, his cousin. William McDowell was married to Justice Maxwell's daughter, Mary, and his brother Nathan was married to Catherine Maxwell. James, William McDowell, Jr. and the miller John McDowell would later be placed in awkward positions interacting with the Smiths and Maxwells due to the future actions of James Smith and their tangled family lives. Years later Smith's Town would be renamed Mercersburg in honor of Dr. Hugh Mercer, a noted area physician and military leader who had a farm south of that town.

Peters Township, north of Smith's Town was given its name in 1751 to honor Richard Peters, the Colonial Secretary of the Province under Governors Thomas, Palmer, Hamilton, Morris and Denny from 1743–1762. The area was taken out of the larger Antrim Township. Peters Township at this time covered the current areas of Peters, Montgomery and part of St. Thomas Townships west of Campbell's Run.³ The burst of Ulster-Scots in the township now included Daniel, Arthur, Andrew and Hezekiah Alexander; William, and Adam Armstrong; John Baird, Sr. and Jr.; William and Robert Barnett; Thomas Barr; Widow Ann, John, and James Black; John and James Blair; Thomas Boal; David Bowel; Joshua Bradner; Widow, Alexander, George, and Samuel Brown; William Sr. and Jr., Michael, and Charles Campbell; Michael Carsell; Samuel Chapman; Thomas Calhoun; William and Thomas Clark; Robert Clugage; Robert Crawford; Patrick Clark; Robert Culbertson; John and James Dickey; Widow and Arthur Donelson; William Dunwood; John Docherty; Samuel, David, James, Philip, David, Nathanel, Joshua, Thomas and Widow Davis; Joseph Dunlop; James Erwin; Widow Farier; John and James Flanaghin; Moses Fisher; James Galbreath; ; James Galaway; Widow Garison; John Gilmore; Samuel Gilespie; John Hamilton; Joshua, John, Charles and Jeremiah Harris; James Holland; Joseph How; John Holiday; Alexander Hotchison; Widow and John Huston; Mesech James; Hugh Kerrell; Henry Larkan; William Lowrie; John Martin; William Maxwell; James and John Mercer; William Marshall; William Moor; Widow McFarland; James Mitchell; John Morlan; Andrew Morison; John, and William Sr. and Jr. McDowell; Alexander McKee, Robert, James and William McClellan; James McConnell; Robert McCoy; William McIllhatton; James McMahon; James Murphy; William Morrison; Robert Newell; Victor Neely; James and Nathan Orr; Thomas Orbison; Thomas Owins; Matthew and John Patton; Francis Patterson; David Rees; James Rankin; Alexander Robertson; William Semple; James Sloan; Richard Stevens; Andrew Simpson; William and Hugh Shannon; Widow Scott; Alexander Staret; Collin Spence; John Taylor; James Wright; William Wallace; Moses White; John Wasson; Joseph Williams; John Wood; Joseph White; Thomas Waddle. Freemen listed were Robert Anderson;

McDOWELL'S MILL FORT

David Alexander; Robert Banefield; James Brown; James Blair; Gavin Cluggage; James Carswell; James Coyle; Willaim Gueen; Alexander Huthison; Edward Horkan; John Laird; Alexander McConnell; Samuel Templeton; William Tayler; James Wilson; James Wallace, Andrew Willabee; Oliver and David Wallace.[4] Some of these names would repeatedly surface in reports of Indian attacks and those serving in the militia. The

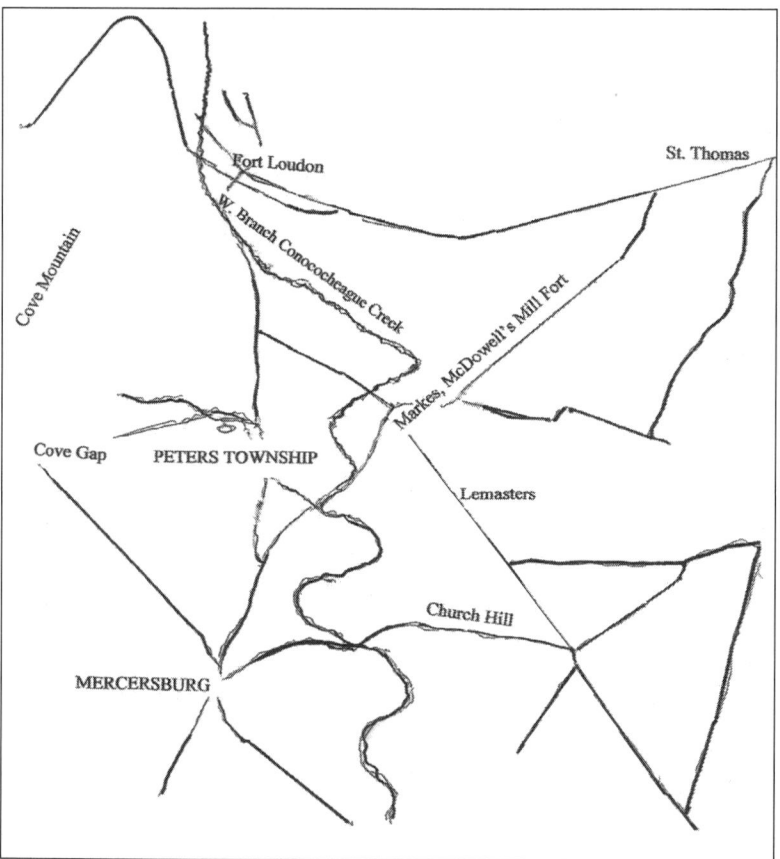

McDowell's Mill Fort was located on Mercersburg Road, just north of the crossing of Mercersburg Road and Lemar Road along the West Branch of the Conococheague Creek in what was called in 1751 McDowell's Mill, Peter's Township. That same area was later called Bridgeport when a bridge was constructed over the Conococheague Creek and then Markes, after it had been confused with another town in Pennsylvania called Bridgeport. Map by author.

area of Peter's Township by McDowell's Mill was formally called the village of McDowell's Mill until 1825.

Things in the area were initially calm. Trade with Indians was relaxed until activities in the western part of the state began to heat up. Fur traders had been working in the Ohio region now known as Pittsburg, traveling on paths which led past Mt. Parnell. The British government had given The Ohio Company of Virginia the right to trade in the Ohio Country in 1749 and they were to settle 100 families by a certain date and build a fort. The Proprietary of Pennsylvania had also proposed some form of protection for its own colonial fur trade interests to the west in 1750. The Governor had called for construction of a colonial fort or block house on the Ohio River but that was rejected by the pacifistic Provincial Assembly. The Assembly still believed that if any danger existed to the colony, it would be Britain's responsibility to send troops to defend the British colonies. The British government, however, viewed things differently and seemed to be more focused on protection of trade along the Atlantic Ocean arena of their colonies showing no interest in protecting the western frontiers.

The Pennsylvania government still believed that through treaties and fair dealings, there would be no trouble with Indians. Unlike other colonies, no forts were constructed by the government before 1755. While Pennsylvania procrastinated, Christopher Gist negotiated with Indians at Logstown in 1750 for The Virginia Ohio Company. The 1752 Treaty of Logstown with ½ King Tanachari and Iroquois Representatives resulted in the Indians giving permission for Gist to build a stone house at the mouth of the Monongahela River.

The Delaware Indians on the Ohio River had been relatively peaceful up to that point. The Pennsylvania government firmly believed that peace would continue because the Indians were dependent upon British trade goods which were of better quality than the French. The Six Nations, who had conquered the Ohio lands and made the Delaware subordinate to them, had once again allowed white settlements.[5] Dealing with only the Six Nations had gone well for the British, but not for the Delaware. Things intensified rapidly as the French began to incite western American

Indians into resentment against the British based upon unfair land losses, brokers by the Six Nations, also seen as enemies of the French.

There had been conflicts within the different Indian tribes in the west with some supportive of the British and some the French. They had not galvanized as yet. The Ohio area had had a relatively small cluster of tribes in 1731: 300 Delaware, 260 Shawanese, 100 Asswekalaes, and some Mingoes. There were a few Seneca on the Upper portion of the Allegheny River. By 1748 Conrad Weiser had reported 789 warriors, with the largest group being Delawares, then Senecas and Shawnees. Iroquois (Senecas and others) made up the rest. Their configuration had changed. They were hunters rather than established settlers, with Europeans infringing in their area, and their numbers were increasing as dissatisfied tribes clustered together, forming their own alliances.[6]

On March 17, 1752 the Governor-General of New France, Admiral Jacques-Pierre de Taffanel de la Jonquière, died. He had only served for three years. A temporary replacement was put in charge until Michel-Ange Duqesne de Menneville (1700–1778) could arrive. The French continued establishing trade with the western tribes. Many of the French traders inter-married with daughters of chiefs, and began guiding individual tribes towards the French interests. Promises of having help recapturing lost land by their new family members was appealing. On June 21, 1752, a party of Chippewa and Ottawa Indians led by a French officer, Charles Langlade, attacked the Miamis at Pickawillany. They killed and ate the pro-British Indian chief, scattering the tribe and traders. The Pennsylvanian province was unable to protect the friendly tribe.[7] This caused concern among the settlers as they looked in shock at the native's behavior. It caused concern among the Indian tribes in alliance with the English as well. Would the English be able to really protect them from their enemies?

The French had begun construction of a line of forts to connect New France/Canada with the Mississippi River and Louisiana, beginning at Fort Presqu'Isle on Lake Erie near Erie, Pennsylvania, and then moving south. They constructed Fort LeBoeuf near Waterford and Fort Machault on the Allegheny River in Venango County. In 1753 they set up posts on the upper Ohio River. They penetrated through the St. Lawrence River to the Great Lakes and beyond the Mississippi River.

Forts which were established also ran from Montreal to Niagara, Detroit and the Maumee and Wabash Rivers on to Ohio.[8] Pierre-Joseph Céloron de Blainville (1693–1759), French military leader and explorer, had led an expedition from Montreal down the Allegany River to the head waters of the Ohio River and then down the Ohio river to claim it in 1749 for France. He had buried up to six plates as proof of ownership, establishing friendships with western Indians in the process. He was unsuccessful in driving off the British traders at that time. Now the massive French undertaking in building forts, despite the October 1748 Peace of Aix-la-Chapelle which had ended the King Georges' War, was seen as an outright invasion. The French were administering these assertive moves in North America under the direct orders from the French King.

The Ohio Company which had attempted to lay claim to the Pittsburg area for themselves and had sent a young George Washington to survey land for his brother Lawrence Washington who was the first chairman or manager of the Company needed quick action. Lieutenant-Governor Robert Dinwiddie of Virginia, also a partner in the company, set things in motion. Twelve families headed by Virginia scout and surveyor Captain Christopher Gist (1706–1759) were busy trying to establish homesteads on the Monongalia River. A two story log storehouse had been built for the Company at the headwaters of the Potomac River opposite the mouth of Wills Creek. Roads had begun to be cleared along the trail from Wills Creek towards Redstone Creek on the Monongahela River. Families were setting up log cabins called "Gist's Plantation."[9] Virginia's actions were troubling to the Pennsylvania Assembly which saw that land as part of Penn's Woods. The Proprietary wished to protect their own trade and treaties but everything just stood still in the Assembly.

Virginia Governor Dinwiddie, on October 31, 1753, commissioned Major George Washington Adjutant of the Southern District of Virginia. He was to carry a communication of protest to the French Commander Jacques Legardeur de Saint-Pierre (1701–1755) at Fort Le Boeuf.[10] The Fort was located about 15 miles from Lake Erie in current Waterford,

Pennsylvania, at the fork of French Creek on the banks of Le Boeuf Creek. It was a trade fort. The letter demanded to know by what authority the French occupied British land and asked them to leave British territory at once. Washington was to wait for a reply.

Washington began his journey the end of November of 1753, joined by Christopher Gist. They moved toward Fort Venango in Franklin and traveled through rough country to Fort Le Boeuf were he delivered the governor's letter only to be rebuffed by the French Commander who said such a request should go to the Major-General of New France in Quebec City. While at the fort, however, Washington took notes about the structure and the strength of the French. It seemed to him that the French were determined to hold the territory by force.

Twenty-two year old Washington arrived back in Virginia in mid-January having failed his mission only to be sent out again as a newly promoted Colonel with a regiment of 400 Virginia volunteers to build Fort Prince George at the forks of the Ohio where the Allegheny and Monongahela Rivers feed into the Ohio River at present day Pittsburg. The Virginians were to construct the fort at the spot used by fur trader William Trent (1715–1787) who then became the commander of the fort for a short time. The French responded by strengthening their posts and on April 18th they arrived at Fort Prince George with a superior force. The Virginians were forced to surrender the fort which was promptly dismantled by the French. The French then proceeded to construct Fort Duquesne/Du Quesne in the same area to honor the Marquis Du Quesne, current Governor-General of New France. The fort was intended to control the three rivers, however it was prone to flooding and swampy. It was also surrounded by the high ground of the Monongahela River enabling an enemy the vantage point of looking down on it, making it difficult to defend.

George Washington's party of about 40 soldiers and Indian allies was at the Great Meadows on May 24, 1754, when they learned that a French patrol was in the area. Washington's men attacked the Canadian scouting party at Jumonville Glen, Union Town, Pennsylvania, on May 27–28, killing ten French and taking twenty-one prisoners. The commander of the French party, Joseph Coulon de Jumonville (1718–1754), was killed during this action[11] and the engagement was named the Battle of Jumonville Glen after his loss. Many of Washington's men were also killed by Indians. This is considered the beginning of the French and Indian War. Washington ordered the rapid construction of a fort called Fort Necessity at Great Meadows in early June, however on July 3rd a superior French force arrived with 600 French and 100 Americans Indians. Washington only had 300 Colonial and British troops at that point and they were forced to surrender Fort Necessity on July 4th. Washington's troops marched sadly towards Wills Creek and Fort Cumberland in Maryland. The French now held both Fort Duquesne and Fort Necessity.

The French and Indian War, or La Guerre de la Conquête (the War of Conquest) as French Canadians called it, was part of the Seven Years War. The Seven Years War was a global conflict involving Sweden, Austria and France allied to crush the rising power of the King of Prussia, Frederick the Great, who was in alliance with the King of England. The French and Indian War, however, was fought on the North American continent.

Indian attacks on frontier settlers had occurred prior to this but they were isolated to a few abductions and murders. Things began to change rapidly after the fall of Fort Necessity and they would increase over the next ten years.[12] This loss by Washington resulted in great concern on the part of those living on the frontiers, which at the time was mainly the east side of the Appalachian Mountains. Pennsylvania voted money for militia following the loss, but the bill was not signed as the French sent more reinforcements to New France.[13]

During 1754 both the French and English tried to strengthen their positions. The English colonies had a larger population of settlers than the French but they were scattered along the Atlantic coast. England had focused on fostering homesteads and trade. The French were more concentrated, and most were military personal, united in faith, Roman Catholic. New France had been established as a naval venture for the fur trade.

With the possibility of an escalating conflict, British Governor William Shirley of Massachusetts (1694–1771) ordered two forts constructed on the Kennebec River to protect the northern Colonies from

French Quebec.[14] A Congress of the Colonies met with members of the Six Nations on June 19, 1754, to design a plan for defense. The English King learned of the Congress of Colonies and expressed concerned that the power in the hands of representatives of the people in North America was becoming too great. In Pennsylvania, Governor Hamilton resigned and was succeeded by Robert Hunter Morris (1754–1756), son of Lewis Morris, Chief Justice of New York and New Jersey, and Governor of New Jersey.[15] He succeeded his father as Chief Justice of New Jersey. It was not uncommon for British officials to hold multiple offices. The British Government called for 3,000 Pennsylvania volunteers but their focus was again on protecting the Atlantic coast from the French navy.

The new Governor of Pennsylvania addressed the Assembly in August of 1754 with concerns he had received from those on the frontier. It seems the people of the Cumberland Valley and upper Lancaster County were afraid of French and Indian attacks and they lacked an ability to protect themselves. They needed arms and ammunition. Those with money did not have access to weapons to purchase them. They requested aid but the governor's hands were tied because the Assembly refused to release money.[16] Had this plea from those on the frontier been acted upon by the Assembly at this early date, it may have avoided some of the needless blood shed that followed.

Some of the accounts of McDowell's Mill Fort mention John McDowell fortifying his mill as early as 1753. If that date is accurate, it would have been in response to the loss of Fort Prince George and Fort Necessity, in anticipation of attacks by the French to the west. His mill and house are described as having a liberal amount of loop holes through which one could fire. The log mill with log home thirty yards from it may have offered some type of defense combined. It would seem likely that the mill had some type of modest enclosure, Members of the same Presbyterian connection were also enclosing other properties. McDowell's Mill Fort was referenced as a fort in 1754 by John Armstrong, so the mill was functioning within the community in that role at that time.

John Armstrong of Carlisle (1717–1795) is credited as designing the 1754 militia plan for the Cumberland Valley. It was called a *Plan for*

Becoming a Chief Fort in Gen. Braddock's Campaign

Defence of the Frontier of Cumberland Co. from Philip Davies to Shippensburgh, 1754. It would be enacted upon later and reads as follows:

> Let one Company cover from Phillip Davies to Tomas Waddel's; And as John M'Dowell's mill is at The most important Pass, most exposed to Danger, has a Fort already made about it, and there provisions may be most easily had, for these Reasons let the Chief Quarters be there; let five men be Constantly at Phillip Davies's, William Marshall's, and Thomas Waddle's, which Shall be relieved every Day by the patrolling Guards; let Ten men be Sent early every morning from the Chief Quarters to Thos. Waddle's, and Ten return from thence back in the Evening. A likewise Ten men Sent from the Chief Quarters to the other Extremity daily, to go by William Marshal's to Philip Davie's and return the Same Way in the Afternoon. By this Plan the whole Bounds will be patrolled twice every Day, a watch will be constantly kept at four most important Places, and there will be every Night fourty-five Men at ye Chief Quarters ready for any Exigence.
>
> Another Company may cover as much more of the Frontier, beginning where the first Ends and reaching towards and back of Shippensburgh, by fixing a Chief Quarters in some convenient Place about the Middle of Said Bounds, and from Thence patrolling the Ground twice a Day, and keeping watches at ye most proper Places, as above; One of which watches may be constantly at Mr. Armstrong's, and another at the proper Place at ye othe Extremity.
>
> This Plan Supposes each of ye Companys to consist of 60 men in all, as fewer cannot So patrol, keep Watch, and leave any Force together to answer Such Exigencies as may occur. These may be furnished by deducting 17 out of Each of ye four Forts back off our Frontier. This leaves 60 in each Fort, and makes up a new Company of 60 men, and Eight to be added to Cap. Peter's Company.[17]

It was clear that McDowell's Mill was at an important pass and well known in that region in 1754. The phrase "fort already made about it," implies some type of enclosure, perhaps less sophisticated than the one later added. The fact that the plan was designed for it to be the "chief quarters" shows that it was capable of sustaining a small force of men even at that point. The phrase "there provisions may be most easily had" means that it had a type of sustainability due to water access and a mill for grinding grain. The McDowell family was quite large, and many of them served in the volunteer militia. They were also elders in the community and public leaders which might have given them influence. They, with neighbors, may have made some type of enclosure which could not only protect family members but would be capable of assisting their community which were largely congregants.

The governor, however, was at loggerheads with the Assembly. He tried to establish some type of voluntary militia, but the Assembly was set on not providing for the bearing of arms. He greatly feared the defection of friendly Indians under French influence. Conrad Weiser was sent in September to Aughwick to meet with George Croghan, Indian agent, and the Indians under Croghan's charge. Shortly after the giving of gifts to restore the "chain of friendship," an Indian of the Six Nations named Izerall/Israel killed Joseph Campble/Campbell, a trader, at the house of Anthony Thompson near Parnall's Knob at the foot of the Tuscarora Valley.

George Croghan, writing to the governor with poor spelling from Aughwick on September 27, 1754, mentioned that he traveled to "Antoney Thomsons" with several Indian chiefs. He met William Maxwell, Esq. there but Israel had escaped. Depositions were taken, speeches made by the chiefs, and all testimonies were then forwarded to the governor.[18] John McDowell's niece Mary, daughter of his brother James, would later marry Captain Thomas Campbell who was the son of James and Rebecca Brown Campbell of this family. They would have been tightly tied to the events occurring near their homes.

Croghan went on to state in his letter that the French, according to his sources, had received reinforcements and provisions from Canada at their fort in the Ohio territory. He mentioned Indians gathering there as well. He felt his own life was in danger. He reminded the Governor that the back country of Virginia and Maryland were protected by the English Camp, but not Pennsylvania. He felt that the friendly Indians were uneasy since they did not see the English making preparations to attack the French. He warned that if the friendly Indians joined the French, then the back settlements would be in danger. He proved correct in his assessment.

The Duke of Cumberland, back in England, believed that war with the French in the colonies would be inevitable, but the King did not want to send his regular troops to America, instead he pushed for raising two regiments in America and sending only two regiments of British regulars with an officer. Major-General Edward Braddock III (1694–1755) of the Coldstream Guards was chosen to lead the action. Braddock, a commoner, had worked his way up the military ladder serving the crown in Europe. He purchased his commission like most commoners, since the highest ranking officers in the royal army were nobles. Braddock had served as acting governor of Gibraltar and there was some speculation that he might become a colonial governor.[19] He was to assume the command of the British troops in North America.

Braddock had no concept of the wilderness terrain into which he would march or understanding of American Indian warfare. He was used to conflicts in Europe in areas surrounded by villages with those schooled in the gentlemen's type of warfare. His understanding of the economic conditions in the colonies was limited, feeling that they should have materials in place for his campaign which they clearly did not. He seemed unaware of the aggressive competition between the colonial governments and their lack of unity.

Braddock was instructed: "You will not only cultivate ye best Harmony & Friendship possible with ye several Governors of our Colonies & Provinces, but likewise with ye Chiefs of ye Indian Tribes . . ."[20] This he was never able to do. Sir John St. Clair was to serve as the Deputy Quarter Master General in America and he left early on. Two regiments of Foot, with 1000 men raised in the colonies, would be commanded by Governor Shirley of New York and Sir. Colonel William Pepperell.

The colonies were to provide fresh food and provisions for the troops. Governors were ordered to supply transports and other necessities.

The two British regular Foot Regiments, 44th and 48th, had been raised in Ireland in 1741 and fought Scots in the second Jacobite rebellion. They were to be enlarged from 500 to 700 men each. The 44th was commanded by Sir Peter Halkett and the 48th was commanded by Colonel Thomas Dunbar. Dunbar was a weak commander and suffered from bad health, yet he was chosen as second in command even though some felt Halkett would have served better in that office.[21] The recruits in these two regiments were not the best examples of British military organization. Lee McCardell, in his book *Ill-Starred General: Braddock of the Coldstream Guards*, went so far as to state that they came from "jails, slums, and gin shops, the majority of the privates in the regiments of the line were dirty, discontented, and debauched, insolent and insubordinate, drinking when off duty until blind drunk. The Forty-Fourth and the Forty-Eighth were two of the most worthless regiments in the army."[22] Strict discipline was enforced on the men, but their rebellious natures would surface later when put to the test.

The movement of troops to the colonies was not kept a secret. The London papers printed full reports of Braddock's plans. The French had no trouble tracking the soldiers as they departed for America in the fall of 1754, and had ample time to prepare for battle and observe their progress. Major-General Braddock was confident he would succeed, and do so quickly. The two Royal Irish regiments, and colonists from Virginia and other colonies would address the French in proper order. Indians would prove to be no problem to his way of thinking when compared to well-trained British forces.

Sir John St. Clair was ordered to establish a hospital in Hampton, Virginia, since some of the troops coming from the West Indies were sick. He was also to oversee recruitment with the best going into the British regulars. He was to assemble the wagons and horses for transport and check out the buildings at Fort Cumberland on Will's Creek in Maryland. He also was to check on the navigability of the upper Potomac River as the plan was to use the river for transport.

While the two nations were preparing to dominate each other, the Cumberland Valley Presbyterians called Reverend John Steele to be the minister of the Upper West Conococheague Church at what was is known as Church Hill. Rev. John Steel actually had two charges; East Conococheague Presbyterian Church in Greencastle and the Upper West Conococheague Presbyterian Church in Smith's Town. Two locations had been discussed for the log meeting-house of the Upper West Conoocheague Church. One location was Church Hill and the other was at Gardners, also know as Waddell's, Eckerts and now Spring Grove Cemetery near Lemasters. A cemetery was established at that location

Most of the descendants of patriarch William McDowell are buried at Spring Grove Graveyard in Lemasters, Pennsylvania. The area was one of two spots members of the Upper West Conococheague Presbyterian Church evaluated for their church home. Though not chosen, the cemetery was established and first called Waddell's and then Etters. Row upon row of McDowell tombstones can be seen beneath the shade of the large trees. Agnes McDowell, John's wife, is reported to be the earliest recorded burial, though many were buried without stones in the mid-1700s due to fear the bodies would be desecrated by Indians and scalped for the reward offered by the French. Burials often took place at that time at night under guard.

with the intention of servicing the church but the location was not chosen by the congregation. The McDowell's and others, however, used the cemetery for generations of family burials. The Upper West Conococheague Church at Church Hill came under the Presbytery of Donegal in Lancaster County.

The Rev. John Steel was a calm religious man who gradually stepped into military leadership in order to protect members of his congregations. He was formally installed as pastor of the White Church in 1754. He was known during the period of conflicts with the French and Indians to have entered his church with his rifle in hand. He placed his hat and rifle on the wall behind him before preaching, picking them both up after the benediction, ever ready to meet a crisis. He once ended a service early to go after intruders with men from his congregation. He became a galvanizing force in both of his congregations with membership which spread for miles in all directions, encouraging them to protect themselves and their neighbors.[23] Services generally took most of Sunday with worship in the morning from 10:00 A.M. to 12:00 P.M., lunch brought by the members, and another service, perhaps focused on the catechism and denominational confessions, took much of the afternoon. Most of the valley was Ulster-Scot Presbyterian. One did not visit an Ulster-Scot on the Sabbath, it was a holy day.[24] The Church would not only meet the spiritual needs of a wide radius of families, but also supply the area with civic leaders and military forces. Rev. Steel would soon lead a company of men through the Indian Wars and during the Revolutionary War. His elders would do the same.

The colony of Virginia had parleyed heavily at court to have Braddock advance through their colony, encouraging the building of a military road towards their commercial interests in the Ohio Valley. This was accepted. Braddock's orders from the crown had been to drive the French from Fort Duquesne and to garrison that fort. From there, he was to reduce the French forts at Niagara, Ontario, Champlain, Crown Point, and Beausejour on the Nova Scotia isthmus. Braddock could name his own subordinate officers for this campaign.[25] Colonel St. Clair was ordered to establish a magazine, park of artillery, and a hospital at Fort Cumberland. A better equipped hospital was to be at Hampton, Virginia.

Sir John St. Clair arrived in Virginia in January of 1755 but he found no buildings to use for a hospital at Hampton, only two small warehouses which became the hospital. The colony was poor, relying primarily on tobacco crops. There were no quarters for troops and no lumber had been set aside for that purpose. The roads were also in poor condition. There were no horses, wagons or supplies anywhere. Worse still, there were no places troops usually frequent when off duty. The upper Potomac River had rapids and could not be used to transport material, and Fort Cumberland at Wills Creek in Maryland was rustic and had nothing in place for the army.

Major-General Braddock arrived from England later in February ready to lead an enlarged force of 2,200 men, including the two British troops of 700 men each, with provincials from Virginia, Maryland and North Carolina. Pennsylvania had sent only volunteer frontiersmen led by George Croghan and Andrew Montour with 100 Indians.[26] The colonies, by King's order, were not only expected to provide volunteers for a colonial regiment, but supplies, wagons and horses for transporting goods. Braddock expected these items to be in place when he arrived and for there to be adequate housing for his troops. This caused friction between the British army and the colonial governors. General Braddock was within his legal rights to impress wagons for the army's service, which he often threatened to do, but there were none to be had in Virginia. British soldiers looked around in dismay and their dislike of their colonial cousins began to grow.

Pennsylvania, on the other hand, was considered the bread basket of the colonies but Braddock did not enter via Philadelphia.[27] Pennsylvania was prospering but it had a frugal pacifistic Quaker Assembly which held the purse strings tightly. New England was focused on the protection of its own colony from French Canada. Carolina had no money and Maryland, largely Catholic, was under suspicion by Braddock. He needed to increase his provincial regiments quickly, but many of the recruits from the log fort at Wills Creek were between ages 60 and 70 and semi-crippled. Eighty from Maryland were deemed fit, but forty from New York were called invalids and were dismissed. Some were referred to as "idle, drunken fellows."[28] Those who were less fit were assigned to be carpenters and rangers.

Braddock was frustrated as he sent out recruiting officers to Maryland, Virginia and Pennsylvania. He was particularly pointed against the Quaker led Pennsylvania Assembly who were not willing to provide defense for their own colony. He was shocked as he wrote about "one of the Principal Colonies preserving a neutrality when his Majesties Dominions were invaded, when the Enemy is on the Frontier."[29] Governor Morris undercut his own Assembly's conduct to Braddock calling them "absurd."[30] The Pennsylvania Assembly held back money, and later the Governor was forced to take matters into his own hands, contributing to the loss of control of the Quakers in the government of Pennsylvania.

The Governor of Pennsylvania was mortified by his Assembly's lack of assistance. He wrote to Sir John St. Clair on February 10, 1755, to cover himself. He had ordered the best maps made for the venture. He stated that there was an open wagon road to the Mouth of the Conocochegue but no wagon roads from Carlisle west through the mountains, only a horse path that the Indian traders used. He would sent a copy of a map of that path right away. He wrote that the Assembly had agreed to send flour to the mouth of the Conocochegue.[31] He then ordered a survey for a road from Shippensburg to intercept the army road from Will's Creek to Fort Duquesne. The task was given to George Croghan, John Armstrong, James Bird, William Buchanan and Adam Hoops. The men were to examine "all the Marshes, Swamps, Rivers, Creeks, and Waters, together with the Passes in the several Ranges of Hills . . . carefully and as secretly as my be to survey and lay out such Roads as you shall judge most direct . . . with all possible Expedition . . ." including distances and where they might need "causeways and Bridges" with an estimate of cost.[32]

Braddock had been given incomplete maps of the territory from Virginia to Duquesne which did not have accurate distances and did not show the many obstacles he would meet. What appeared to be a direct route for construction of a road through Maryland became a long arduous process hacking out brush through the wilderness, with numerous rivers and creeks to cross. The shortage of horses and wagons prevented rapid movement of material. The lack of materials meant soldiers without supplies. The construction of the military road would be a slow process because Braddock expected his road to be perfectly level and wide enough for his fancy carriages and large cannon. This proved not possible. He also had bridges constructed over the many waterways and seemed to creep along which frustrated George Washington, his aidde-camp, who recommended a quick attack on the French with material carried by pack-horses. While Braddock's men inched along, the French watched the whole process and used the time wisely.

By the time Braddock finally reached Fort Cumberland, he was shocked to find a simple rustic fort with no supporting taverns and shops. To make matters worse, meat coming from the colony of Maryland had spoiled reroute and there were no cattle at the fort. Braddock ordered a public market be set up with fixed prices but the settlers in that area had no food to sell, only whiskey.[33] While at the fort, Braddock was briefed by friendly American Indians about the strength of the French, but he discounted much of their intelligence. Washington, acquainted with the territory who might have provided helpful information, became sick during this period and had to temporarily leave, re-joining the army later.

Braddock was furious with the colonies, particularly Pennsylvania, for disobeying the King's orders to supply the troops. Edward Shippen wrote a fearful letter to his father on March 19th, 1755, about Braddock's charges of "faction and disaffection" and he mentioned Braddock's blustering: "he shall take due care to burthen those colonies the most, that show the least loyalty to his Majesty; and lets them know that he is determined to obtain, by unpleasant methods, what it is their duty to contribute with the utmost cheerfulness. The Assembly know not how to stomach this military address, but 'tis thought it will frighten them into some reasonable measures, as it must be a vain thing to contend with a General at the head of an army, though he should act an arbitrary part; especially as in all probability he will be supported in everything at home."[34]

Governor Morris ever pointed to his rebellious Assembly. He also mentioned that the recruiting happening for men in Philadelphia was done by Governor Shirley's son and those men were to go to his father's regiment up north. Benjamin Franklin of Philadelphia, the Deputy Postmaster General of the North American Colonies, was listening to the growing problem and finally took it upon himself to intercede. He would secure Pennsylvanian goods, wagons and horses for the British forces. Franklin had gone to Frederick County, Maryland, under the guise of setting up mail posts for General Braddock's army and after seeing the anger of the British officers, he diplomatically commented that had Braddock landed in Philadelphia, he would have found a partial road in place and plenty of supplies for his venture.

> Our assembly, apprehending from some information, that he {Braddock} had received violent prejudices against them as averse to the service, wished me to wait upon him, not as from them, but as post-master-general, under the guise of proposing to settle with him the mode of conducting with most celerity and certainty, the dispatches between him and the governors of the several provinces, with whom he must necessarily have continual correspondence; and of which the proposed to pay the expense. My son accompanied me on this journey.[35]

Franklin tried to break down Braddock's "prejudices" and seeing that there were only 25 wagons in Maryland, most not serviceable, Franklin proceeded to print hand bills and distribute them in Lancaster, York and Cumberland Counties in Pennsylvania. He called for 150 wagons with four horses each and 1500 pack-horses to assist the campaign. All would be under a contract for hire and were to gather at Lancaster and York. Each wagon with driver would receive 15 shillings per day and horses with pack-saddle or saddle would receive 2 shillings per day. A horse without saddle would fetch 18 pence per day. These would proceed to Will's Creek about May 20 and travel would be counted from the stated date to the date of discharge with a price set for loss. Braddock's paymaster would give a seven day pay advance to make it more desirable and they would not be considered soldiers. Anyone coming with extra oats, Indian corn or forage would receive additional compensation.

Many locals from the Cumberland Valley contributed wagons and horses to the campaign, after all the service was promised to be "light and easy" with only 12 miles per day.[36] Local flour was to be delivered to the Conochocheague by March 20th. Mills like McDowell's might have also been used to process flour. Franklin's son William was the one who contracted people in Cumberland County.

Franklin mentioned to Braddock that Indian ambushes were a real threat to the army campaign. He felt that proceeding in a long and slender line was dangerous. Braddock, however, dismissed this, feeling that well trained British troops would be more effective than "raw American Militia" at addressing the Indians and French.[37]

The maps, at the time, showed no direct way to connect the Pennsylvanian goods to the advancing army, so a Pennsylvanian military road was commissioned. The existing road west from Philadelphia would be widened. Construction would also begin at McDowell's Mill and extend west over the mountains through Raystown (Rea's Town/Ray's Town/now Bedford) to the three forks of the Youghiogheny River, also called Turkey Foot or Crow's Foot, where it would meet with Braddock's road. The Pennsylvania military road would be a shorter, parallel route to Braddock's wandering road. It would allow for faster communication back east, and delivery of supplies west.

A road already existed from Carlisle south through the Cumberland Valley via Shippensburg. It had been extended to McDowell's Mill as a rough wagon road. Colonel James Burd would be in charge of cutting the new road ten to thirty feet wide using 300 Pennsylvanian men who hacked out the ground using picks, hatchets and explosives.[38] Sir John St. Clair would be in charge of the supplies on this route.[39] This proved to be a difficult task with continual shortages of men and supplies.

Governor Morris reported to Sir Thomas Robinson on April 9th that the recruits ordered in America had nearly met their quota. He had pressed his Assembly to grant supplies, provisions and necessaries and had opened roads and provided carriages for the expedition. He was still fighting with his Assembly over access to their proceedings and he wrote about the "Danger of such Powers in the Hands of any Assembly, and especially of one annually chosen by a People, a great part, if not a Majority of whom are Foreigners, unattached to an English Government, either by Birth or Education. And as none of these things are warranted by the Proprietary Charter, under which the Assembly act. Or in the least countenanced by the Proprietaries themselves, I think them the more extraordinary, and very worthy the Notice of the Government."[40] The struggle over self-government would only increase in cities like Philadelphia.

The commissioners for the road west in Pennsylvania reported to the Governor that they had ridden west from Carlisle through the wilderness on March 29th with difficulty and had reached the Youghiogheny on April 11th. They learned of Indians in the area and their Indian guides fled. They wrote about the difficulty of travel over the mountains and that St. Clair was giving them trouble, complaining that the road should have been approved by the Pennsylvania Government back in January.

The road crews were being mistreated and soldiers were ordered not to lift an axe. They reported issues between the Soldiers and Virginian men. Soldiers threatened the inhabitants with the possibility of killing cattle, impounding horses and burning houses. They told the road crews that if they were defeated by the French due to Pennsylvania's delays, then soldiers while returning with sword drawn would "pass through it, and treat the inhabitants as traitors to his master; that he would, to-morrow, write to England by a man-of-war, shake Mr. Penn's proprietaryship, and represent Pennsylvania as a disaffected province; that he would no hesitate to impress our Assembly, for his hands were not tied."[41] They were told to tell the Governor and Assembly just that. Burd communicated that he would forward drafts of the road proposal to the Governor on April 27th but Armstrong would report in May that the road choppers would not go beyond Raystown without some type of armed cover. The Indians in the area were active.[42]

General Braddock urged Governor Morris of Pennsylvania to hurry supplies to his army along the military road that was to pass near McDowell's Mill in the spring of 1755. Morris in turn wrote to Thomas Penn in May about the opening of the road to the Forks of the Youghiogheny. He hoped to have it finished with 100 men working at that time. Mr. Peters was charged with hiring more men.

Morris wrote to Col. James Burd at Sideling Hill from Mr. Maxwell's on May 27, 1755. The General had okayed the narrowing of the width of the road but wanted it "good and easy for wagons, in every low, stony, or hilly place."[43] Morris mentioned that if his Assembly did not pay for the road, Braddock promised to repay him. He had 150 wagons and 600 horses ready.[44]

Peters wrote to the Governor shortly after this from Shippensburg, after speaking with John Armstrong, and commented that only 60 men were working on the road. Mr. Burd was called "equal to such a task, tho' a very good man, & well disposed."[45] Having cleared seven miles in ten days, he did not feel that they would finish in time. Peters requested more men from Mr. Shippen and he reported that 200 enlisted as a result. Peters also commented that he had rejected half of the horses collected from York County.

On May 20th there was a meeting near Sugar Cabins, between John Armstrong, James Bird/Burd, John Smith, William Buchanan, Joseph Armstrong, Richard Peters, and 108 workers, overseers and waggoneers. The road was then 30 feet wide and now reached 38 miles west from Shippensburg. They discussed making it 20 feet wide and in stony or marshy places only 10 feet wide to move the process along. They needed supplies to finish the project and they voted to consult Braddock on the matter.[46] Supplying the road crew seemed to be a difficult process and there were repeated requests for food, pay and material. Governor Morris, later that month, wrote to Peters encouraging him to place ads for road laborers amongst the Dutch (maybe also Deutsch/German) and English.

Working on the new road was not without danger. The men were attacked by American Indians. One event involved eighteen year old James Smith who had been born in Cumberland County in 1737. His relative and later brother-in-law, William Smith, Esq., was one of the Conococheague Commissioners, overseeing men in the construction of the Pennsylvanian military road. In May of 1755, James was sent from Raystown (Bedford) back eastwards towards McDowells Mill Fort to see how far the supply wagons were progressing on the new road. When he began his return trip to Raystown to tell the others of their progress, he was captured by a Canasatauga and two Delaware Indians near Ligonier and taken to Fort Duquesne. His partner, Arnold Vigoras, was shot. Smith was badly beaten by the Indians at the French fort and his wounds were dressed by a French doctor. He would learn of the fate of Braddock while at that fort as a prisoner.

Smith was eventually adopted into the Caughnewaga tribe and was kept with them until his escape in 1759. During that time, he learned Indian customs and warfare practices. He would use his new skills when released, becoming a Lieutenant under General Bouquet for the expedition against the Ohio Indians in 1764. James was also a Captain of a Company of Rangers in Lord Dunmore's War, and in 1775 would be a Major of a regiment of militia, serving the Continental Army and then serving in the Assembly.[47]

John McCollough, and Richard Bard with his wife, were also taken during the 1755 period. Most of these people were part of the Reverent John Steel's congregation. John McDowell's niece Jane, daughter of James, would later marry Isaac Bard.

The supplies for Braddock's army were slowly accumulating in Pennsylvania. On June 3rd Governor Morris reported that 100 head of cattle, 112 barrels of Pork, 20 barrels of rice, 200 bushel of peas, with 240 more barrels of the finest cured pork coming. The rest of the meat in beeves was on its way. He hadn't decided at that point if it would go to Shippensburg or McDowell's Mill. Mr. Peters would later make the final decision. He would build store houses and get receipts for the items. Good pasture land was needed for the 300 head of cattle and the plan was to fatten them up as much as possible. In York, Lancaster and Cumberland County 1,200 barrels of flour had been secured which would be stored either at Shippensburg or McDowell's Mill. The rest would soon be sent. He went on to say:

> "Mr. Peters, who on his way from the Camp came through Cumberland county, judges that a Place called McDowell's Mill

situated upon the new Road, about twenty miles Westward of Shippensburg, is much more convenient for the magazine than Shippensburg, which, if you approve of, you will let your Secretary notify your Approbation by the Return of this Express, to Charles Swain, at Shippensburg, who, by my Instructions, is to wait that Approbation before he begins to build or hire Shore-Houses, and in the mean Time he is to employ himself in procuring Pastures and purchasing the Flower."[48]

Morris also weighted the issue of sending bread rather than flour. Flour would need to be baked which would need to happen at a magazine. That would require bakers which he would secure. The bakery would need to be capable of supplying a large army. Unfortunately, the harvest in Pennsylvania for hay and corn would not be complete. He could only send a partial order until the crops were ready. Corn would not be ready until the beginning of August.

Much of the flour from the Assembly going to the Conocochegue had been placed in green casks which caused the flour to sour. He ordered each one checked to try to recover unspoiled flour and to repack it in seasoned barrels. The next day he reported the good news that forage had been purchased from Lancaster County. There were 1,000 bushels of oats, 1,000 bushels of Indian corn from Philadelphia, and wagons, oxen and sheep were making their way to the storage area. The road was now open to Sideling Hill but the workers would need a guard beyond Raystown.[49]

It appears that the construction of the store houses with the supplies to fill them began at McDowell's Mill Fort prior to the establishment of a formal stockade. In a June 12th letter to Richard Peters from William Allison and William Maxwell at the "Conegochege" we learn that the road crews were out of provisions and that wagons filled with bacon had left from John McDowell's on the 9th. They were being supplied from that fort before the Governor's stockade was in place. This also points to a temporary stockade.

The complaint in the letter was that the supplies were exhausted and all the salted meat in the county was gone. The laborers needed help and nobody had been empowered in that area with money to buy material. Wagoneers were also needed and those in service wanted to stick closely to their contracts, expecting the pay promised and would not take less. The line of supply was a major problem.[50]

Governor DeLancey of New York sent a letter of warning to Governor Morris on June 13th stating that he had learned through his sources that the French had incited Indians against General Braddock. They had warned him that the French would send the whole force in Canada against him. Governor Morris, in turn, addressed his Assembly, telling them that General Braddock had also warned him about French and Indians intending to sweep behind the army to attack the back country, killing the inhabitants. Morris told the Assembly to prepare and urged the establishment of a militia. "I must also recommend it to You, Gentlemen either by establishing a Militia or otherwise to enable me to protect the Inhabitants of the Back Country against the Incursions of the French and their Indians."[51] They did not respond favorably.

On the same day, Edward Shippen wrote to the Governor offering the use of "a Strong Stone House 30 feet square" at Shippensburg to store local supplies.[52] Shippen had felt a magazine ought to be constructed to house at least 20, or 30 soldiers within a stockade.[53] The town did not have a formal fort at that time. Shippen related that the military supply road was creeping along. Laborers were slowly coming forward to construct it and Burd had 200 men.

Though Shippen had pitched the use of Shippensburg, Charles Swaine's assessment in June and Mr. Peter's findings seemed to have swayed the Governor away from that town. Both had felt that the town lacked sufficient buildings for storage. There were only a few pastures but it did have water for cattle. There was little of what he "cellaring" to keep dried pork with theft of pork a real issue. There were also no bricks for ovens and little lime. Swaine went on to tell the Governor that money would be needed for a magazine, to pay cattlemen, and to create a watch for stores. Coopers in the area had their own plantations and would not be able to devote their skills fulltime to a fort. Mills in that area only provided course flour. Morris decided to send oxen there, but to not establish his Chief Fort for this campaign in that town.[54]

General Braddock gave his affirmation to having the magazine at McDowell's Mill on June 11, 1755. The army supplies from Pennsylvania would be gathered there and from that point they would be sent to Fort Cumberland in Maryland via Winchester, Virginia. Colonel Conrad Weiser would be able to enlist farmers from Lancaster, York and Cumberland County to provide supplies.[55]

The Pennsylvanian military road, running parallel to Braddock's road, extending west from McDowell's Mill over the mountains via an old Indian trail to Raystown. It was to intersect with Braddock's road at the place of the great crossing, by the forks of the Youghiogheny River. Raystown was located along the current route 30 and named after a fur trader named John Ray/Rae/Wray. The area had only begun to be settled in 1751.[56] The town would later be re-named Bedford after the Duke of Bedford. Colonel James Burd was the one overseeing the construction of the Pennsylvania military road, so it was referred to as Colonel Burd's Road. It was scheduled to be completed to Raystown by June,[57] but the men constructing the road complained about lack of money to feed their families back home.

The Pennsylvania Governor traveled to the Cumberland Valley with the intent to oversee the construction of a wooden stockade at McDowell's Mill and to secure the magazine which already existed there. He would hear about Braddock's fate while in the Cumberland Valley. While construction at the fort was underway, on June 21st through the 22nd, Indians killed and scalped 13 men, women and children on the border of Pennsylvania about four miles from Fort Cumberland at Wills' Creek. McDowell's Fort was close to that border. Edward Shippen in a June 30th letter to William Allen, Esq., a cousin, mentioned it as "last Monday" {22nd}. He stated that on Wednesday Indians had killed 7 more settlers. Shippen went on to write that General Braddock was a few miles beyond the Great Meadows at that time and that attacks behind the army movement had begun. Braddock only had 30 days of provisions for his men and needed the supplies from Pennsylvania as soon as possible. Some of his supply was at Will's Creek, Maryland, but the Indians were trying to cut off his communication and supply from that fort. Braddock lacked sufficient men to guard his own supply route.

Shippen also mentioned in his letter that Captain Hogg was with the Pennsylvania road-cutters and that Mr. Burd was at the Conococheague trying to secure wagons to carry provisions to feed those men and soldiers. They only had one and one-half days provisions and recently 14 road-cutters had deserted. Burd was unable to send fuses to the cutters to help fell trees and blast through rock. Sherriff John Potter had sent his son with forty head of cattle to try to help feed the cutters and Captain Hogg's men, but the Indian incursions were frightening people, and they were unwilling to venture out to the wooded area alone. Shippen was seeking in his letter money to pay the road-cutters for three months in order to keep them in place.

Conrad Weiser at Paxton, writing to John Harris at Harris' Ferry, related his version of the recent Indian attacks mentioning twenty inhabitants who had been killed or taken near Fort Cumberland. He called it a "desolation on the Potomac." Both Weiser and Harris had heard the settlers voice their suspicions of friendly Indians because English arms and goods had been found on Indians who had done the attack at Will's Creek. Those arms and goods had just been given to Indians who swore allegiance to England. He also stated a need to raise men for defense.[58] The settlers in their communications with each other came to the same conclusion, prepare. Colonel James Burd recommended the erection of a fort at Raystown which would happen in the future but not for Braddock's venture.

General Braddock wrote to the Governor on June 30th who was then in Carlisle, "My Chief Defendance must therefore be upon your Province, where the Road will be secure from Insults or Attacks of that kind. And lest it should not be in My Power to send a sufficient Number of Waggons or Horses, to bring up from the Magazine at M'Dowell's Mill, the Provision I may have Occasion for, I must desire You to direct Mr. Swaine or some proper Person, to have in view such a Number of 'em as may answer that Purpose, which shall be conducted to the camp under a proper Escort . . ."[59]

Braddock left Wills Creek on the Potomac River the end of June with 2,500 men. Supplies from McDowells had been formally requested. On July 3rd, 1755, Pennsylvanian Governor Morris wrote to Sir Thomas Robinson his compliance to Braddock's request. Morris confirmed the choice of McDowell's Mill Fort to Robinson because it was closer to Braddock's position. He told Robinson,

> I am laying in a magazine of Provisions in the back parts of this Province, and opening a road from hence to the waters of the Ohio. I wish my Assembly would have enabled me to have done these things at the expence of the Province, or even have regulated the Hire of wagons and price of provisions, but they have done nothing but promise to bear the Charge of opening the road, which I much doubt whether they will perform, and as to everything else are stil in the same ungiving temper, & will raise money upon no terms but such as will increase and render permanent their own power and lessen the authority of the Crown & Government.[60]

The same day he wrote Braddock about supplies gathered at Shippensburg: fifty-six thousand weight of "flower," and 100 oxen were ready

> . . . and will remain at Shippensburgh till I go up into the Country, which will be on Tuesday next, and then I shall form the Magazine at or near McDowalls Mill, and put some stucado's round it to protect the Magazine, and the people that will have the care of it; for without something of the kind, as we have no militia, and the Assembly will mentain no men, for or five Indians may destroy the Magazine whenever they Please, as the inhabitants of that part of the Province are very much scattered. Inclosed I send you a plan of the fort or stucado, which I shall make by setting Logs of about ten foot long in the ground, so as

to inclose the store houses. I think to place two swivel guns in two of the opposite Bastions; which will be sufficient to guard it against any attack of small arms . . .[61]

John McDowell most likely had done some type of fortification prior to the provincial plan, beginning in 1753 or 1754.[62] The log mill with loop holes and log home functioned as a type of simple fort and might have had a rustic enclosure. We also know that John's mill served as a store and that the store houses were now in place. Here we learn that the fort would have a ten foot high stockade surrounding the store houses, with two swivel guns in opposing bastions. Swivel guns were small cannons attached to a swiveling post or stand which were able to arc in different directions as needed. They were usually mounted on sailing ships and fired at short range and were about three feet in length. The bore diameter could be up to 1¼ inches, using small caliber rounds.

The above pen and ink drawing of Fort McDowell was created by Charles J. Stoner and featured on Eugene Etter's *History of Lemasters, Pennsylvania* book. Used by permission from Paula S. Reed, PhD, daughter of the artist. Also see the author's drawing of the fort later in the book.

Swivel guns could not stand heavy recoil and were limited in their use. They would not hold up to larger French artillery, but would discourage light troops. These were to be placed on "opposite Bastions" at the fort. The bastions may have been constructed at this point, but we learn much later of the arrival of the swivel canons.

Simple forts were usually stockaded by digging a four or five foot deep ditch around the area to secure the logs. Oak logs were placed vertically in the trench, usually cut to be 17 to 18 feet long though these would be shorter. The tops were pointed. The upright logs were cut flat on two sides to abut each other. They were then secured near the top with a horizontal piece which was spiked on the inside. The ditch was filled with soil to hold the logs perpendicular, and platforms were constructed on the inside of the enclosure four to five feet off of the ground. Those defending the fort were stationed on the platforms and fired through loop holes near the top of the enclosure. There were usually a few gates attached which were strong and could be secured when closed.[63] That would allow access to the fort when open and protection when closed. Block houses stored material and barracks housed men. It would have been a simple structure without frills. The issue of baking bread versus providing flour had been addressed. The fort had stores of flour and may have had a simple bakery, though most of the bread appears to have been baked at Fort Cumberland.[64]

Croghan's orders of December 1755 mentioned building some "stockadoes" in Cumberland County which were "Fifty feet square, with a Block-house on two of the corners, and a Barrack within, capable of Lodging Fifty men." McDowell's, however, served as a Chief Fort and was described as rectangular. It was built by a water source with a mill.[65] The fort would be called by many names: "McDowell's Fort," "McDowell's Mill," "McDowell's Mill Fort," "Fort at McDowell's Mill," "John McDowell's Mill," and just plain "McDowell's."[66] The spelling of McDowell varied greatly in reports, mainly because the colonies did not have standardized spelling and the settlers had a variety of educational levels. The fort was ready to supply Braddock, but would soon find itself in an entirely different role.

CHAPTER FIVE

1755–1756

McDowell's Mill Fort in the Defense of the Frontier

While the Pennsylvania Governor was busy with preparations in the Cumberland Valley, British officers in various colonies were preparing to follow their orders to assault the French at various points. Massachusetts Governor William Shirley was strengthening fortifications at Fort Oswego, Fort Bull and Fort Williams by Rome, New York, with preparations to attack Fort Niagara. Sir William Johnson was to capture Fort St. Frédéric at Crown Point, New York, and fortify Fort Edward on the upper end of the Hudson River where he would unsuccessfully engage the French in the Battle of Lake George between Forts Edward and William Henry. Fort William Henry would come under siege later. The French ultimately withdrew to Ticonderoga Point and began construction of Fort Carillon (later named Ticonderoga by the British). Colonel Monckton would be the only successful officer in this campaign with the capture of Fort Beauséjour on the border of Nova Scotia and Acadia in June. He was able to cut off land reinforcements to the French located at Louisbourg. Nova Scotia's Governor Charles Lawrence then deported French-speaking Acadians and American Indians.

McDowell's Mill Fort in the Defense of the Frontier

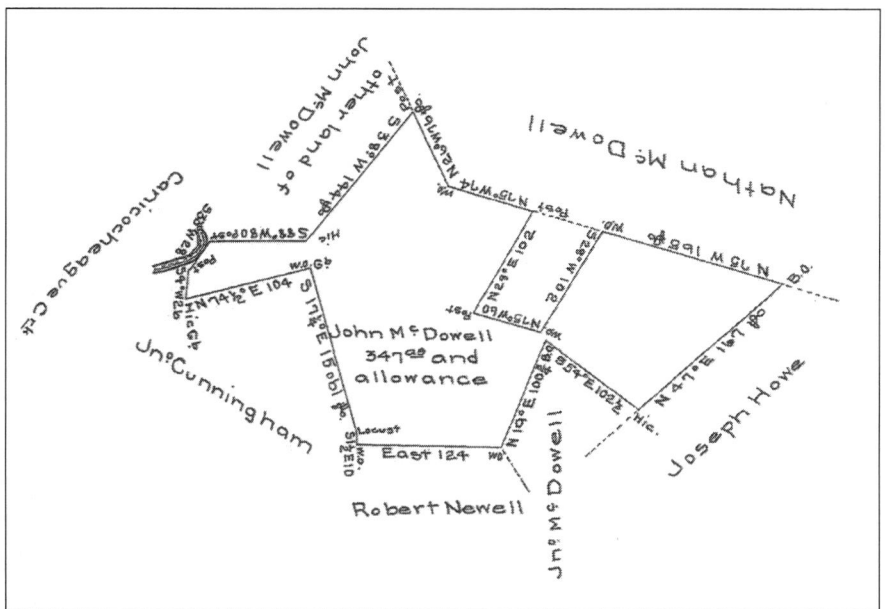

This March 17, 1769, survey of a 347 acre tract of land by John McDowell's mill was done by John Armstrong, Deputy Surveyor, who surveyed much of the McDowell's land. The tract was being added to John McDowell's existing property with an easement. The new tract has odd angles including a triangle pointing upward and the imprint of a rectangle all of which may mean unique land features. Though the fort is not listed on it, the precise rectangular shape, excluded in the purchase, cannot be a natural feature. It is part of the preexisting McDowell property. We know that the fort was a rectangular structure. This may very well be its outline.

This survey gives dimensions in perche or rods. According to Marty Curfman of Curfman and Zullinger Surveying, Inc. in Chambersburg, Pennsylvania, the perch measurement follows the bearing. This rectangle is 60 perches by 102 perches. One perch equals 16.5 feet making the rectangle 990 feet by 1,683 feet. The West Conococheague Creek to the left has one of its many spellings. The survey is available at the Pennsylvania State Archives and no permission was needed to reproduce it here. The warrant and survey information are H, 47, 681, C141, 223. To see this survey location in a modern context, see the author's illustration which follows.

General Braddock's army was headed to Fort Duquesne to drive out the French and he expected it would go well. His troops crossed the Monongahela River on July 9th with great fanfare, marching in their crisp red uniforms to fife and drum in single file. They did not see the

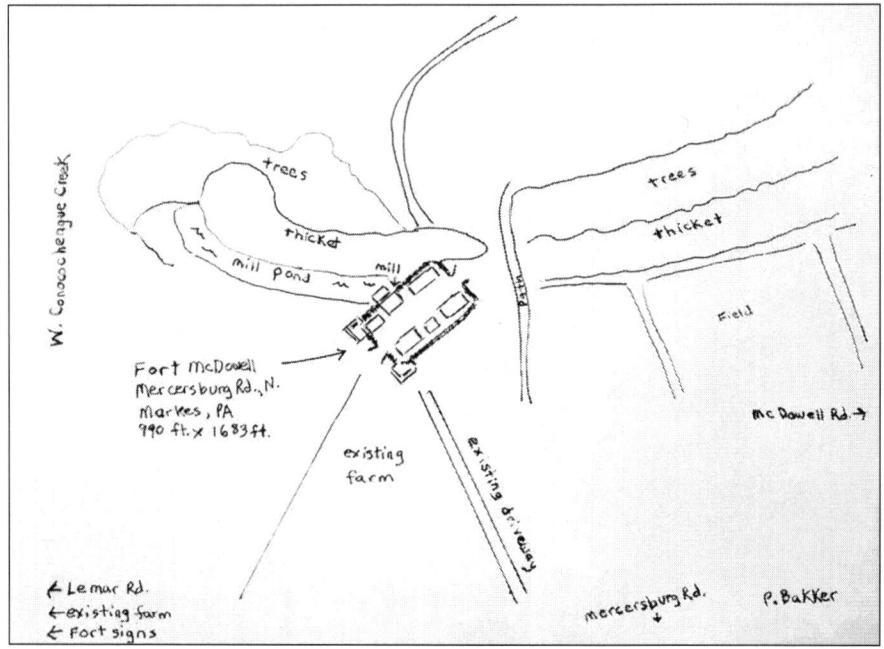

The author has attempted a drawing of the fort in its original location on Mercersburg Road.

ambush set before them. The French, with Indians, lay hiding in the bushes and woods. They found the British easy pickings. The Battle of the Monongahela would last only three hours.

As the attack commenced, Braddock's troops were in disarray with many deserting. Withdrawal was called but the forward retreating soldiers then collided into the rear advancing troops with many shot by friendly fire. Farmers in horse drawn wagons filled with supplies turned and fled homeward. It was a terrible loss with the British suffering about 900 casualties which included many of Braddock's officers among the wounded and dead. The French with their Indian allies suffered less than 50 casualties.

George Washington had two horses shot out from beneath him during the action. The fact that he was not wounded led some western Indians to believe that he had spiritual protection as a warrior. Braddock, however, was mortally wounded and carried from the scene back to Dunbar's

McDowell's Mill Fort in the Defense of the Frontier

This is an aerial view of the current location of the fort by the pond.

Camp.[1] Dunbar had stayed back with the baggage. Braddock died four days later on July 13th about one mile west of the Great Meadows and was buried in the road under George Washington's supervision. The men then marched over the grave to disguise it so that his body would not be desecrated by Indians. The French retained Fort Duquesne.

The costly venture came to nothing and the blame for its failure was dispersed on provincial governments and Braddock himself. Governor Shirley of Massachusetts blamed the battle's failure on the conception in England, appointment of the commanders, and the delays and expenses. England covered the failure with reports that European troops defeating Braddock, failing to mention American Indians.[2] George Washington blamed the slow pace of road construction as Braddock chose to ignore his desire to make a swift march using pack horses. Governor Morris received the news of Braddock's defeat while supervising Braddock's depot at McDowell's Mill Fort. He had laid up the stores at Shippensburg and McDowell's Mill without the aid of the Assembly.[3]

On July 20th Governor Morris wrote Governor Sharpe telling him that he had just returned from that area

> where I have been regulating the Magazine and putting the people into the best posture of defence I could, without money or any Militia Law, and have prevail'd on some of the inhabitants to arm themselves in defence of their familys. It was there I received the first accounts of the defeat-and the death of the Gen., which I collected from frighted Waggoners who had left the army, a number of whom are returned into this Province, and all I have seen agree in the same story, that the Gen. and many officers are kill'd and his whole division defeated, or rather destroyed; but their accounts are mostly hearsay from people that fled from the Gen.'s division, so that I am still at a loss to form a Judgmt. Of the state of our Army, but at all Events think it right to send all the men in our power, either to aid the retreat of our forces or to protect the Back Inhabitants, for this Purpose I have appointed my Assembly to meet on Wednesday next; but they have hitherto been deaf to the Calls of the Crown, I fear they will now be regardless of the present danger, or of the distress of the army sent to protect us . . . [4]

He was correct. Braddock's loss was a complete shock to everyone. The main body of troops returned to Fort Cumberland but some injured soldiers straggled along Burd's Road and sought refuge at McDowell's Mill Fort, Shippensburg and Carlisle, Pennsylvania. Morris asked Colonel Dunbar to post the remains of Braddock's army at those three posts.[5] Governor Shirley of Massachusetts, the new Commander of the British forces in North America, initially ordered Dunbar to move west to fix Braddock's mistakes but added that in case of defeat "to make the most proper Disposition of his Majesties' Forces to cover the Frontiers of the

Provinces, particularly at the Towns of Shippensburg and Carlisle, and at or near a place called McDowell's Mill, where the New Road to the Allegheny Mountains begins in Pennsylvania, from the Incursions of the Enemy until you shall receive further orders."[6] Governor Shirley initially had encouraged a strong presence at McDowell's Fort, but he never enforced it.[7]

Governor Morris wrote to General Shirley on July 30th asking him again to keep troops at the frontier through the winter. "you will, therefore, give me leave to propose to you to order that such parts of the troops as shall not be wanted for the Garrison of Fort Cumberland be posted in the Towns of Shippensburgh and Carlisle, and at or near a place called McDowell's Mill, where the new Road to the Allegheny Mountains begins, at which places there are numbers of houses for the soldiers, and where they can be well supply'd with every thing necessary . . ."[8] He warned that without them there the French and Indians would be able to penetrate into the settlement beyond the Susquehanna.

Morris estimated that Colonel Dunbar would be at the mouth of the "Conogogee" by August 7th. He also had heard reports through his sources that the loss was due to the bad conduct of the commanders. He fully expected Dunbar to stay in the Cumberland Valley, in fact he contacted the Justices and Sheriffs in Cumberland County the same day about his plan for Dunbar's troops with his desire for them to be posted at Carlisle, Shippensburg and McDowell's Mill. He asked the Justices and Sheriffs to take care of those troops.[9] He even wrote to Colonel Dunbar on the 31st asking him to continue on in the frontier. He pleaded, stating that if the grain in that area was lost and the inhabitants driven off that would hinder a future march against the French which everyone, even the French, expected. It would be difficult to supply an army without food from those inhabitants. He again requested that Dunbar post troops from the great road on the Potomac to Philadelphia "at or near the place called McDowell's Mill, at the Town of Shippensburg and town of Carlisle."[10] These three places were repeated often during the weeks following Braddock's terrible loss.

By August, the Governor was shocked to learn that Dunbar planned to withdraw his men to Philadelphia, leaving the frontier unprotected.

The soldiers had already expressed their disdain for the colonists. British military focus was again on the Atlantic seaboard rather than the frontier and Western Indians. When Dunbar's troops arrived in Philadelphia, they caused trouble there by loitering, drinking and fighting. Meanwhile, Governor Shirley designed his plans for the next campaign while in Albany. He would renew the plans to capture Fort Niagara, Crown Point and Duquesne. He would attack Fort Frontenac on the North shore of Lake Ontario and send an expedition through the wilderness of Maine, down the Chaudière River to attack Quebec, but his plan had little support. He ultimately informed the Pennsylvania Governor that he had his own plans for the British troops in Philadelphia. They would travel on to New York. Pennsylvania, Maryland and Virginia would have to defend themselves.

Governor Morris frantically tried to persuade his Assembly to create a militia but the Assembly adjourned without a vote. Governor Shirley was then replaced as Commander-in-Chief of the British troops in North America by John Campbell (1705–1782), the 4th Earl of Loudoun, in January of 1756 with Major-General James Abercrombie as his second. Lord Loudoun would also serve as the Governor General of Virginia but be recalled in 1757. Parliament was closely watching events in the colonies.

Col. James Burd (1726–1793) had been busy cutting the road in Pennsylvania to meet Braddock's road when on July 17, 1755, he learned the news from Fort Cumberland of Braddock's earlier defeat. Construction on that road abruptly ended at the summit of the Allegheny Mountains where Burd buried his tools. Indian war parties soon used the road for their assaults on the frontiers. Fort McDowell and other places in the Conocochegue Settlement were exposed and the road led war parties straight to the community. Indian bands with French soldiers were bolstered by their recent wins against the English. They began attacking the back settlements in Cumberland, Lancaster, York, Berks and Northampton Counties. The leaders of these raids on the Cumberland Valley were Chief Shingas (Shinges/Shingask/King Shingas), meaning bog meadow, and Indian "Captain Jacobs." A reward of seven hundred dollars was subsequently levied on each of their heads.

McDowell's Mill Fort in the Defense of the Frontier

Chief Shingas (1740–1763) was the leader of the Delaware Indians in the Ohio Country. They were based in Kittanning on the Allegheny River northeast of what is now Pittsburg. He was called "Shingas the Terrible" by Indians and settlers. Shingas was small in stature but considered a courageous and bloody warrior.[11] He had actually traveled with George Washington to Fort LeBoeuf in 1753. His uncle was Sasoonan, the Delaware King in alliance with the British, who had died in 1747. Shinga's brother, Pisquetomen (born about 1700), became the successor as leader but the British found him too self-empowered for acceptance, even though he spoke English very well. Disillusioned, Pisquetomen with brothers Tamaqua/Beaver (died 1769) and Shingas led their people west to Kittanning where they were caught between the British, French and Six Nations. They settled for an alliance with the French which gave them freedom from the Six Nations. The failed British Indian policies would have destructive consequences.

Captain Jacobs (died September 8, 1756) was actually Indian Chief Tewea. He was given the strange European name by an Englishman who felt he resembled a German living in Cumberland County. Jacobs allied with the French by default after being unable to secure trade goods from the Governor of Pennsylvania. He and Shingas made a deadly pair on the frontier.

70 settlers in the Cumberland Valley "heartily" joined as a company under Joseph Armstrong, Esq. in preparation for defense. They sent a letter to the Governor. In it they wrote, "Your Pettioners are at present in A most Dangerous Situation, as we live upon the frontiers, Expos'd to the Inhuman Cruelty of Barbarous Savages, and Nothing to Impede them or Defend Us, but the Sovereign Benignity of Almighty God, for we are in A Defenceless Condition, having Neither arms nor Amunition, and in this Lamentable Case . . ."[12] The same plea would be repeated often.

The Rev. John Steel was also watching over the Ulster-Scots in the valley. He encouraged his two congregations to construct strong houses for protection. He organized a company of voluntary rangers and was elected Captain. Reverend-Captain Steel had been staying at McDowell's Mill Fort.

Steel was out with a guard watching over harvesters near McDowell's Mill Fort on July 19th when Indians led by Shingas and Jacobs raided the group. One person was killed and two were taken prisoners.[13] A committee met in response on July 25th and supplied elder William Maxwell, Esq. with 50 guns, 1 ½ hundred weight powder and 2 ½ hundred weight lead for Peters Township.[14] Some of that material may have gone to McDowell's Mill Fort and some to Maxwell's house now converted into a log fort.

On July 30th the Upper West Conococheague Church began construction of a stockade around their building. Fourteen foot long logs were placed in a five foot deep ditch around the churchyard. The lower end of the logs were then covered with earth. The church/fort was re-named Fort Steel/Steele, or Fort at Steel's Meeting-House. It would be used to protect families, particularly women and children, from November 4, 1755 to about 1758.[15] The fort was three miles east of Mercersburg.

Below is a list of militia officers in voluntary Pennsylvania Provincial Service in 1755.

Officers of the Provincial Service, 1755[16]
Lieut.-Colonels James Burd, Benjamin Chambers, Conrad Weiser, and Timothy Horsfield
Major William Parsons
Captain George Croghan, at Aughwick
Captain Alexander Culbertson, at Lurgan twp., Cumberland County
Rev. Captain John Steel, at McDowell's Mill
Captain Christian Busse
Captain "Hans" Hamilton
Captain Jacob Morgan, Forks of Schuylkill
Captain James Wright
Captain William Trent, mouth of "Conegochege"
Captain Isaac Wayne, at Nazareth
Captain James McLaughlin

Officers of the Provincial Service, 1755[16]
Captain Frederick Smith, at Tolebaio and Monody
Captain Jonas Seely
Captain Adam Reed, on Susquehanna
Captain John Van Etten at Upper Smithfield, Northampton County
Captain _____ Craig at Lehigh twp., Northampton County
Captain _____ Trexler at Lyn and Heidelberg twp, Northampton County
Captain Nicholas Wetherholt
Captain Charles Foulk at Gnadenhutten
Captain Thomas McKee at Hunter's Mills
Captain James Patterson
Captain Rev. Thomas Barton
Captain Adam Hoopes (commissary)
Captain Dr. Mercer at Fort Shirley
Lieutenants _____ Davis, James Hyndshaw, William Spearing, James Hays

This is an additional list of settlers who joined as a company under Joseph Armstrong:

A Number of the Inhabitants of Cumberland County Heartily Joined as a Company, August 7, 1755

Captain Joseph Armstrong

Privates: John Armstrong, Thomas Armstrong, James Barnet, John Barnet, Joshua Barnet, Thomas Barnet, Sr., Thomas Barnet, Jr., Samuel Brown, Samuel Bown, John Boyd, Alexander Caldwell, Robert Caldwell, James Dinney, William Dinney, Robert Dixson, William Dixson, James Eaton, John Eaton, Joshua Eaton, James Elder, George Gallery, Robert Groin, James Guthrie, John Hindman, Abram Irwin, Christopher Irwin, John Irwin, John Jones, James McCamant, Sr., James McCamant, Jr., Charles McCamant, James McCamish, John McCamish, William McCamish, Robert McConnell, John McCord, William McCord, Jonathan McKearney, John

Machan, James Mitchell, John Mitchell, Joshua Mitchell, William Mitchell, Jon Moore, James Norrice, John Norrice, James Patterson, Joshua Patterson, William Rankin, William Rippey, Barnt Robertson, Francis Scott, James Scott, Patrick Scott, William Scott, David Shields, Matthew Shields, Sr., Matthew Shields, Jr., Robert Shields, Sr., Robert Shields, Jr., Jon Swan, Joshua Swan, William Swan, Charles Stuart, Daniel Stuart, John Stuart, Devard Williams, and Jon Wilson

Lieutenant-Colonel Conrad Weiser, Indian agent, was also concerned about settlers harassing and abusing friendly Indians. He complained to the Governor that rougher settlers, "curse and damn them to their faces, and say, 'Must we feed you, and your husbands fight in the meantime for the French?'"[17] He tried to keep treaties intact, but saw a growing problem. He defended settlers militarily but would often express the injustices done to local Indians and criticize the British Indian policies.

Petitions were also sent at this time to the Governor from the settlers in Lurgan Township in Cumberland County. They had formed a company of men under Alexander Culbertson, but were "destitute of arms and ammunition."[18] They asked the governor to "strengthen their hands with such a quantity of arms and ammunition, and upon such terms as your Honor sees fit . . ." Many within these communities were willing to fight but they were ill equipped.

Plans for the defense of Cumberland County were formally adopted on August 5th, but on the 6th two soldiers were killed within two miles of McDowells's Mill Fort with another wounded. The frequent attacks resulted in many settlers fleeing to the fort for protection or medical assistance. In response, Lieutenant-Colonel John Armstrong sent more soldiers to guard that fort.

Indians attacked settlers near the mouth of John Penn's Creek (Mahahany Creek) on the west side of the Susquehanna on October 16, 1755. They killed, scalped or carried away about twenty-five settlers in what is now Union. Their homes were burned and the area deserted.[19] One of those killed was Jacob King (Le Roy) from Switzerland. The inhabitants of the area sent a petition to Governor Morris, and on October 20th

John Harris wrote the governor about it stating that friendly Indians were also afraid and sought a meeting.

Forty-six inhabitants on the Susquehanna by Harris' Ferry met at Shamokin to speak to the Indians on October 23rd but were ambushed on their return with four killed, and four drowned.[20] Harris mentioned on October 28th that the Indians on the west branch of the Susquehanna were responsible. He also mentioned intelligence given him that French with 1,500 Indians were coming, composed of "Picks, Ottaways, Orandox, Delawares, Shawanese, and a number of the Six Nations."[21] Conrad Weiser had brought "500 weight of flour" to Indians at Aughwick in mid-July to try to appease them.[22] The stress on both settlers and Indians was mounting.

The same day settlers at Penns Creek were attacked, Indians were seen near William Maxwell's place on the Conococheague. There was another near-massacre of area settlers on October 25th as the Cumberland Valley was busy trying to organize itself for defense. More stockades were raised and log houses, churches and mills became fortified. Even with all this preparation, John Harris wrote from Paxton to Edward Shippen, Esq. on October 29th stating that the inhabitants were abandoning their plantations. He complained that there was "no sign of assistance" for the settlers. He was forced to cut loop-holes in his own house and he felt the Susquehanna Indians had turned towards the French. He urged for the construction of a fort in his town to counter work being done by a French officer in the area. He also suggested that local Indians should be made to take an oath of allegiance. Enemy Indians were spotted in the vicinity of Shamokin the end of October into November, with several murders. He questioned whether local Indians would remain faithful.[23]

Sheriff John Potter called a meeting at Edward Shippen's house on October 30th to discuss defense. Sheriff Potter lived by the Old Brown's Mill graveyard in a limestone house in what is now Franklin County. His house was also used for protection.[24] Present at that meeting at Shippen's house were William Allison, John Irwin, Adam Hoops, James Burd, William Smith, James McCormick, Benjamin Chambers, Robert Chambers, H. Alexander, John Findlay, John Potter, Rev. Ray, John Mushell, Samuel

Reynolds, Rev. John Blair, John Smith, Alexander Culbertson, and John Armstrong. They resolved to construct five large forts at Carlisle, Shippensburg, Chambersburg, Rev. Steele's Meeting-House (already begun on Church Hill) and William Allison, Esq.'s near Waynesboro. Women and children would be protected in these forts, and they would communicate with each other by patrols.

Small private forts already being used by people in the valley were voted to be strengthened. Colonel Benjamin Chamber's Fort in Chambersburg would have a stockade by 1756. Philip Davis' Fort would be constructed in 1756 eight miles south of McDowell's Mill Fort by the Maryland border on Fort Davis Road in Sylvan. Davis was a local Welsh tax collector and church leader. His fort was built on a small knoll known as Casey's Knob which overlooked Welsh Run, a stream.

John McDowell's Mill Fort was in place. On November 25, 1755, a delivery would be made to James Burd, Adam Hoops, John Potter and Joseph Armstrong of "Four swivel Guns; 5 Quarter Casks of Powder; 5 hundred w't of Lead; 2 Quarter Casks Powder; 2 hundred of Lead, for Chambers and McDowell's Mill."[25] It appears the swivel guns in the original plan had not been in place at McDowell's before Braddock's expedition but would now be installed.

William McCord's Fort was erected between 1755 and 1756. It was at the base of the Kittatinny Mountain, north of Parnell's Knob. Thomas Waddle's Fort, a fortified house, was in St. Thomas (then Peter's Township). Justice William Maxwell's Fort in Welsh Run was a fortified house with log stockade south of McDowell's. Elliott's Fort was in Path Valley at Springtown. Baker's Fort was near Dry Run.

The construction of strong houses ran from what is now Bedford, through Franklin, Cumberland and Dauphin Counties.[26] This strengthening of the valley with block houses and private forts by colonials amidst a passive government and disinterested crown began to develop a sense of independence in the settlers from British affairs and continued the resentment they felt toward Parliament for past wrongs done. It was heightened when the British troops verbally abused settlers and then left Pennsylvania for the safety of New York with little thought of

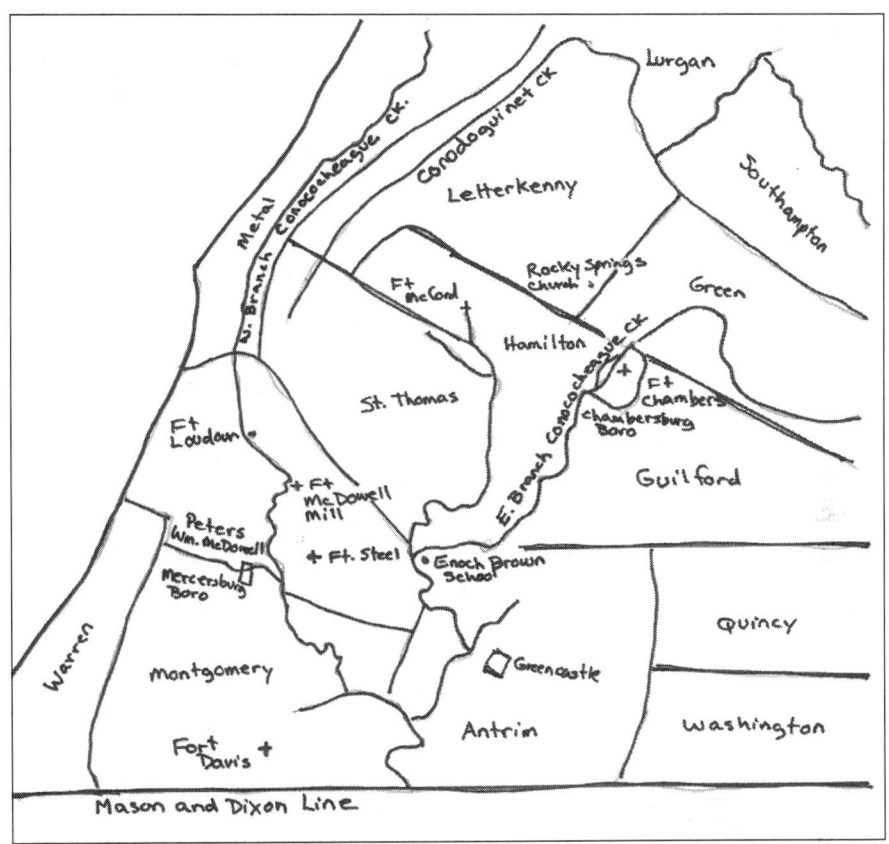

This map of the forts of the lower Cumberland Valley during the 1750s and 1760s shows the location of McDowell's Mill Fort within that structure. Map by author.

the protection of the western line of defense. The frontiersmen, assisting each other, slowly adopted Indian customs in hunting, trading and warfare. They adapted to behaviors which fit the frontier better and looked to their neighbors for aid.

Following Braddock's defeat, the Governor also called for the construction of a wooden fort at Carlisle and the formation of four companies of Militia. The Carlisle militia was commanded by William Buchanan. Lurgan Township militia was commanded by Alexander Culbertson who also had a private fort. Hamilton Township was commanded by Joseph Armstrong. Peters Township militia was commanded by Justice

William Maxwell, Esq.[27] People on the frontier either fled the area or began their own preparations for defense as their farms were converted into mini-forts.

Delaware Chief/King Shingas with Captain Jacobs returned with warriors to Cumberland County on November 1, 1755. They attacked the Big/Great Cove area west of Markes, close to William Maxwell, Esq.'s property. This is in present day McConnellsburg in Fulton County, Pennsylvania. Twenty-seven plantations were burnt, cattle destroyed, settlers killed or taken prisoners. One twenty-nine year old woman had their breast torn off. Settlers were attached to stakes and mutilated.

Of the 93 families, largely German, in the Little Cove, Great Cove and the "Conolloways" (Tonoloways Creek near the Maryland border), forty-seven persons were killed or taken captive and the rest deserted the area, fleeing into the forts for protection.[28] McDowell's Mill and Steel's Forts housed many of those fleeing and the wounded. The Tonoloways Settlement spread over the current borders between southern Pennsylvania and northern Maryland. It was situated with the Big and little Coves to the north, the Potomac River to the south, the Big Tonoloways creek to the east and the Little Tonoloways Creek to the west. Among those people taken was the wife of one John Martin with his two sons and two daughters.[29]

Adam Hoops from Conococheaque wrote to the Governor on November 3rd, sending the letter and a tomahawk which was found sticking in the breast of David McClellan to Philadelphia with Patrick Burns. The letter read:

> Gentlemen,
> I am sorry I have to trouble you with this Melancholy and disagreeable News, For on Saturday, I recd. An Express fro Peters Township, that the Inhabitants of the great Cove were all Murdered or taken Captive, & their Houses and Barns all in Flames, some few fled, upon notice brought them by a certain Patrick Burns, a Captive, that made his Escape that very Mourning before this Sad Tragady was done. Upon information as

afores, John Potter, Esq., and Self, sent Expresses through our Neighbourhood, which included many of them to meet with us as afores, at John McDooles' Mill, where I with many others had the unhappy prospect to see the Smoke of two houses that was set on Fire by the Indians, with all the Expedition Immaginable, but to no Success; these Indians have likewise taken two women Captives, belonging to said town ship. I very much Fear the Path Valley has undergone the same Fate . . .

He went on to describe the cries of those with loses and the homeless.

Hoops mentioned that Mr. Burd with 40 men had just left his house in "Cannogogig." He would join them on the 4th at McDowell's Mill with added forces to check damage and to offer assistance. He complained that there were no other magazines to supply guards or scouts (Braddock's material had not yet been opened).

> "The whole weight of their maintenance lies Chiefly upon a few Persons . . ."[30] Smoke from the houses of Matthew Patton and Meshech James were visible. Their cattle were shot, with horses bleeding from Indian arrows. A group of 100 men led by Rev. Steel, and John Potter, Esq., went after the Indians, but were unsuccessful.

Men staying at McDowell's would have been in that search party. The Governor reported to the Assembly on November 3rd that the Indians were within 80 miles of Philadelphia. He praised the frontiersmen:

> The people of the back counties have on this important Ocassion behaved themselves with uncommon spirit and activity, but complain much of the want of Order & Discipline, as well as of Arms and Ammunition. As we have no Militia it is not in my power to Form the people into such regular Bodies as the present Exigency requires, and you must be sensible that I have neither Money, Arms, or Ammunition at My disposal; all I have, therefore been

able to do has been to issue commissions to such as were willing to take them and to encourage the people to defend themselves and their Families till the Government was enabled to protect them.[31]

On November 6th Hoops wrote again reporting that:

"The People of Path Valley are all gathered in a small fort, and according to the last account were safe. The Great Cove and Conolloways are all burned to ashes, and about fifty persons killed or taken-Numbers of the inhabitants of this county have moved their families, some to York County, some to Maryland.

"Hance Hamilton, Esq., is now at John McDowell's mill w upwards of 200 men {from York County} and about 200 from this County, in all about four hundred men, and to-morrow we extends to go in to the Cove and to the path Valley, in order To Bring what cattle and horses that the Indians Hath Left alive; we are informed by a Dolleway {Delaware} Indian, which Lives amungths us, on the same day The murder was cummitted, he seen four hundred Indians in the Cove; and we have sum Reason to Believe the are a bout there yet; the people of ShearMan's Crick and Juneate {Juniata}, is all cum a way and Left there houses, and there is now about 30 miles Of this Country lead weast {waste}, and I am afraid there will Be soon more."[32]

He added that George McSwane had been taken captive 14 days prior but made his escape carrying two scalps and a tomahawk with him.

Thirty-three year old Justice William McDowell, Jr., brother of the 39 year-old miller John McDowell, was serving in Captain Hance Hamilton's Company as a Sergeant. He would have been in this cluster of men. Hoops also made mention of a Delaware who lived within the community. It seems likely that the presence of friendly Indians would have been a common site up to this point but then fear and confusion set in: who could you trust?

Sheriff John Potter writing from Conocochegue to Richard Peters on November 2, 1755, also referred to the attack at the Great Cove from his perspective.

> On Saturday last about three of the clock in the afternoon, I received intelligence in conjunction with Adam Hoops, and sent immediately and appointed our neighbors to meet at McDowell's. On Sunday morning I was not there six minutes till we observed about a mile and a half distant one Matthew Patton's house and barn in flames; on which we sat off with about forty men, though there were at least one hundred and sixty there; our old officers hid themselves, for aught I knew, to save their scalps, until afternoon when danger was over. We went to Pattons with a seeming resolution and courage, but found no Indians there, on which we advanced to a rising ground, where we immediately discovered another house and barn on fire belonging to Mesach James, about one mile up the creek from Thomas Bars. We set off directly for that place; but they had gone up the creek to another plantation, left by one widow Jordon the day before; but she had unhappily gone back that morning with a young woman, daughter to one William Clark, for some milk for her children, and were both taken captives; but neither house nor barn hurt. I have heard of no more burnt in that valley, which makes me believe they have gone off for some time; but I much fear they will return before we are prepared for them; for it was three o'clock in the afternoon before a recruit came of about sixty men; then we held council whether to pursue up the valley all night or return to McDowell's; the former of which I and Mr. Hoops, and some others plead for, but could not obtain it without putting it to vote, which done, we were out-voted by a considerable number; upon which I and company was left by them, (that night I came home) for I will not guard a man that will not fight when called in so imminent manner; for there were not six of these men that would consent to go in pursuit of the Indians. I am much afraid that

Juniata, Tuscarora, and Sheerman's valley hath suffered; there are two-thirds of the inhabitants of this valley who have already fled, leaving their plantations; and without speedy succor be granted, I am of opinion this county will be laid desolate and be without inhabitants. Last night I had a family of upwards of an hundred women and children who fled for succor. You can form no just idea of the distress and distracted condition of our inhabitants, unless you saw and heard their cries. I am of opinion that it is not in the power of our representatives to meet in Assembly at this time. If our Assembly will give us any additional supply of arms and ammunition, the later of which is most wanted. I would wish it were put into the hands of such persons as would go out upon scouts after the Indians, rather than for the supply of forts.[33]

Sheriff Potter and Adam Hoops had summoned neighbors to meet at McDowell's Mill. They scouted among the plantations which were still burning. Some of those who had been attacked were pacifists, Quakers, Mennonites and Dunkards (German Baptists), and would not bear arms. The fear in the locals was evident. Even if a few had the will to fight, they were without arms and they were facing a type of violence the Europeans had never witnessed before. James Burd and Hanse Hamilton had gone to McDowell's with 400 men but returned without success. Ben Chambers wrote that Delaware and Shawnese were those who did the destruction.[34] They knew their enemies and they knew where they lived but had no arms to formalize a counter-assault.

Meanwhile Col. James Burd in Lancaster wrote to Edward Shippen, Esq., on work being done at the Shippensburg Fort and the number of refugee families who had fled there. Four to five families were crammed into each house and others were in barns and every imaginable space. He mentioned in his letter that forty men had left to join others on November 4th at "Mr. McDowell's mill." All the force could do was check on the level of damage in the area and design a plan for the relief of the settlers. He complained, "As we have no magazines at present to supply the guards, or scouts, the whole weight of their maintenance lies chiefly upon a few persons. I pray your Honor to excuse what blunders there are by reason of haste."[35] Volunteers were trying their best. They did not have permission to open Braddock's stores at McDowell's at that time.

John Armstrong mentioned sixty men with Mr. Hamilton from York County with those who were collecting to address the issue but the Indians had headed west by this time and were no longer in the area. Armstrong reinforced the need to keep inhabitants safe and to make sure that they did not drive off their cattle. Cattle were necessary in that remote area. He reported that there were no inhabitants on the Juniata or Tuscarora at that time. As a precaution, he sent his own wife away to safety.[36]

The style of warfare used by the Indians was unknown in Europe. Warriors had been hardened by the environment and could go days without food, hiding under cover in quiet preparation for an assault. They performed quick violent raids and then disappeared into the woods. Many of them desecrated bodies in a frightening manner. Settlers developed deep seated fears about the spooky appearances made by warriors with faces painted red, black and yellow who had shaved heads, except for a long section with feathers attached, and pierced ears with things dangling from them. Their war woops were ghostly sounds in the woods. Repeated requests were sent to the Assembly for formal militia but the Assembly votes were endlessly delayed. The Assembly seemed to be unable to visualize what was happening to their west and how it might put all the colonies in danger.

The small warrior bands were attacking the entire British frontier, experiencing little resistance. They swarmed over the mountains murdering, dismembering and scalping settlers, looting and burning homes, and killing cattle from the Hudson River to the Potomac. Settlers fled in large numbers due to their inability to defend themselves. Friendly tribes were also placed in an awkward position. They began to doubt the British ability to protect them from their own tribal enemies. In addition, peaceful tribes were suddenly unable to trade with the English. They were threatened by both French and western Indians and waffled in loyalty.

INDIAN DEPREDATIONS ON THE FRONTIERS.

This engraving, "Indian Depredations on the Frontiers," comes from William H. Engle's, *An Illustrated History of the Commonwealth of Pennsylvania, Civil, Political and Military, from its Earliest Settlement to the Present Time* (1876).

Colonel John Armstrong from Carlisle had written to the Governor on November 2nd encouraging the construction of a chain of blockhouses along the south side of the Kittatinny Mountains spanning from the Susquehanna River to the southern temporary borderline.[37] The 1754 "Plan for the Defense of the Frontier of Cumberland County" which was to run from Philip Davies' to Shippensburg had been accepted but was not fully in place yet.[38] The plan called for McDowell's Mill Fort to have 45 men garrisoned with men leaving on patrol in the morning and returning in the evening. We do see this beginning to happen by November with a certain type of order. Communication between Philip Davies', William Marshall's and Thomas Waddle's Forts would have been part of the daily routine for the men at McDowell's Mill Fort with each area reporting events as they happened within their regions.

Written records and letters were kept. They show an attempt by the local people to address the problems in a systematic way, working through their County Justices and the Sheriff. Other companies of men covered from those points back to Shippensburg. John Armstrong monitored everything from Carlisle, the county seat. Reports were sent directly to the Governor who read them before the Assembly, and the Pennsylvania newspapers printed the stories of the losses, so Philadelphia was fulling informed of the distresses happening at the western front, but the Governor's hands were tied.

Though Governor Morris had called out the militia on November 3rd to respond to the needs of those on the frontier, the Assembly was slow to approve money which prevented the actualization of relief. The people in the valley eventually became so enraged by the lack of response by the Assembly that they hauled the dead and mangled bodies of the victims to Philadelphia and carried placards declaring them victims of the Quaker-led policy. A mob soon surrounded the House of Assembly as the dead bodies were placed in the doorway of the building with demands for relief of those on the frontier.[39] The pressure was mounting and ultimately led to a loss of political power by the Quakers.

Among those fleeing the Indian attacks in the Cumberland valley in 1755 were the elder patriarch William McDowell, Sr., and his wife Mary

Irvine McDowell. They sought refuge at Wrights Ferry/Wrightsville in York County. William's home and fields had been burned like others in his community. He was aging and unable to fight off natives. Wrights Ferry was on the west side of the Susquehanna River, in the Susquehanna Valley, south of current Route 30. John Wright, a Quaker and Justice of the Peace, had been running the ferry between Wrights Ferry and Columbia on the east bank since 1733, having received a license to do so from the Penn family. That crossing was considered the most important point on that river. It was also the eastern end of the Monocacy River trail which extended southwest into Maryland. The trail was used originally by American Indians and had been enlarged by settlers to carry wagons.

Wright's ferry most likely had been used by the McDowells when first traveling west. Pioneer William McDowell would never returned to his Franklin County property, instead he turned it over to his sons. He lived an additional four years in Wrights Ferry. The sons of William McDowell, Sr., appear to have stayed close to their plantations and some of them brought their families into McDowell's Fort to live for a number of years. Some also retreated to Lancaster, and some of the women and children may have gone east to stay with cousins because records of them are sketchy.

We do know that John and Agnes Craig McDowell's family were at the fort. The family of William, Esq. and Mary Maxwell McDowell was there. William's son John (born February 11, 1751) reported spending his childhood in the fort when his home was burned twice by Indians.[40] Nathan had the farm next to John and would have likely been in the fort with his family. James McDowell was a local constable. Thomas was in the militia. They may have all been at the fort with some of their sister's families. The McDowell children would witness numerous Indian raids. A number of them would later marry community leaders and military men who had also grown up within the Cumberland Valley fort system.

One of those listening in Philadelphia was Benjamin Franklin who served under a Committee of the Assembly. He mentioned in a letter to James Reed, Esq. on November 2, 1755, that he had tried to purchase some arms to supply the frontier. Arms and ammunition had been placed under the care of Mr. Reed and Mr. "Wiser" with the understanding that it would be returned once peace was achieved.[41] He also recommended that families begin stocking grain and fodder. He still had to deal with the fall-out of losses of wagons and horses which had been contracted for "light and easy" service to Braddock. General Shirley had to release money due wagoneers, and commissioners were sent out to pay them for their service.[42]

A small group guarding Tullyhoe's Gap at night on November 8th were attacked resulting in five settlers killed with two wounded. John Elder from Paxton also wrote to Mr. Peters, Esq., on November 9th that

> within these few weeks upwards of forty of his majesty's subjects massacred on the frontiers of this and Cumberland counties, besides a great many carried into captivity, and yet nothing but unseasonable debates between the two parties of our legislature, instead of uniting on some probable scheme for the protection of the province. What may be the end of these things, God only knows; but I really fear that unless vigorous methods are speedily used, we in these back settlements will unavoidably fall a sacrifice, and this part of the province be lost.[43]

Permission was finally given on November 19th to open some of Braddock's flour supply at McDowell Mill Fort which was then distributed by Joseph Armstrong and John Smith to inhabitants in distress. Powder and lead were also distributed by Edward Shippen in Cumberland, York, Lancaster and Berks Counties under a "lend-lease" agreement.[44] The stingy Assembly finally granted some funds for a paid militia. Twenty-five companies of 1,400 men, were raised and equipped to defend the frontier, most had already been serving.

Forts like McDowell's Mill were overwhelmed as they served a number of community needs. They were places of refuge for defenseless settlers driven from their homes, serving a social services and housing need. They were regional hospitals for the wounded. They were store houses for military material and ammunition. Militia was recruited and garrisoned there. They were rallying points for those tracking Indian movements and reporting on property damaged as a type of local police force or National Guard.[45] Men serving there also were called on to guard harvesters to prevent regional starvation.

The year rounded out with an attack on the Woolcomber family on Shearman's Creek the end of December. Most of the inhabitants there were clustered at Robison's Fort (both George and Robert Robison had block-house forts) but Woolcomber, a Quaker, believed his peaceful dealings with the Indians would keep him safe. The Indians who arrived, unfortunately, knew that they could make money selling scalps to the French. Husband, wife and a number of children were killed with one boy escaping.[46]

The next year was no better. Indians attacked along the lower Juniata River, close to Fort Patterson at the mouth of the Tuscarora Valley, opposite Mexico, and again at Sherman's Creek on January 27, 1756. James Patterson, an Ulster-Scot, had settled near there in 1751 and his log house had been converted to a fort. A family of seven on the creek lost their lives, a man was wounded and a horse killed.

Mrs. Boyde, her two sons and a daughter on the Conodoguinet Creek were also killed. There was the murder and scalping of James Leaton in what is now Bedford County on the 28th. Catharine Stillwell and one of her children were also killed and scalped, and two other children ages eight and three were taken by the Indians. Her husband, Elias, had been at a neighbor's house and after finding his family members dead and missing, he entered Coom's Fort distraught. Cooms/Coombs' Fort was in the Tonoloways settlement which was spread between current Fulton County, Pennsylvania and Washington County, Maryland. Fulton County at the time was Cumberland County. The fort was near Warfordsbury.

John McKenny's house was also robbed and burned, and his cows killed. Samuel Eaton's barn was burned with the cows in it. Samuel Hicks, his cattle and mare were all killed, and his house burned. The tracks of seven Indians, a child and horses were spotted which led towards Aughwick.[47]

McDowell's Mill Fort in the Defense of the Frontier

A German man on a wagon in what is ow Dauphin County was killed. The rest of those in the wagon fled to a nearby fort. The men at the fort, responding to a report of Indians, saw a crying woman running towards them. The wagon was found pillaged and destroyed. The next day twelve men sent to alert the fort were fired upon and either killed or wounded with only two escaping.[48] Mrs. Boggs also was fired upon while on horseback. The horse was killed and she and her infant child were taken prisoner. The child was later murdered and scalped.

Attacks on the Conococheague settlement were intensifying as settlers fled to eastern communities. Indian bands were on the prowl and also swept through the Susquehanna and Potomac River regions. Between 1756 and 1758 the Conococheague would suffer at least 40 raids with hundreds killed, captured and property destroyed. McDowell's Mill Fort was soon surrounded by abandoned and burned plantations.

Governor Morris wrote a letter to Governor Dinwiddie on February 1st detailing his plan to build a new chain of forts along the frontier and a proposed Indian treaty at Harris's Ferry.

> This Chain of Forts & Block hos, is to extend from Delaware along ye Kittahteny Hills, to ye new Road opened on our Southern Frontier towds. ye Allegany Hills; those on ye West side of Susquehannah are already erected, at abt 20 miles a sunder. One of them is placed at a River called Matchetongo, abt 12 miles from Susquehanah, whc I have called Pomfret Castle, another near Juniata, where Kishikoquillos falls into it, call's Fort Granville; a 3d at Auchquick, call'd Fort Shirley, & a 4th at ye Sugar Cabbins upon ye new Road, call'd Fort Littleton. At each of these I have placed a Garrison of 75 men, & ordered them to range ye woods each way. Those between Delaware & Susquehanna, are to be abt 10 or 12 miles a sunder; ye most considerable of them is built at an important Pass thro' ye Kittahteny Hills, on our Northern Frontier, & I have called it Fort Henry. The whole of them I expect will be completed in abt 10 days, & will be garrisoned by 800 men actually raised & taken into ye Govts pay for ye purpose . . .[49]

These forts were added to the small forts originally established as private forts. The militia of 1756 included 1st Battalion of the Pennsylvania Regiment, led by Captain Lieutenant-Colonel Weiser and 2nd Battalion of the Pennsylvania Regiment, led by Captain Lieutenant-Colonel John Armstrong. Officers commissioned with Armstrong at Carlisle were Lieutenant William Thompson and Ensign James Potter. Regiments under Armstrong included Captain Hance Hamilton with Lieutenant James Hayes, Ensign John Prentice and Sergeant William McDowell; Captain John Potter with Lieutenant William Armstrong and Ensign Thomas Smallman; Captain Hugh Mercer with Lieutenant James Holladay/Holliday[50] and Ensign William Lyon; Captain George Armstrong with Ensign Nathaniel Cartland; Captain Edward Ward; Captain Joseph Armstrong and Captain Robert Callander.[51] Many of the men under Armstrong would carry out important duties which brought them to McDowell's Mill Fort for various periods of time.

The frontier suffered a raid on Saturday, February 11, 1756, when two boys named John and Richard Cox were abducted from Widow Cox's home by nine Delaware. The home was just under Parnell's Knob by McDowell property and two miles north of McDowell's Mill Fort. The house was burned and the cattle shot. John and Richard were taken to Kittanning by Indians.

John Craig and another man were sent from McDowell's Mill Fort to look for them but they were also captured by Indians. The other man was killed and Craig later escaped from Kiskiminetas to Fort Augusta.[52] John McDowell's wife was a Craig but it is unknown if they were related. Both Cox boys also later escaped.

William Trent at Carlisle, writing about the matter to Richard Peters in Philadelphia the next day, mentioned:

> a Lad who went from McDowell's Mill to see what fire it was never returned, the Horse coming back with the Reins over his Neck; they burnt the House and shot down the cattle. Just now came News that a Party of Indian Warriors were come out against the Inhabitants from some of the Susquehannah Towns, and

yesterday some People who were over in Sherman's Valley, discovered fresh Tracts; all the People have left their Houses betwixt this and the mountain, some come to Town and others gathering into little Forts; they are moving their Effects from Shippensburgh, every one thinks of flying; unless the Government fall upon some effectual Method, & that immediately, of securing the Frontiers, there will not be one Inhabitant in this Valley one Month longer. There is a few of us endeavor to keep up the Spirits of the People. We have proposed going upon the Enemy to-morrow, but whether a Number sufficient can be got cannot tell . . . [53]

Trent recommended a fort at Carlisle which was in the plan.

Captain Patterson with his scouting party encountered Indians at Middle Creek, now in Union County on February 29th. They scalped one Indian, and one of his men was wounded. Patterson had reports of settlers seeing Indians in the woods from the Juniata to Shamokin. During the raids, Hugh Mitcheltrees' wife was killed. The war party proceeded to William Wilcox's home where his wife and eldest son were. John Wilcox, and James Armstrong's wife plus two children were taken. The Indians killed Edward Nicholass and his wife, and took Joseph, Thomas, and Catharine Nicholass. William Sheridan and his family of thirteen were also killed along with three elderly persons named French.[54]

Two more boys were fired at by Indians by David David's Fort in Little Cove on February 29, 1756. One boy was killed and the other escaped to alert others at the fort. Twenty Indians proceeded to fire on that fort. The Indians were driven off by soldiers but four soldiers were lost in the process.

On the same day a man with the last name of Alexander and another unnamed man discovered a band of 50 Indians by Thomas Barr's place in Peters Township and they sounded an alarm, seeking reinforcements at McDowell's Mill Fort. It resulted in an engagement with several Indians. Barr's son and a soldier were killed. There were Alexanders living locally who were members of the Presbyterian Church: Daniel, Arthur, Andrew and Hezekiah are listed. It is not clear which Alexander this was.

The men were pushed into a retreat as reinforcements came from McDowell's Mill Fort, but they lost the Indians. Meanwhile the Indians had doubled back and attempted to surprise the fort. Two Dutch boys were also referenced in documents who were feeding cattle during this. They discovered the Indian band by McDowell's Fort. One was killed and the other reached the fort in time to alert the garrison. The fort was soon surrounded by the band of Indians who fired from the thicket. The men of the fort fired back from within the stockade between the loop holes. Two additional men crossing to the fort's gate made it into the fort, one again named Alexander. The group of soldiers who had been at the Barr's home then traced back to the fort and spotting the attack, drove the Indians from the thicket.

Retreating, Indians then met five men from Hoop's Company riding towards the fort. One of the company was killed and another severely wounded. The sergeant at the fort, who lost two men, wouldn't follow the Indians until his commander, Commander Crawford, returned from Mr. Hoop's. This may have been Captain Samuel Crawford who was a Captain of a company of Associators from 1747 to 1748. He had served at that time with Lieutenant William Rowland and Ensign Richard McDonald. We later learn of McDonalds in the area of McDowell's Mill Fort involved in another raid. No first name was given in the report, however.

On this particular day thick snow was falling which hindered the process. The Indians burned Barr's house with their dead inside before heading west. Mr. Crawford on the morning of March 2nd took a force of 50 men after the Indians but was unable to apprehend them.[55] Indian Chiefs Shingas and Captain Jacobs were named as the ones leading the warriors who attacked both David Davis' Fort and McDowell's Mill Fort. The Barr's property would later be a suggested spot for a new fort, but not chosen and would be a location associated with a settler revolt against British regulars.

Community stories later circulated about these assaults at Fort McDowell after the defeat of Braddock. One was about John McDowell's hat. It seems he was out checking his cows by the creek (tax records only record him having a few) when his hat blew off. He reached down, picked it up and put it on. It blew off again and he repeated putting it on. The third time it blew off he took it as a divine warning and returned quickly to the fort only to learn that Indians had been hidden and were ready to pounce on him.[56] They soon made their presence known in the area. He would have been forty in 1756.

Another story was related by Thomas Creigh in his 1877 *History of the Presbyterian Church of Upper West Conococheague*. He wrote that settlers were seeking shelter at McDowell's Fort on "a clear and lovely morning" when an assault was made by Indians, but "suddenly, about ten o'clock in the morning there was a fall of snow. The Indians abandoned their purpose, fearing, lest by their tracks in the snow they would be pursued to their lurking place."[57] It was taken as another act of providence.

As the winter continued in February, William Sheridan and a family of 13 living by Sherman's creek were killed. More families exited the area resulting in a drop in the numbers of men available to fight. In addition, more Indians who had professed friendship with the English defected, trying to see if they could recover land from the British with the help of the French.[58]

The Governor complained to Indian agent Sir William Johnson that the enemy who came at first in small parties was penetrating deeper and deeper into the colony in larger and larger groups. They had defeated several detachments of armed men and burned property in many counties. Terror among the settlers was mounting because they lacked arms and ammunition to protect themselves. He feared the total desertion of the back counties. If York and Cumberland were evacuated, the Susquehanna River would soon be the frontier. His plan was to offer rewards for Indian prisoners and scalps as a last ditch effort to keep settlers in place.[59]

About this time John Craig escaped from captivity by Delaware Indians. He wrote a letter on the 30th in which he briefly described McDowell's Mill Fort at that time: "Inhabitants of Peters township contiguous to McDowell's mill erected a Fort which included the Mill and with it several little Houses that they built themselves and retired into it with their families . . ."[60] The addition of "several little houses with families," also mentioned later by Justice William McDowell's son John. This points to a cluster of civilians now using the fort as their regular home.[61] Justice McDowell and other brothers were serving in the militia and it seems that the wives, nieces and nephews may have been among those clustered at the fort stockade while the men served in military and judicial duties. Other wives and children may have also been housed at the fort. Those women may have helped out by doing laundry, cooked and tended the sick.

McDowell's Mill Fort, we read from record, had a large rectangular stockade and it was nestled by the east side of the West Conococheque Creek. Riflemen would have daily kept watch through loop-holes while standing on clapboard attached inside to the stockade logs, a few feet off the ground. Inside the enclosure were blockhouses which may have contained munitions and other storage, and a barracks which housed at least 50 or more men. Storage houses were often placed in the four corners of a stockade but there was an existing mill with the miller's two story home thirty yards from it which might have changed the inner configuration a bit. There were two bastions in opposite corners constructed to house two swivel guns. The mill was by a mill pond and it also served as a store. There was an old block house, which was said in 1840 to have been part of the fort, on and slightly west of what was called the old Loudon Road.[62] It may have been constructed to protect the troops ranging between mini strong houses.

There were several additional little houses for families which may have been either attached to the outer wall of the fort or within the stockade. There was a thicket by the fort. At times up to 100–400 men with horses were gathered around the fort along the road cut to the west. It would likely have make-shift tents set up inside and outside the stockade with small fires continually burning. It was a center of activity with detachments coming and going. Settlers also fled into its gates seeking protection. Some arriving may have needed medical attention. American Indians with French officers ran regular raids into the area.

The exact supplies kept at McDowell's might have been barrels of food such as cured beef, pork, and clams, peas, flour, rum, and salt. We do know that the creek had a steady supply of fish, particularly bass,

This simple tent is an example of the make-shift tents used by soldiers at this time. It is from the re-enactment of the Battle of Monmouth in June of 2015. Photo by author used by permission, the Division of Parks and Forestry, Trenton, New Jersey.

which could have been added to the men's diet. There was also a great deal of live game in the area, though they may have been frightened off by the engagements and homes burning.

    A formal fort would have also had tools like pick axes, grubbing hoes, round eyed hoes, maul rings, falling axes, broad axes, spades, shovels, drawing knives, wedges, calking irons, whip saws, pole sockets, drag chains, tap borers, nails, bar iron, ploughs, files, plains, gimblets, chizels, jointers, gouges, trowels, augers and hammers with pad locks, and rope.

    McDowell's, however, was not well stocked in arms by the government and would have most likely been dependent upon the tools owned by local farmers. Items for horses like saddles, bits, reigns and blankets would have belonged to the individual soldiers as would have muskets, rifles, bullets, lead shot, and powder. They may have later had grape shot, and gun powder for the swivel canons but the Assembly was resistant to providing military arms. By March officers there were under the pay of the province, but the fact that they had served for free prior to that says something about the dedication of the men in the valley and their determination to protect their families and property.

The list of officers at that time is as follows:

Officers in the Province Pay, with the Dates of Their Commissions, 1756
Commissary General of Musters Elisha Saltar, March 28, 1756
First Battalion
Lieut. Colonel Conrad Weiser, May 5, 1756; Major William Parsons, May 14, 1756
Captain Conrad Weiser, (L.C.) May 5, 1756; Lieut. Samuel Weiser, Capt. Lieut., July 3, 1756; Ensign–Henry Geiger, Dec 20, 1755
Captain William Parsons, (M.,) May 14, 1756; Lieut. Jacob Wetterholt, Dec 20, 1755; Ensign Martin Everhart, Dec 20, 1755
Captain Frederick Smith, Nov 14, 1755; Lieut. Anthony Miller, Dec 29, 1755; Ensign Nicholas Conrad, Dec 29, 1755
Captain Jacob Morgan, Dec 5, 1755; Lieut. Andrew Engle, Jan 5, 1756; Ensign Jacob Kern, Jan 5, 1756
Captain John Nicholas Wetterholt, Dec 21, 1755; Lieut. James Hyndshaw, Jan 12, 1756; Ensign Daniel Harry, Jan 26, 1756
Captain Christian Busse, Jan 5, 1756; Lieut. Samuel Humphreys, Jan 25, 1756; Ensign William Johnson, Mar 12, 1756
Captain Jacob Orndt, April 19, 1756; Lieut. Philip Marsloff, April 27, 1756, Dec 1757; Ensign Jacob Kreider, May 19, 1756
Captain John Van Etten, May 1756, Lieut. Samuel Allen, May 19, 1756, Ensign Jacob Snyder, Sergeant, color, John Van Etten Jr., Sergeant Leonard Derr
Captain George Reynolds, May 17, 1756, Lieut. Philip Weiser, July 3, 1756, Captain James Patterson, Lieut. Hugh Crawford, Ensign Thomas Smallman
Captain Charles Foulk, Lieut. Michael Beltz, Sergeant John White, Sergeant Dewalt Bossing, Corporal Christian Weirick, Privates Michael Laury, Killian Long
Second Battalion
Lieut.-Colonel John Armstrong, May 11, 1756; Surgeon Dr. William Jamison, killed by the Indians near McCord's Fort, April 1756; Commissary of Provisions Adam Hoops

Officers in the Province Pay, with the Dates of Their Commissions, 1756

Captain John Armstrong, Jan 1756, (a Lieut.-Colonel, wounded at Kittanning Sept 7, 1756); Lieut. Robert Callender (Capt. Lieut.), Jan 16, 1756; Ensign James Potter, Feb 17, 1756; Privates James Caruthers (wounded at Kittanning), Thomas Forster (wounded at Kittanning), Thomas Power (killed at Kittanning), John McCormick (killed at Kittanning), John Strickland (wounded at Kittanning).

Captain Hance Hamilton, Jan 16, 1756; Lieut. William Thompson, Jan 16, 1756; Ensign John Prentice, May 22, 1756; Sergeant William McDowell; Privates John Kelly (killed at Kittanning)

Captain John Potter, Feb 17, 1756; Lieut. William Armstrong, May 10, 1756; Ensign James Potter, April 17, 1756 (wounded at Kittanning); Privates Andrew Douglass (wounded at Kittanning), James Corkem (captured by the Indians, Nov 1756), William Cornwall (captured by the Indians, Nov 1756), Bartholomew McCafferty (killed near McDowell's Fort, Nov 1756), James McDonald (killed near McDowell's fort, Nov 1756), William McDonald (killed near McDowell's fort, Nov 1756), Anthony McQuoid (killed near McDowell's fort, Nov 1756)

Captain Hugh Mercer, March 6, 1756 (wounded at Kittanning); Lieut. James Hayes, May 22, 1756; Ensign William Lyon, May 22, 1756 (resigned); Ensign John Scott, July 1756 (wounded at Kittanning); Privates John Baker, John (killed at Kittanning), Thomas Burke, Thomas (missing at the capture of Kittanning), Bryan Carrigan (killed at Kittanning), Richard Fitzgibbins (wounded at Kittaning), Dennis Kilpatrick (killed at Kittanning), John McCartney (killed at Kittanning), Cornelius McGinnis (killed at Kittanning), Emanuel Minskey (missing at the capture of Kittanning), Robert Morrow (missing at the capture of Kittanning), Patrick Mullen (killed at Kittanning), Philip Pendergrass (missing at the capture of Kittanning), Francis Phillips (missing at the capture of Kittanning), John Taylor (missing at the capture of Kittanning), Theophilus Thompson (killed at Kittanning)

Captain George Armstrong, May 22, 1756; Lieut. James Hogg, May 1756 (killed at Kittanning); Ensign Nathaniel Cartland, May 22, 1756; Privates James Anderson (killed at Kittanning), George Appleby (missing at the capture of Kittanning), William Baker (missing at the capture of Kittanning), Thomas Camplin (wounded at Kittanning), William Findley (wounded at Kittanning), John Ferral (wounded at Kittanning), Anthony Grissy (missing at the capture of Kittanning), James Higgins (killed at Kittanning), William Hunter(missing at the capture of Kittanning), John Lasson (killed at Kittanning), John Lewis (missing at the capture of Kittanning), Edward O'Brien (killed at Kittanning), Charles O'Neal (wounded at Kittanning), Robert Robinson(wounded at Kittanning), Holdcraft Stringer (killed at Kittanning), Thams Swan (killed at Kittanning)

McDOWELL'S MILL FORT

Officers in the Province Pay, with the Dates of Their Commissions, 1756

Captain Edward Ward, May 22, 1756; Lieut. Edward Armstrong, May 22, 1756 (killed at the capture and burning of Fort Granville, July 30, 1756); Ensign John Lowdon, April 19, 1756; Privates Ephraim Bratton (wounded at Kittanning), Samuel Chambers (missing at the capture of Kittanning), Lawrence Donnahow (missing at the capture of Kittanning), Patrick Myers (missing at the capture of Kittanning), William Welch (killed at Kittanning)

Captain Rev. John Steel, March 25, 1756; Lieut. James Holiday, March 25, 1756; Ensign Archibald Irwin, April 1756; Privates Terence Cannaberry (missing at the capture of Kittanning), Captain Alexander Culbertson (killed by the Indians near M'Cord's Fort, April 1756)

Captain Joseph Montgomery, Oct 5, 1756; Ensign Thomas Smallman, May 22, 1756

A detachment of 14 from George Croghan's unit with 12 locals engaged the enemy on March 1st by Fort Shirley/Aughwick Fort. The natives were armed with guns which had been captured previously from the Braddock campaign. The Indians fired on the soldiers and attempted to rush the fort but then withdrew.[64] A few days later on March 5, Benjamin Blyth in Shippensburg wrote a quick letter with heavy accent to Captain Burd about this engagement:

> I just give you a Short account of our afears I Came home Last knight from McDowels mill where we ware going to thire assistance {Fort Shirley} but was too Late ye Indians being gon where we found ye Pople in grate un easy ness ye Indians having killed two of Colanol Crohans men and one Cuntry man killed wounded Aran Rily and bar a yong Lad. had not providence prevented by Snow it being ye first of this instant the wholl Vally would have Sufred there bing about 80 of ye inamy I am going of to morrow to Lancaster County to get help if psable to Act Either one ye A fencife ore Defencif as ned Requires I am inphormed that ye have takne of horces equel to thire number they had beset all ye Rods in to the fort of said mill ye people have sent apiticion to the govinor

which pitician Rev Mr Steel and Mr Armstrong Carres doun in ordure to Call in you of ye block houses to oure Vally . . .[65]

Doctor Hugh Mercer took up headquarters as Captain of a group of rangers at McDowell's Mill Fort. We know some of those men from the prior report were Lieutenant James Hayes; Ensign William Lyon who was replaced by John Scott; Privates John Baker, Thomas Burke, Bryan Carrigan, Richard Fitzgibbins, Dennis Kilpatrick, John McCartney, Cornelius McGinnis, Emanuel Minskey, Robert Morrow, Patrick Mullen, Philip Pendergrass, Francis Phillips, John Taylor, Theophilus Thompson. They would have been in the barracks. Mercer's patrol area was from Welsh Run and Smith's Town to the foothills.[66] Mercer became a local hero, much beloved, and Smith's Town would ultimately take his name, Mercersburg. He lived just south of that town.

John McDowell took an interest in medicine at some point, serving later as a surgeon during the Revolutionary War. He might have been influenced during this period by university educated Mercer.[67] During the colonial period doctors were either trained as proper surgeons with a degree like Mercer, or apprenticed. Some were also what we would consider quacks. John most likely fell into the apprentice slot, or he may have just pitched in as the doctor directed.

The fort had repeated reports of injured persons seeking cover. Having some type of medical training would have been imperative. John's mill was used to grind flour, but it would not have been running daily, especially during the winter and spring. He was most likely stationed at the fort and would have been serving in a multitude of tasks beyond farming and milling, like ranging, garrison duties and perhaps medical assistance. He is not listed with any type of rank but he later served the Pennsylvania line as a Lieutenant, so he must have had some type of service record within the militia that enabled him to step into an officer's role. His brothers are listed as serving in early militias. It would not be unlikely that he had some type of rank as owner of the mill fort.

He also served as an elder and would have carried out that function within the community while the attacks were under way and the pastor off leading a company of men. Elders were highly regarded by the people and elected to office. Each elder had an area of responsibility. John McDowell's wife and daughters might have also contributed to patient care and nurture at the fort. John's daughter, Mary, would later marry Dr. Richard Brownson (1737–1790) in 1765. Brownson would serve as a Surgeon during the Revolutionary War in the 6th Battalion under Colonel Samuel Culbertson. A number of John's nephews also later became doctors, so they may have all been put to work out of necessity.

Captain John Steel, former pastor of the log meeting-house, also was given official orders on March 25, 1756, to take formal post at McDowell's Mill Fort, though he was already staying there. Governor Morris wrote to Captain Steel:

> With these Instructions you will receive a Commission appointing you a Captain of a Company in the pay of the Province, which is to be made up by Draughts of 13 men out of each of the Companys composed by James Burd, Hans Hamilton, James Patterson and Hugh Mercer, Esq . . . also a commission appointing James Hollowday ({Holliday} your Lieutenant. When you have formed your Company you are to take post at McDowell's Mills, upon the road to Ohio, which you are to make your Head Quarters and to detach patrolling partys from time to time to scour the woods . . . You are to apply to Mr. Adam Hoops, for the Provincial allowance of Provisions for the men under your Command.[68]

Morris followed with instructions to Elisha Salter, Commissary General of Musters, to go to McDowell's and muster a company under Captain Steel. They were to send out patrolling parties to check the woods and to protect settlers. The Reverend Captain Steel with small pocket Bible carried a rifle with him everywhere.

While all this preparation was taking place, plantations, fields and the woods were still dangerous places for the settlers. In Hanover Township on March 7th Andrew Lycan and Ludwig Shut and a man named Revold were feeding animals when they were fired upon by 16 Indians.

Lycan, Revold, and Shut were wounded. Present were Lycan's son John, an African man, and a boy. The Indians also killed Bill Davis, Tom Hickman and Tom Hayes. Those particular Indians were identified as Delaware living 25 miles below Shamokin near Wiskinisco Creek. The same day Samuel Bell and his brother James, living 5 miles south of Carlisle, were hunting in Shearman's Valley. Samuel was at Mr. Patton's cabin on Shearman's Creek when he saw three Indians. All three Indians were subsequently killed.[69] The month rounded out with an Indian attack on March 30th at Patterson's Fort.

One-hundred Indians under Chief Shingas and Captain Jacobs from Kittanning divided themselves into two band between April 1st and 4th. One band arrived in the Conocoheague Settlement at William McCord's Fort. Fort McCord was a private fort near Mount Parnell midway between St. Thomas and Strasburg and a few miles north of Fort McDowell. McCord's two story house with loop holes had been stockade a few months earlier. It was at the base of the Kittatinny Mountain but was not well fortified. It was captured and burned.

Twenty-seven men, women and children were either killed or carried off by Indians. Among those killed were Mary McCord, Mrs. John Thorn and her baby, Mrs. Annie McCord wife of John McCord and her two daughters, Martha a young pregnant woman and a young girl. The Indians took William McCord's wife. They cut off James Blair's head and tossed it into Mrs. McCord's lap saying it was her husband's head but she knew it was not.[70]

One reason the Indians may have been particularly aggressive at McCords Fort might be traced back to 1753. McCord obtained his land grant that year and proceeded to push Delaware Indians out of their hunting area, burning their lodgings. When they tried to rebuild, he burned their lodgings again and the Indians finally withdrew. They may have held a grudge from that event and seemed to have been watching the fort. They knew the schedule of the men, attacking when farmers were out in the fields with less men on guard duty at the stockade.

Upon hearing the news of the loss of that fort, Captain Alexander Culbertson with a company of fifty men pursued. Captain Hance

Hamilton, now Commander of Fort Littleton, also heard about the event and marched east. A two hour engagement with Indians occurred at Sideling Hill and Culbertson was defeated. Each side lost about twenty with many wounded. The soldiers listed as killed included Captain Alexander Culbertson, Ensign of Captain Chamber's Company John Reynolds, with privates Robert and William Kerr, James Blair, John Layson, William Denny, Francis Scott, William Boyd, Jacob Paynter, Jacob Jones, Robert Kerr, William Chambers, Daniel McCoy, James Robertson "a tailor", James Robertson "a weaver", James Peace, John Blair, Henry Jones, John McCarty, John Kelly and James Lowder. Those wounded included Lieutenant Jamieson, Abraham Jones, Francis Campbell, William Reynolds, John Barnet, Benjamin Blyth, John McDonald, Isaac Miller, Engisn Jamieson, William Hunter, Matthias Gaushorn and William Swailes.[71] A surgeon was desperately needed from Carlisle and Dr. Prentice was requested. Some of the men retreated to Fort Littleton and some to McDowell Mill Fort.[72]

Chief Shingas and Captain Jacobs with forty warriors also streamed into the Coves, burning property, scalping settlers and taking prisoners like Hugh McSwine who later escaped. William Mitchel from the Conocoheague Settlement was also shot and killed while taking in his harvest.[73] Chief Shingas was also wounded on April 18th near Fort Cumberland, but raids continued under the leadership of Captain Jacobs.

At McDowell's Fort, Reverend Captain Steel had problems filling the governor's orders in building his company. The companies under Burd and Patterson, from which he was to take men, had men whose terms were expiring and they in turn were short staffed. Other companies also lacked guns and relied upon men bringing their own weapons. He could not at first secure men, arms or blankets.

> But we are in a great measure supplied by the arms the young men had brought with them. Captain Patterson had received but 33 fire-arms. Captain Mercer has not so many, but is supplied by Mr. Croghan's arms, and Captain Hamilton has lost a considerable number of his at the late skirmish at Sideling Hill. As I can neither

have the men, arms, nor blankets, I am obliged to apply to your Honor for them, the necessity of the circumstances has obliged me to muster before two magistrates the one-half of my company whom I enlisted and am obliged to order guns. I pray that with all possible expedition 54 arms and as many blankets and a quantity of flints, may be sent to me, for since McCord's fort has been taken and men defeated and pursued, our country is in the utmost confusion, great numbers have left the country and many are preparing to follow. May it please your honor to enlist me an ensign, for I find a sergeant's pay will not prevail with men to enlist in whom much confidence is reposed. I beg leave to recommend Archibald Erwin to your honor for the purpose.[74]

Col. Burd wrote to Governor Morris on April 19th from Carlisle. He had tried to recruit volunteers for his company but found few. He only had four new ones for 12 months service. Captain Mercer also was there recruiting for Fort Shirley. Burd wanted to march on the 19th for Fort Granville but the creeks were too high for the carriers to transfer the horses and loads over water. Fort Granville was without provisions at the time, enduring enemy assaults. He asked for a surgeon and medicine for the fort stating that "we shall loose one half of our men with perhaps slight wounds, purely for want of assistance."[75]

The conflicts in the American colonies with the French and Indians pushed the British to formally declare war on the French on May 18th. The Cumberland County suffered more loss on May 20th when John Wasson, a farmer in Peters Township, was scalped and his body was left horribly mangled.[76] His house was burned and his wife abducted. A posse of Steel's men followed the Indians but were unsuccessful in finding them. Armstrong wrote to Captain Burd on May 29th that he had been told by Captain Mercer on the 26th about the family and that three men from McDowells Mill had also been killed. A detachment of Captains Steel and Potter's men had gone on a search of the area.

In the midst of the devastation, the stagnant Commonwealth began to slowly move. Five large forts were constructed and connected to smaller private forts by patrols. In the spring of 1756, more than a dozen Pennsylvanian forts were established and staffed with paid troops.[77] Many of the settlers at those forts were tightly connected to each other ethnically, religiously and in many cases by marriage.[78] They would produce military and community leaders for generations to come.

John McDowell's Mill had functioned as a private fort until the Governor of Pennsylvania made it into a Provisional Chief Fort. This had marked the beginning of a Provincial defense system in Pennsylvania. It was part of the 1754 plan of defense for the Cumberland Valley and set on the old road into Virginia and the new road to Raystown/Bedford.[79] This western extremity of the early colonial roadway had marked the beginning area of the packers' or trader's path. Both Captain Steel, Mercer and Potter had their company headquarters at McDowell's Fort for a time. They detached scouts from there into the surrounding woods and patrolled the area.

Back east Benjamin Franklin urged the Assembly to continue to fund militia to protect the western frontier of the state. He accepted command of that frontier for a short time, and raised a force. The line of forts and block-houses along the Kittatinny Hills from Delaware to the Potomac were not, however, given artillery and not expected to be able to withstand a formal French assault with cannon. These forts were also widely separated. Twenty-five companies of militia were recruited and organized and stationed along the line of posts.

Pennsylvania finally had forts functioning well with paid troops by the spring of 1756. McDowell's Mill Fort, as a Provincial garrison for Militia, had men furnished with a rifle, ammunition and a blanket. Their weekly ration per man was 3 lbs. beef, 3 lbs. port, 1 lb. fish, 10 ½ lbs. bread/meal with one gill of rum per day.[80]

The towns of Carlisle and Shippensburg became centers where refugees gathered because they had functioned as a county seat at one time or other. Benjamin Franklin ultimately gave command of the area over to Colonel Clapham and he returned to the Assembly where he continued to be of great help.[81] The Earl of Loudoun was the Commander-in-Chief of His Majesty's Forces in the North Atlantic, and Governor Morris, who

McDowell's Mill Fort in the Defense of the Frontier

had formally declared war on the Indians and tried to stop the killing spree, was replace by William Denny as new Governor of Penns Woods (1756–1759).

While the colony tried to reorganize, soldiers in the forts took on their various duties. They patrolled and scouted for the enemy. They performed construction within their garrisons. They guarded settlers during harvest time which was paramount to survival on the frontier. Settlers had to rely on their protection and on their own provisions due to their distance from ports. They were no longer trading with the West Indies but were keeping the precious little they had to prevent starvation. The people in the valley tried to stabilize while protecting property and each other.

The French understood the importance of the harvest season for the British colonies. Western Indians were instructed to destroy it and to drive the hungry settlers out. In July, Indians surprised Captain Steel's men who were guarding reapers in the fields four miles from McDowell's Mill. The Indians killed and scalped one man, and another was taken. The reapers fled in terror. The same day one soldier by Maxwell's mill was guarding two women gathering water at the spring. The women made it back to the fort, the soldier was reported missing. At about the same time, a man and woman were scalped a few miles on the other side of the mill.[82]

Eight Indians arrived at the house of Jacob Peebles near Great Spring and McClure's Gap which was ten miles from Carlisle on the 21st. They killed an old woman and carried off two children. An old man went missing and the Indians chased a boy on horseback who was able to escape.[83]

Joseph Martin was killed on July 26th as two brothers, James and John McCullough, ages five and eight, were playing in the road along Muddy Run. Their two-year old sister was sleeping in the house while their parents and oldest sister were pulling flax with a neighbor, John Allen. Five Indians and one Frenchman arrived at the McCullough plantation in the Conocheague settlement. The war party attacked and scalped the parents, older sister Rebecca and a neighbor. Killing the youngest child and capturing the remaining children, the band took the two brothers to Fort Duquesne and then on to "Shenango and Saol Licks." They were held captive for eight years while John lived as an adopted son with the Delawares on the banks of the Muskingum River.[84]

That month the French and Indians also besieged the garrison of Fort Granville a few miles west of Lewiston, Pennsylvania, on the Juniata River. It was captured and John Armstrong's younger brother was killed. He had been an inspiration to the settlers during the early days of the engagements.

The governor spoke solemnly to the Assembly in Philadelphia on August 6th, "The people to the West of the Susquehanna, distressed by the frequent incursions of the enemy, and weakened by their great losses, are moving into the interior parts of the Province, and I am fearful that the whole country will be evacuated, if timely and vigorous measures are not taken to prevent it."[85]

Frightening reports circulated telling of the attack on August 8, 1756, of the Walter Family in a meadow along the Muddy Run near Rankin's Mill. The father, Casper, was killed by Indians and the house was set on fire. Five children were taken. The youngest was killed near the site and the oldest, Rebecca, was scalped. Inhabitants of Cumberland County wrote to the Governor about the attacks and the "large numbers of captives with settlers fleeing." They wrote that they were "finding that it is not in the power of the troops in pay of the government (were we certain of their being continued) to prevent the ravages of our restless, barbarous and merciless enemy." They reasoned that the loss of settlers was against "his Majesty's interests in general, and to the welfare of the people of this Province in particular."[86]

The government decided to address the issue at its source. Colonel John Armstrong was commissioned to lead an expedition in 1756 to the Indian village of Kittanning on the east bank of the Allegheny River, twenty miles north of Fort Duquesne, and to destroy it. Kittanning from the Delaware word Kit-han-ink means "at the great river" or "the big mountain river." The Allegheny and Ohio Rivers were considered the same river by the natives. Kittanning was the home of a number of

McDowell's Mill Fort in the Defense of the Frontier

Delaware from 1730–1756. It also had served as a recruiting station for bands of warriors who attacked the frontier settlements.

Armstrong raised 280 Provincial troops and prepared to march through the wilderness from Fort Shirley by August 31st. His troops were largely from the Cumberland Valley.[87] Armstrong's battalion included men in the companies of Captains Hance Hamilton, John Potter, Hugh Mercer, George Armstrong, Joseph Armstrong, Edward Ward and Joseph Callendar. William McDowell served as a Sergeant under Captain Hance Hamilton with Lieutenant William Thompson and Ensign John Prentice. The officers in the Cumberland Valley continually made pleas for blankets, arms and ammunition for their men.

Hance Hamilton wrote to Col. John Armstron at Carlisle on August 19th that he was on his way to the "two forts" with a part of Captain Mercer's company.[88] They were driving cattle and packhorses. The rest of the supplies were to be brought west by Captain Potter and Steel's men. Armstrong then wrote to Robert Hunter Morris from Carlisle on August 20, 1756, the following:

> To-morrow, God willing, the men march from McDowell's for Fort Shirley, and this afternoon some part of my own company, with the provisions here, set out for Shearman's valley, there to halt till the residue come up. This night I expected to have been at Fort Shirley, but am much disappointed in getting in of the strays, for collecting whereof we shall not wait longer than this day. Hunter has got about half a score, and commissary Hoops about a dozen. The commissioners (for which your Honor will please to make them my sincere compliments) have sent every thing necessary except the canteens wrote for by Mr. Buchannan, which I am persuaded they have forgot, and which we must supply by tin quarts. They were probably right in keeping back the tents, as they might have proven an incumbrance, and there is not one shilling laid out on this occasion that does not give me sensible uneasiness, but through the want of experience, and

fewness of our numbers, the good end proposed should fail of being obtained.

"The harvest season, with the two attacks on Fort Granville (Lewistown) has left us bare of ammunition, that I shall be obliged to apply to the stores here for some quantity, for the expedition. The Captains, Hamilton and Mercer, having broken open the part I sent to McDowell's for Fort Shirley, and given them receipts as for the expedition, though I know it for the particular defence of those two posts: nor will it be in my power to prevail with double the number of men, and a double quantity of ammunition to keep a Fort, that would have done it before the taking of Fort Granville. I hope the first opportunity of conveying ammunition to this town will be taken. For farther proofs of the numbers of Indians among us and waste of this country, I shall enclose your Honor some letters lately received."

McDowell's Mill Fort served as the gathering place with the provisions for the campaign. Hamilton and Mercer opened stores there for army use. Fort Shirley was to serve as the staging area for the actual raid on the Indians. It was located in Southern Huntingdon County by Shirleysburg. That fort was originally a trading post used by George Crogan. He had fortified his home and store houses, renaming it Fort Shirley. The fort was then taken over by the Pennsylvanian government and set within a chain of forts: Shirley, Granville, Lyttelton, and Patterson.

Mentioned in the above letter was a Peter Walker who had escaped from Granville and stated that there were about 120 enemy there and that a McDowell was serving as an interpreter. That "McDowell" spoke to Walker and warned of a possible attack on Fort Shirley coming by 400 men. It is unclear which McDowell this was. Captain Jacobs had threatened to burn Fort Shirley, which was taken seriously. Armstrong mentioned that he felt Fort Shirley was not easily defensible. Their access to water could be jeopardized. He also evaluated McDowell's Mill Fort.

He continued,

> Lyttleton, Shippensburg and Carlisle (the two last not finished) are the only forts now built that will, in my opinion, be serviceable to the public. McDowell's, or thereabouts, is a necessary post, but the present fort not defencible. The duties of the harvest have not admitted me to finish Carlisle Fort with the soldiers, it shoud be done, and a barracks erected within the fort, otherwise the soldiers cannot be so well governed, and may be absent or without the gates, at a time of the greatest necessity.[89]

Lieutenant-Colonel Armstrong's assessment that McDowell's Fort was "not defencible" would later result in the construction of a new fort two miles north. At that time McDowell's Mill Fort would returned to a private fort status. The new fort would be called Fort Loudoun/Loudon, named after Lord Loudoun the Commander-in-Chief of the British Army in North America from 1756 to 1757.

The Indians may have caught wind of the forthcoming attack because on August 27th bare chested American Indians in breech clothes, leggings, moccasins and caps attacked the mouth of the Conocheague Creek. What was called another "slaughter at Potomack" left 39 killed or taken.[90] Settlers had been attending a funeral when the attack began. It left fifteen persons killed and scalped, and the rest wounded or captured. William Morrison was captured and his house burned.

At another area six men on a scouting mission from Isaac Baker's were attacked with one returning wounded, four killed and other captured. More areas also were attacked. Militia scouting parties and settlers alike came under a gruesome assault. It continued into the next day when on August 28th Betty Ramsey, her son and a cropper were killed. Her daughter was taken prisoner.[91]

Thomas Barton, writing from Reading Township to the Governor on that day, stated that "Marsh Creek is now the frontier . . ."[92] The east side of the Susquehanna was abandoned. The intrusions of Indians and

McDOWELL'S MILL FORT

Fort Loudon/Loudoun was constructed in 1756 to replace Fort McDowell as McDowell's was deemed indefensible. This re-construction was done in 1993. Fort Loudon was two miles closer to the new road being constructed by General Forbes for his campaign to clear the French from Fort Duquesne (Pittsburg). The picture gives an idea of what McDowell's Mill Fort would have looked like. Photo courtesy of the Fort Loudon Historical Society.

the flight of settlers was impacting the function of the entire western part of the state.

A few days later William Morrison went to his home in the Conococheague Settlement and five Indians found him. He put up a fight and pretended to call in re-enforcements from both of his flanks. It worked, the Indians were startled as he escaped.[93] The settlers in these struggles were not aware of the arrival of Swiss born Henry Bouquet in New York. He was busy recruiting a regiment of Royal Americans for a forthcoming advance. Bouquet had entered military service at age 17, serving the Dutch first and then the British. He was highly trained in military tactics and drew from the Swiss and German populations in America for his regiment.

Colonel John Armstrong's column continued their march towards Kittanning to avenge the defeat at Fort Granville on September 7th. What would be called the Kittaning Expedition/Armstrong Expedition/Battle of Kittaning began with an advance group under Lieutenant James Hogg who had been sent to scope out the village. Two dozen Indians had left the day prior to attack the unit under Hogg. Hogg died of his wounds and a number of his men were lost.

Armstrong's forces launched their main attack on September 8th. A number of Indians had fled with prisoners prior to his arrival, but those who remained defended themselves. Their homes were burned by soldiers and the Indians were then killed and scalped by the soldiers. Captain Jacobs would not surrender. His home was set on fire with his family in it. He would not leave it. Gunpowder was stored within the structure. His home and other buildings exploded as they burned.[94] Both Chiefs Jacobs and Shingas were killed during this action. Newly delivered French war goods were also discovered in the tribal town.[95]

Armstrong returned to the Conocoheague on September 13th with 11 freed English captives. Prisoners re-taken from the Kittaning assault included Ann McCord, the wife of James from Fort McCord, and Martha age seven from same; Barbara Hicks from the Tonoloways Settlement; Catherine Smith a German child taken near Shamokin; Margaret Hood taken near the mouth of "Connegochieg," Maryland; Thomas Girty taken from Fort Granville; Sarah Kelly taken near Winchester, Virginia; and an unidentified woman, boy and two little girls.[96]

A peace treaty was later signed by Shinga's brother Tamagua called the Treaty of Easton, but the issue of Indian raids was far from settled.[97] Lieutenant-Colonel John Armstrong returned, a hero, to Carlisle where he busied himself reforming the 2nd Battalion of the Pennsylvania Regulars using men in Potter, Steel, Hamilton, Mercer, Burd and Patterson's companies.[98] Captain Mercer was one of those severely wounded at Kittanning by a bullet to the shoulder. He was carried from the field only to be forced to hide from Indians and slowly walk alone back to Fort Cumberland where he recovered. Mercer was then sent to command Fort Shirley with 75 men.

While that was going on, a petition was presented to the Assembly written by Rev. John Steel, Captain of a Company at Conococheague, related to the ravages of Indians. The conditions in the valley were said to be miserable. Others letters were read from those in distress in Shippensburg, and those suffering in Lurgan and Hopewell townships. Joseph Armstrong, a member of the Assembly, and Adam Hoops, commissary of provisions for Cumberland County forces, also presented their cases.[99] One petition after another spoke to the loss and suffering west of Philadelphia. The devastation was headline news even with the win at Kittanning.

The Pennsylvania Archives has a letter written by James Young to Harris's Ferry in October in which he mentions McDowell's Mill Fort in passing, showing that it was well known as a local landmark within the entire region. His focus, however, was on the possibility of the cannon located at Chamber's Fort being taken by the French and used against the community. This was a great concern because none of these forts in the Cumberland Valley could withstand large artillery barrages. They were made for simple defense and not against sophisticated assaults by trained European artillerymen.

> In our journey to Fort Lyttleton we stoped at Mr. Chamber's Mill, 10 miles beyond Shippensburg, towards Mckdowels, where he

> has a good Private Fort, and on an Exceeding good situation to be made very Defenceable; but what I think of great Consequence to the Government is, that in said Fort are two four Pound Cannon mounted, and nobody but a few Country People to defend it. If the Enemy should take that Fort they would naturally bring those Cannon against Shippensburg and Carlisle, I therefor Presume to recommend it to your Honor, Either to have the Cannon taken from thence, or a proper Garrison Stationed there.[100]

The cannons in what is now Chambersburg would not be relinquished by Ben Chambers and they continued their defense of the fortress. McDowell's Mill Fort, with two swivel canon, was in a similar situation of possible capture by the French. The guns could then be used against the British forts. In his report we see that the canon in question were four-pounders.

Throughout the fall atrocities continued with murders, scalping and abductions in the area. Houses were plundered and burned, animals killed and fields set on fire. Bands of Indians roamed as soldiers tried their best to protect settlers and guard those attempting to harvest remaining crops. In October in Bethel, Jacob Farnwal was fired on by two Indians and wounded. Frederick Henly and Peter Sample, on wagons, were killed. Indians tended to refer to these actions as raids, while settlers called them massacres. On November 4, 1756, Robert Callender wrote to Governor Denny from Carlisle:

> this day I received advice from Fort McDowell that on Monday or Tuesday last, one Samuel Perry and his two sons went from the Fort to their plantation, and not returning at the time they proposed, the commanding Officer sent there a corporal and 14 men to know the cause of their stay, who not finding them at the plantation, they marched back toward the fort, and on their return found the said Perry killed and scalped and covered over with leaves: immediately after a part of Indians, in number about 30, appeared and attacked the soldiers, who returned the fire,

and fought for some time until four of our people fell, the rest of them made off-six of them got into the Fort, but what became of the rest is not yet known; there are two families cut off, but cannot tell the number of people. It is likewise reported that the enemy in their retreat burnt a quantity of grain and sundry horses in the Cove.[101]

Listed as murdered soldiers in Captain Potter's company were James and William McDonald, Bartholomew McCafferty, and Anthony McQuoid. Those missing were James Corkem and William Cornwall. Inhabitants killed were John Culbertson, Samuel Perry, Hugh Kerrell, and John Woods. The wife and mother-in-law of Woods and Elizabeth Archer were also killed. John Archer's four children were missing as was a boy named Samuel Neely and a child named James McQuoid.[102]

John Armstrong, in his letter from Carlisle to Governor William Denny on November 8, relayed information:

> May it please yr Honor,
> Last week a party of Indians has been in the upper part of this County, but a few Miles from McDowel's Mill, where they have Barbarously Mangled a Number of the Inhabitants, and as is supposed taken some Children Captive; enclos'd is a list of the kill'd and Mission.
> A Certain Samuel Peary, mention'd in the List, left McDowel's Fort on Wednesday afternoon, only going to put his Horse to Pasture about a Mile & an half from the Fort, and had with him a little boy, but Neither returning that Night, fourteen men was Sent from the Fort belonging to Cap. Potter's Company, who found S. Perry scalp'd & his body cover'd with leaves; and on their return were waylaid by about thirty Indians, the Soldiers discovering the Enemy on every hand, gave the first fire, and says they wounded some, but were soon broken and put to the Rout, four of the Soldiers being kill'd on the spot, and two missing; this misfortune is happen'd thro' the weakness of the Garrison,

neither Potter's nor Armstrong's Company being compleat, and the latter having been Station'd in different parts of the Frontier was not convenient enough to assist, but they shall be no longer Separate. This week, God willing, we begin the Fort at Barr's There are general Complaints of the Powder here.[103]

Armstrong mentioned McDowell's Mill Fort again in a letter to the Governor on the 11th, stating that he had wanted to be there by that time to begin a new fort in the area close to it, but had to send 100 men to escort cattle and provisions to Lyttleton. He planned to visit McDowell's on his return trip.[104] Armstrong gave a report to the Governor on the status of McDowell's Fort on the 12th.

> . . . As we had nineteen people, soldiers and others, kill'd & taken near McDowells Mill, every Post in this Cn. Naturally expecting an attack at that time, we cou'd not even come up with these Murderers, tho' in our own Country.
>
> At present we have 100 men at McDowells, Guarding and Escorting the Publick Provisions to Fort Lyttleton, and are now on their way there, and as the residue are not near supply'd with proper Arms, its Utterly impossible for us to come up with the Enemy so far to the Northward, as in all Probability they will pass, as 'tis highly Probable they will return some 30 or 40 miles from Shamokin, up or across the East Branch of Sasquehanna, and so make the Ohio near Winnanggo. Some of them may return on this side Sasquehanna, about Ten or Fifteen Miles from Augusta, yet not so Probable; but in either of the Routs 'tis altogether out of our power to intercept them, yet I hope Colo. Claphams People will be successful. I am with a Detachment from each Fort to meet the Escort now set out for Lyttleton on Tuesday next, at Barrs place, where it's very Probable the Red Caps will soon pay us a Visit. We want about Sixty Blankets, and those we have are not near large enough.[105]

The men in Armstrong's charge who had been allotted 1 ½ pounds of fresh meat per day were now receiving 4 pounds of beef, 3 pounds of pork and 10½ pounds of flour a week, and a gill of rum or whisky per day. He complained to the governor about the cut in rations stating that some unscrupulous persons were selling goods to the men for a profit.[106] The beef were "ill fed" and men were given the leftover parts of the cow like necks, shins and the like. He wanted better beef so that the men did not lose weight and warned of scurvy. One hundred hungry men clustered around a small fort for any extended time was not a good thing.

He mentioned having been at McDowells in another letter to the Governor in which an incident involved deserters Philip Pather and Frederick Croft. They were suspected of having turned to the French as Catholics, though one professed to be Protestant. Pather had been intercepted on his way to Fort Duquesne by Captain Ward of Fort Lyttleton. Armstrong received the information "being then at McDowel's Mill," and he detached a party of men to apprehend Frederick Croft. Both men were sent on to the Carlisle Jail awaiting the Governor's orders in the matter.[107] The larger Cumberland County had only six Irish Catholics recorded in 1757, Lancaster County had 108 German Catholics and 22 Irish Catholics.[108] Protestants were the definite majority under the Protestant Colony and Crown.

Armstrong, reflecting on November 30th in a letter written to the Governor, "I'm sensible to the loss of the Soldiers near McDowels was owing to ye defects {numbers} of Potters Company, and Joseph Armstrong's being with 20 of his men then at his own House, but not ye murders then done in ye neighbourhood, for these might have happen'd had ye Fort been ever so well Garrison'd."[109] Though Captain Potter's men had served well, Armstrong had already assessed that the fort, though necessary, was indefensible. Another site had been proposed on the Barr property to the north but after examination, Armstrong claimed that he could not find a proper situation for a fort there. The soil was "too Strong to admit the Ditch, and the spot it self, Overlook'd by an adjoining Hill."[110] He found property belonging to Mr. Matthew Patton more agreeable. Patton's house had been burnt by Indians in prior raids. The property was near the new road being constructed, two miles north of McDowell's. The new fort would be named Fort Loudoun/Loudon after the current commander of the armed forces in the colonies and would connect communications between Shippensburg and Fort Lyttleton by Sugar Cabins. The fort, also referred to as Fort Conococheague, would have a 127 foot square palisade with two wooden buildings on stone foundations and a stone-lined well. The gate would be on the north wall. It also would have a jail. One of the two buildings may have been the existing log house. Armstrong over-saw the work on the project. They were still in need of arms and blankets.

Armstrong informed the Governor on December 22, 1756, that "The Publick Stores are safely removed from McDowels Mill to Fort Loudon, the barracks for the soldiers are built, and some proficiency made in the stockade, the finishing of which will doubtless be Retarded by the inclemency of the weather, the Snow with us being upward of a foot deep."[111] He requested the "colours" {the British flag}, and stated that the new fort would need at least 50 men garrisoned with two commissioned officers. With the establishment of the new fort, even though not completed, John McDowell's Mill Fort returned to a private fort status.

CHAPTER SIX

1757—1759

McDowell's Mill Fort during Gen. Forbes' Campaign

McDowell's Mill Fort returned to the function of a private fort in 1757 but still housed companies of men. A report had circulated that the French and Indians had an encampment at Raystown/Bedford and that they were still moving in small bands through Pennsylvania. One hundred men under Captain Lieutenant-Colonel Conrad Weiser's 1st Battalion were sent to reinforce the Cumberland Valley. Some of those men were stationed at McDowell's Fort from February to April of 1757.[1] It would be another cramped setting.

Officers in 1st Battalion included Captain Lieutenant-Colonel Weiser with Captain Lieutenant Samuel Weiser and Ensign Henry Geiger; Captain Major William Parsons with Lieutenant Jacob Wetterholt and Ensign Martin Everhart; Captain Frederick Smith with Lieutenant Anthony Miller and Ensign Nicholas Cunrod; Captain Jacob Morgan with Lieutenant Andrew Engle and Ensign Jacob Kearn; Captain John Witterhold with Lieutenant James Hyndshaw and Ensign Daniel Harvey; Captain Christian Bussee with Lieutenant Samuel Humphrys and Ensign William Johnson; Captain Jacob Orndt with Lieutenant Philip

Marsloff and Ensign Jacob Sneider; Captain John Vanetton with Lieutenant Samuel Allen; Captain George Reynolds with Lieutenant Philip Weiser; and Captain James Patterson with all their companies.[2] Captain Schmitt wrote on March 21, 1757, from McDowell's Mill Fort that the people at the fort needed attention. Lack of pay was the main issue and some of the reinforcements later left the fort discontent in April.[3]

Indians had attacked at Rocky Springs on March 29th with one woman killed and 11 taken prisoners. This was followed by attacks April 2nd on William McKinley and his son. Both were killed and scalped while trying to reach home having left the safety of Chamber's Fort. *The Pennsylvania Gazette*, April 7, 1757, mentioned more deaths at the Conococheague settlement with three families killed by Indians, two of which were the Campbells and Pattersons.[4]

Jeremiah Jack was taken captive on April 17th near the Potomac River and his two sons were killed. Another man and one woman were drowned in the Potomac. On April 23rd another John Martin and William Blair were killed with Patrick McClelland wounded in the shoulder, dying later near Fort Maxwell.[5] In May the abductions and murders continued with 11 people killed at Paxton, and then Colonel John Stanwix was sent by Lord Loudoun with members of the 1st Battalion of Royal American Regiment to strengthen Cumberland County, establishing his headquarters at Carlisle on May 30th. Five companies of his battalion constructed an entrenched camp northeast of that town.[6]

Two men were killed and five taken near Shippensburg on June 6th and on the 9th Lieutenant James Holiday/Holliday and 14 men were either killed or taken by Indians. James, killed, was serving in Captain Hugh Mercer's Regiment in the 2nd Battalion. He had served under Captain Steel in the Kittaning Campaign of 1756. His wife was Elizabeth McDowell, daughter of the pioneer William and sister of the miller John McDowell.[7] Seventy-five of his men had been sent to reconnoiter in the woods. Half the men were at a local spring when surprised by 100 Indians while the other half were at the deserted house of Mr. McClellan in the Great Cove.

The tension in the valley grew as news arrived stating that James Long's son and another man were killed in a quarry at Fort Frederik, nineteen men were killed in a mill at Quetapahely and four men were killed in Shearman's Valley. One man was additionally killed on June 17th at Cuthbertson's Fort. Four men in the fort had shot at the Indians while they scalped the man. Alexander Miller was killed on June 24th and his two daughters were taken from the Conococheague, and John Kennedy was badly wounded, and Gerhart Pendergrass' daughter was killed at Fort Littleton.

July was even worse. One woman and four children were taken from Trent's gap on July 2nd. The same day a man with the last name of Springson was killed near Logan's Mill in Conococheague. Men were killed on the 4th while driving a wagon to Fort Frederick. On the 8th, two boys were taken from Cross' Fort in Conococheague. The next day Trooper Wilson's son was killed at Antietam Creek, and on the following day ten soldiers were killed at Clapham's Fort. Six men were either killed or taken on the 18th near Shippensburg. They had been out cutting crops in John Cisney's field. Among those killed were John Kirkpatrick, Dennis Oneidon and those missing were John Cisney and three boys, two of which were Cisney's grandsons and the other was Kirkpatrick's grandson.

Men were also killed and taken while reaping a field near Shippensburg on July 19th. Joseph, James and William Mitchell, John Finlay, Robert Steenson, Andrew Enslow, John Wiley, Allen Henderson and William Gibson were among those killed and Jane McCommon, Mary Minor, Janet Harper and the son of John Finlay were among those missing with only one Indian killed, and on the 27th a man named McKisson was wounded and his son taken from South Mountain.[8]

John Armstrong wrote to the Governor from Carlisle in late July reporting on the tracking of small parties of Indians at Raystown. He was covering the area from Fort Duquesne to Fort Cumberland with his men. He mentioned their "extreme fatigue" with the daily pursuits of small bands of Indians. The combination of ranging, protecting settlers trying to harvest crops and recovering items dispersed during raids was

McDowell's Mill Fort during Gen. Forbes' Campaign

taking a toll on his men.[9] He went on to say that on Wednesday of the past week he and forty soldiers with Mr. Smith, Indian interpreter, and ten Cherokee Indians had marched into Shearman's Valley along with 30 inhabitants who were trying to remove their cattle from there. The friendly Indians detected tracks in the area moving west. The Cherokee were afraid of the Western tribes and would later defect.

Armstrong went on to describe attacks near Carlisle, and repeated the fact that Colonel Stanwix was sending out "fatigued men" with the Cherokee to save the harvest. The excessive rains were not helping and had swollen the creeks making them hard to cross.[10] Armstrong complained to the Governor of a lack of provisions. All the forts needed meat. He and a local doctor were concerned that the men were not having nutritious diets. He also mentioned that the surgeon had not been paid, and that there was a need for an exchange of old arms for new.

> May it Please your Honr,
> For the Security of the Inhabitants in the Harvest, I have strenuously recommended the people's working together in partys as Large as possible, and have from Willm Maxwel's, near the Temporary line, to John McCormick's, near Sasquehanah, plac'd out about twenty Guards, altering and Changing the Station as well as the Number of Each guard, according to the necessity and Conveniency of the people. Where a Number of Women and children happen to be in any Fort, the guard Stays with them, by which Means all the Men belonging to such Garrison are enabled to Labour; but where women and children are not wth the party, then the soldiers are Station'd with the Reapers, keeping Centry around the field, whereby some of the Sculking Enemy have been discover'd & repuls'd; but such is the infatuation of a Number of the people that they can't be prevail'd on to convene in proper partys for their Own Safety, in consequence where of the following Melancholy accidents have happen'd . . . [11]

He reported 12 men with flux at Fort Loudon and the lack of meat there. Mr. Hoops was out trying to secure provisions in Carlisle. Dr. Blair had attended the sick and some were beginning to recover. He focused again on the poor diet. It would be likely that the same held true two miles south at Fort McDowell.

While the letter was read by his superiors, the settlements were still under attack and a severe illness hit near Hanover in Lancaster County. It disabled most of the inhabitants leaving them without sufficient men for protection and on August 15th, William Manson and his son living near Cross's Fort were killed.

Twenty guards were on watch from William Maxwell's Fort to John McCormick's near the Susquehanna, additional people were serving as guards, but on the 17th the bands of Indians kept moving east and in Tract, York County, William Waugh's barn was burned. James Mackey's son was taken on the 18th and the son of Joseph Barnet with Elizabeth Dickey and her child, and the wife of Samuel Young and her child. 94 people of all ages fled "in one body" and more in smaller groups.

An assault happened on the 19th near Harris' Ferry with 14 either killed or taken from Rev. Cinky's congregation.[12] In Lancaster County six were taken and a man named Beatty was killed in Paxton.[13] In Berks County, Indians were spotted by Fort Lebanon and on the 21st the house and barn of Peter Semelcke were burned. Three of his children were taken. Four additional person were made prisoners by 50 Indians. Four children were taken from Lebanon Township, in addition some type of sickness seemed to be in that area from which people were quickly dying.[14]

By 1757 Lieutenant-Colonel John Armstrong with Lieutenant James Potter and Ensign Frederik Van Hornbeck were in charge west of the Susquehanna River and Commander Loudoun sent his entire 2nd Battalion to the area by September. Seven companies arrived at Carlisle on the 22nd; two others were at Reading; and a third was divided between Lancaster and York. It was a desperate month with James Watson found scalped and James Mullen missing on September 1st. The next day a man was killed near Bigger's Gap along with one Indian.

Daniel Voorhees models a reproduction British uniform worn during the re-enactment of the Battle of Monmouth in June of 2015. Photo by author used by permission, the Division of Parks and Forestry, Trenton, New Jersey.

Two men looking for their horses near Tobias Hendricks' in current Pennsboro Township, Cumberland County, were missing on September 8th and the next day a boy and girl were taken from Donegal. John Andrew's wife was taken by 6 Indians in Hanover, and in Bethel Township John Winkleblech's two sons with a provincial soldier named Joseph

Fischbach were attempting to bring in cows when they were fired on by 15 Indians. The two boys were killed and one scalped. The boy fled to the house where he later died. The soldier was wounded in the hand.[15]

The same morning two miles below Manaday Gap Thomas McQuire's son was bringing in cows when he was chased by two Indians and escaped. The same day in Hanover, Leonard Long's sons were ploughing when one was killed and scalped. The other son was taken prisoner. John Graham near the gap of Indian Town Creek who had lost a steer was killed and John Brown had two cows killed. Rangers tried to follow the roving warriors but seemed to be unsuccessful at finding them. The month rounded out with Robert Rush and John McCraken with five others killed or taken captive near Chambersburg on September 26th.

Peter Wampler's children were taken in in Lebanon on October 1st and on the 17th four were near Hunter's Fort were simply pulling corn. Alexander Watt and John McKennet were killed and scalped and then dismembered. Two other were also scalped. The Captain of the Augusta Regiment met 20 Indians on Peter's Mountain and the enemy ran giving them a slight feeling of victory.[16]

To the east in Philadelphia, James Hamilton was appointed Governor of the besieged Commonwealth of Pennsylvania. The British government finally voted in money for the colonies for five years to cover the expenses related to the French and Indian War. This was largely due to the politicking in London of Philadelphia citizen Benjamin Franklin.[17]

The settlement around McDowell's Mill Fort was attacked once again by Delaware Indians on November 9, 1757. John Woods, his wife and mother-in-law were all killed. His four children were taken hostage, and an additional nine men were killed near the Fort.

Hunter's Fort reported spotting 12 Indians. Soldiers ranged the area and found William Martin dead in the woods. They tried to rally the inhabitants to continue a search but were hindered by rain.

Thomas Robinson and the son of Thomas Bell were killed and scalped in Hanover Township on the 25th. The multiple waves of carnage seemed to be unstoppable. Townships were on guard and the tension seemed to never break while warriors moved freely both east and west of the Susquehanna, attacking soldiers and inhabitants. Scorched plantations lay abandoned with enemy bands roaming through the woods.

Up to that point the Earl of Loudoun had been in charge of the British military in the colonies, but he was recalled in 1758. Scottish born General James Abercrombie (1706–1781) was given command with James Wolfe (1727–1759), Jeffery Amherst (1717–1797) and John Forbes (1707–1759) serving under him. The operations in the American colonies would now focus on attacks of the French fort at Louisburg, Nova Scotia; the New York Hudson River Valley region and across Pennsylvania to Fort Duquesne on the forks of the Ohio.

The British attack in Pennsylvania would be led by Scottish-born Brigadier-General John Forbes with Swiss-born Lieutenant-Colonel Henry Bouquet (1719–September 2, 1765) as second in command. Forbes was the 51 year-old laird of the Pittencrieff Estate near Edinburgh and a doctor of medicine, he was slowly dying. Bouquet was a 39 year-old professional soldier hired by the British to fight in this campaign.

General Forbes increased the number of all the troops under him on March 23, 1758. Nine companies were garrisoned at 11 posts on a line from the Delaware to the Susquehanna Rivers and the numbers were increased at Fort Augusta. General Forbes was ordered to reduce Fort Duquesne using Royal troops, with militia from Pennsylvania and Virginia under highly cultured brunet Colonel Bouquet and tall reddish-brown haired, George Washington, now twenty-six. Forbes' forces would total about 7,000 men. Bouquet had been successful in rallying German and Swiss immigrants from Pennsylvania, Maryland and Virginia to fight in his 60th Royal American Regiment.

While the British plan was being implemented, Teedyuscung, leader of the eastern Delaware was in peace negotiations with Pennsylvania Governor William Denny in Philadelphia. The British plan was to try to keep Indians neutral while the campaign against the French proceeded.

General Forbes wrote to the Governor of Pennsylvania on March 28, 1758, with his plan to have troops assemble at "Conegochie" on April 20th. The winter of 1758 had seen a lessening of attacks on that settlement, but spring and harvest seasons were always the most dangerous time. Sure enough on April 13, 1758, young Hannah McBride spotted 19 Indians outside Richard Bard's home and ran to tell her Father and Mother there. Lieutenant Thomas Potter, brother of General Potter was also there as was a child a 6 month old and a "bound boy," most likely indentured. The Indians rushed the house and killed Potter. The rest surrendered and were taken prisoner.[18] Indians returned on May 21st, abducting a woman and five children from Yellow Breeches and on the 23rd Joseph Gallady was killed and his wife and child taken from Conocotheague.

Negotiations had begun with Cherokee Indians during the summer of 1758 for assistance in fighting the Western tribes. Forty Cherokee gathered at Fort Loudoun to discuss an alliance, but the Indians soon grew tired of the slow pace taken by the British army as they began the construction of another road. Fearful of the power of the Western tribes, the Cherokee would not only leave but later become the backbone of Pontiac's forces against the same settlers in the 1760s.

Forbes' campaign would differ drastically from Braddock's. He planned a line of forts at regular intervals for supply and communication along his new road where troops could find protection. He would enter the forks of the Ohio on Burd's Pennsylvania military road instead of using Braddock's Road, which caused Virginia and Maryland great concern since each had designs on the Ohio area.

Forbes placed elements of the 42nd Royal Scottish Highlander Regiment of Foot, Black Watch, who had arrived from the West Indies, in the Cumberland Valley and some were barracked at McDowell's Mill Fort, awaiting the expedition.[19] Many of those troops were ill and needed time to recover. The Lowlander Ulster-Scots in the Cumberland Valley tended to dislike the Scottish Highlanders, a feeling which would only intensify. They had differing ethnicity, language and traditions even though both claimed to be Scots. Even so, the Cumberland men joined the Highlanders for this campaign. John Armstrong was the Colonel Commandant of the 1st Pennsylvania Battalion and Colonel James Burd commanded the 2nd Pennsylvania Battalion. Armstrong was second under Bouquet. Thirty-three year old Justice William McDowell was promoted to Ensign

McDowell's Mill Fort during Gen. Forbes' Campaign

These men are dressed as Royal Scottish Highlanders who were housed at Fort Loudon and McDowell's Mill Fort for the Forbes Campaign against the French. Photo courtesy of the Fort Loudon Society.

under Captain Thomas Hamilton and Lieutenant Victor King within Hugh Mercer's 3rd Battalion.[20]

Sir John St. Clair, Lieutenant-Colonel of the 60th Foot, was the Quartermaster for the expedition, as he had been for the Braddock campaign. He had a quick temper and both Forbes and Bouquet were uncomfortable with his role in the venture.[21] Food and supplies were gathered at Lancaster, Pennsylvania, in the brick courthouse. Local farmers delivered cattle, forage, flour and other items for military use. The area around McDowell's Mill most likely contributed to this collection of material because the settlers dearly wanted the campaign to be successful. The British wagons, once again, were too heavy for the roads and they needed to be exchanged for Pennsylvania wagons and packhorses. Men like Adam Hoops assisted in the hiring of these.[22]

Local militias were rationed seven pounds of bread or flour, seven pounds of beef or 3½ pounds of pork either fresh or salt brined, six pints of dried peas, ½ a pint of rice, and 6 ounces of butter a week with ¼ pint of rum or whiskey a day. The diet could be supplemented with fresh game, salted fish, oatmeal or beans. They usually carried their provisions in their haversacks. Four to six men formed a "mess" and shared cooking utensils, a single tent with an iron kettle and a hatchet. Officers, of course, ate much better.[23] Most of the Pennsylvania men were dressed in their ordinary clothes.

The Governor was the one who had given the task of overseeing the military road construction to Brigadier-General Forbes, who in turn gave it over to Bouquet. The road begun by James Burd by Fort McDowell was supposed to have connected to Braddock's Road at the Youghiogheny River, called Turkey foot, but Colonel Dunbar had evacuated Braddock's army after Braddock's defeat and the construction had stopped. Colonel Burd's Road wound around Parnell's Knob or North Mountain, passing in a Northerly direction up Path Valley and then over the Tuscarora Mountain by Cowan Gap. It then slid down between Tuscarora and Cove Mountain to Little Aughwick Creek at Burnt Cabins.[24] It had only been completed three miles beyond Raystown.

In the new plan, Fort Lyttleton/Littleton would be linked to Fort Loudoun/Loudon just north of McDowell's for supply and communications. Forbes' forces would marched to Raystown/Bedford and begin construction of the new road to Ohio which needed to be completed for the campaign. Construction on Forbes Road began in June. It would be the chief road from the East to Pittsburgh and would zigzag the current path of the Lincoln Highway or Route 30.

The Burd Road to Raystown had followed the Indian and trader path which was then widened by axe-men under Colonel Henry Bouquet. Forbes could have cut south from Raystown to Fort Cumberland in Maryland and then followed the existing Braddock's Road west but he chose not to do that, a decision which bothered George Washington to no end. Forbes had the road cut from Raystown directly west instead because he felt it was closer to the Forks of the Ohio. It proved difficult to make it accommodate an army of 6,000 men with artillery and took six months to complete.

Lieutenant-Colonel Bouquet also met with the Cherokee and Catawba warriors in June at Fort Loudoun before marching to Raystown to oversee the beginning work on the road from there. Raystown would be renamed Fort Bedford, now simply known as the town of Bedford. That would be a base camp for the campaign. Bedford was in an isolated valley and would have an irregular 400 foot square Pentagon stockade constructed with an earthen moat on the Juniata's rocky bluff.

Meanwhile to the east on July 15, 1758, an envoy with German Moravian Christian Frederick Post and Delaware leader Pisquetomen left Philadelphia on a peace mission to the Ohio Indians after having held council with Governor Denny and others. Post had lived with and married into an Indian family. He and Teedyuscung had been instrumental in diplomatic negotiations. A treaty would assure Indian neutrality in struggles between the French and British, which was key to success in the campaign.

The Forbes Expedition would last from September to October of 1758 with the mission to drive the French from the Ohio country. Colonel Bouquet left from Carlisle in August in preparation as his army was gathered at Fort Loudoun. Pennsylvanian troops joined his regular units there.

Colonel John Armstrong was busy that month hacking out the road across Pennsylvania to Loyalhanna as Colonel George Washington with Virginia troops at Fort Cumberland in Maryland began their route on the old Braddock Road towards Fort Duquesne. They would meet Bouquet at Loyalhanna in August. Forbes, very ill, slowly made his way to Shippensburg behind his men.

Colonel Burd, with his detachment of Pennsylvania militia, arrived at Loyalhanna early in September and began construction on Fort Ligonier with Bouquet joining a few days later. Burd and James Shippen would also built Fort Burd the following year on the Monongahela as a depot for the river transport to Pittsburg.

Forbes arrived at Fort Loudon on September 6th. Though gravely ill, he was still able to not only oversee the road constructed but orchestrated the fortification of forts at Carlisle, Shippensburg, Chambersburg, Loudon, Littleton, and Bedford. He had not studied engineering. He had studied medicine and may have known that this was his last battle.

Current analysis of his symptoms point towards a form of gastroenteritis, an inflammation of the stomach or intestines caused by bacteria, viruses or parasites which blocks the absorption of vitamins and nutrients, resulting in some of the skin disorders and other symptoms from which he suffered.[25] He was carried in distress on a stretcher slung between two horses for the remainder of the campaign. He reached Raystown on September 15th. His great road would become the primary military road from the Atlantic Ocean to the trans-Allegheny region which would be used throughout the Revolutionary War as the main route to reach the western forts.[26]

The seventy-seventh Royal Scottish Highlander commander, Major James Grant, was sent on a reconnoitering mission to Fort Duquesne with 850 men on September 14th. They were beaten back by French resistance and many were taken. Major Grant was among the captured. General Forbes debated waiting for a full scale attack, thinking to winter his troops first, however, the French with Indians attacked Loyalhanna on October 12th. They were successfully repulsed by the British forces and later in the month Colonel George Washington arrived with the Virginia troops.

Christian Frederick Post and Pisquetomen had returned to Philadelphia from the west with items of business which would lead to the Treaty of Easton, Pennsylvania, between the Ohio Indians and the Pennsylvania government. Conrad Weiser had also spent the fall in council at Easton as an arbitrator with the western tribes of the Ohio, trying to encourage their abandoning support of the French. The Western Indians finally agreed to cut off their allegiance to them in exchange for no European settlements in the Ohio Country. It would be a condition that would never be upheld by the British. Post and Pisquetomen then headed back west.

They met General Forbes who had finally arrived at Loyalhanna in November with news of the Treaty of Easton. Both diplomats then proceeded with letters from Forbes to the Western Indian villages. Their role had been instrumental in saving many lives.

The British were twelve miles from Fort Duquesne on November 24th when the French Canadian Commander François-Marie le

Marchand de Lignery (1703–1759) blew up Fort Duquesne and escaped with his garrison on local rivers. The British army took possession of the smoldering French fort the next day with General Forbes arriving on November 26th. He renamed the site Pittsburgh in honor of William Pitt, British Prime Minister from 1766–1768, and declared a day of public thanksgiving. Construction began in earnest on the new Fort Pitt.

Bouquet was ordered to remain at Pittsburg until December and then slowly head back to Ligonier as Captain Mercer took command of Fort Pitt. General John Stanwix succeeded General Forbes on March 15, 1759, when Forbes sadly died. Stanwix went on to Pittsburg in August of 1759.

The fortress at Louisbourg in Nova Scotia was also taken by the British, and Wolfe took Quebec from Montcalm. The British had won Canada from the French. The struggle between the two countries was finally over and the 1758 Easton Treaty with Indians promised a sense of closure to the conflicts for the colonists. It was now possible for settlers to re-claim their plantations and slowly recover from all the loss of life.

Some of the white captives were returned to Fort Pitt by Delaware and Shawnee Indians and then between June 1759 and October 1760 an additional 138 were released. Even with the success of the capture of Fort Duquesne, the area around the Conococheague Settlement was still subject to random attacks by western Indians. Fort McDowell still stood with the promise of refuge for settlers.

The patriarch William McDowell Sr. was able to learn of the end of the conflicts with the French while living in Wrightsville but died soon after on September 12, 1759, at age 77. His body was not returned to his home by Mount Parnell, instead it was ferried across the Susquehanna River and he was buried in the Old Donegal Presbyterian Churchyard in Lancaster County. His funeral was most likely conducted by Rev. Joseph Tate who served the church from 1748 to 1774. The church during that period was made of undressed field stones with a dirt floor and an unpainted interior. Paver bricks would later be laid over the dirt and then a wooden floor. The entrance faced the southeast and the new graveyard where William's grave with horizontal marble slab is still visible today. His weathered tomb reads "In Memory of William McDowell Late of Conococheague who was a tender parent, careful instructor and an example of piety to a numerous progeny, when the settlement was obliged to fly by the barbarous Indian war he deceased in these parts so was interred here September 12th, 1759, aged 77 years." William left a detailed will which included money for his burial, ferry fees for the family, mourning scarfs, gloves, his wife's funeral expenses and refreshments for all at "Mr. Baylies," an inn.[27] Mary Irvine McDowell, his wife, died shortly after him on November 27, 1760. William had conveyed land to his sons as tenants in 1754.

CHAPTER SEVEN

1760—1764

McDowell's Mill Fort during Pontiac's Rebellion

The Cumberland Valley began to fill again with those who had fled during the disturbances following Braddock's loss. Colonel James Smith recounted in his narratives published in the early 1800s, *Incidents of Border Life*, that as "the people were now beginning to live at home again, they thought it hard to be driven away a second time, and were determined, if possible, to make a stand; therefore they raised as much money by collections and subscriptions, as would pay a company of riflemen for several months."[1] At the gathering of the subscribers, a committee was elected to manage the process and James Smith was elected to serve as Captain of the group of rangers.

Smith had been held captive by Indians and had learned Indian warfare techniques. He dressed his rangers with "breech-clouts, leggings, moccasins and green shrouds." They wore red handkerchiefs on their heads and then painted their faces red and black. He recounted, "I taught them the Indian discipline . . . we succeeded beyond expectation in defending the frontiers, and were extolled by our employers."[2] Smith had served as an Ensign in the regular army in the Pennsylvania Line and now was leading his men in a different discipline. Even with the local protection, on May 29th, 1759, a Mr. Dunwiddie and Mr. Crawford shot two Indians in Carrol's tract, York County, and then on July 20th a boy ploughing at Sweetara was shot by two Indians. A horse also was killed and another person wounded by warriors.³

Desires for retaliation inevitably grew among the settlers. They had been distrustful of American Indians, not knowing which band was the clear enemy, and they did not always have a desire to discern the matter. Their frustration would be carried to extremes within the next few years. A Delaware Indian, named Doctor John, who had been considered friendly lived in a hunting cabin on the Conodoguinet Creek with his family. They were killed and scalped in the winter of 1760 by whites. It was called an "inhuman and barbarous murder"⁴ by the authorities. James Hamilton had been installed as Pennsylvania Governor in 1759 and he learned of the murder on February 21st. An inquest was made by Captain Callender who was then to report to the Assembly his findings and a reward of 100 pounds was offered for the apprehension of those involve to avoid retaliation by the Indians.

A search for those guilty took place between the Conodoguinet and Kittatinny mountains, all the way to the Susquehanna River. In the report, some of the settlers referred to the Indian as "insolent" by showing "disrespect" towards area soldiers. Doctor John reportedly bragged that he with a small band could drive the soldiers out. The Indian allegedly said that even though Captain Jacobs had been killed, there were others more powerful able to take his place. He also was reported to have bragged of killing 60 whites himself and capturing six. After careful examination, Callender found that fingers for the murder pointing to John Mason of Cumberland County, James Foster of Paxton, William George and his son with some of the sons of Arthur Foster. The men fled to the forks of the Ohio. A conference was later held with the bereaved relatives of the Delaware at Philadelphia on May 6, 1762. Governor Hamilton, Richard Peters and Joseph Fox extended great sorrow for the loss to the family.⁵ It seemed to have been accepted.

With one potential powder keg extinguished, life in the Cumberland Valley began to take on some normalcy and the education of children was able to continue. In 1760, John King became one of the first formal teachers of boys in what would be Franklin County. His log school was next to Steele's meeting-house at Church Hill and featured a Latin education. John was in his early 20s and served the community teaching for three years. He had studied French, Greek and Latin and would later learn Hebrew. He also had studied logic, metaphysics and philosophy. His sister, Susan, was married to Hugh Cunningham and lived by the White Church. Some of the McDowells attended this school, especially noted was Justice William McDowell's son John (1751–1820) who later became the first Principal of St. John's College in Annapolis and the third Provost of the University of Pennsylvania, as well as serving as a professor. William's other sons would have most likely been in that school along with their cousins. South of King's school Enoch Brown was teaching children males and females, in a log school three miles north of Green Castle/Greencastle. Schools had wooden benches with desks attached to the outer walls.

In the larger McDowell family, Nathan McDowell had fled during the French and Indian War to Lancaster. He wrote to his brother Constable James, who was near Fort Loudon, on April 6, 1761, stating that he was collecting wool for blankets and mentioned 300 men who had enlisted to garrison area forts. He may have been seeking supplies for the Mill Fort. He inquired about the possibility of a market at Carlisle for flour while commenting on the great rain they had received.[6] James was preparing for a wedding and married Jean "Jane" Smith on June 7, 1761. This was one year after the death of his father.

Jane was sister to Mary, the wife of Justice William Smith. He had married his cousin. Jane and Mary were sisters of Captain James Smith who was now leading patrols of men in Indian apparel. William and James Smiths lived just west of McDowell's Mill Fort. It would be unlikely for any of them to have missed this wedding with everyone living so close to each other and attending the same church. Jean McDowell, a sister to the Constable, Justice and Miller, had married Archibald Irwin in 1757. Irwin was an ensign in Captain Steel's company during the Kittaning Expedition. Their daughter, Elizabeth, would later marry Robert Smith, brother of Justice William Smith. In fact, when one looks at the Ulster-Scot families in the valley with each having many children, one begins to see many families tied to each other, often making neighbor kin. It may also explain why they worked well with each other in military formations. They were often defending family members.

John McDowell, the miller, was now forty-four. McDowell's Mill Fort may have still housed some of the local militia or rangers as settlers returned to their properties to rebuild and tend their farms. Those settlers returning may have also needed shelter during this process with so many dwellings destroyed. They could have sought refuge at the fort. Log cabins were slowly raised near the charred ruins of homes and barns as the mill and store returned to their earlier purposes of grinding wheat and selling flour. The McDowell family members would have continued to till their own soil and cultivate crops.

As part of this reconstruction process, the residents of Peters Township gathered and submitted an April 1761 petition to the government for a new road to help them get their items to market, particularly flour. It was now possible to export crops. The only market available to them was Baltimore and there was no easy way to reach the port. There were two mills in the town proposal which connected to the suggested road: one was John McDowell's mill and the other was Justice William Smith's mill. They asked for the road to go from the mills to meet at or near the house of Justice William Maxwell's mill and from there to run towards Baltimore until it met York County. The three in-laws had definite interests involved in this community project. The road would later be granted in April of 1768, but the branches to the mills would be restricted to bridle paths. The road would unite near James Irwin's mill in Peters township and then cross the Conococheague Creek at the mouth of Muddy Run as it ran through Antrim to Nicholson's Gap in South Mountain and then on to Baltimore. It followed a trail which became a bridle path turned to wagon road, and then a turnpike as so many other roads in the colony had done. In 1768 the court appointed Justice William McDowell, Esq., as one of the "viewers" for the road.[7]

General Henry Bouquet (1719–September 2, 1765) was overseeing the construction of forts at Presqu'Isle, Venango and LeBoeuf as the colonies received news of a new king. King George II had died in 1760 and was succeeded by his unstable son George III. During this transitional period in England, Parliament was discussing ways to defray their expenses incurred by the French and Indian War with plans to transfer that burden onto the colonists via assorted taxes.

The ever nagging issue of the boundary line between Maryland and Pennsylvania also resurfaced in court. Even with a tentative solution in place which only addressed the settled portions for taxation purposes, it was still impossible to give out land patents without proper surveys. After years of confusion, mathematicians and surveyors Charles Mason and Jeremiah Dixon were commissioned to determine the final boundary line between Pennsylvania, Maryland and Virginia (now West Virginia). They arrived in November of 1763, working until 1766, and erected stones every five miles between those colonies. One side of the stone had the coat of arms of Pennsylvania engraved on it, and the other side had that of Lord Baltimore. At each intermediate mile, a smaller stone was placed, with one side engraved with a P for Pennsylvania and one with an M for Maryland. The surveyors only reached the summit of the Little Allegheny as work was suspended in June of 1766 due to Indian trouble. The rest of the line would be finished between 1782 and 1784 by other surveyors. A resurvey of the line ordered in 1849 found only a few minor errors. The monumental work as a whole had been very accurate.[8] The Conococheque Settlement abutted this southern border of Pennsylvania.

Colonel Armstrong was busy surveying and laying out the streets at the county seat at Carlisle while serving at the square shaped stockade. He also surveyed property for others like the McDowells. His Indian battles seemed to have ended and his focus was on beginning to rebuild his life and that of his community. Most of the buildings in Carlisle were log with only five formally constructed homes.

Maryland and Pennsylvania had conflicting land grants from different British kings. Mathematicians and surveyors Charles Mason and Jeremiah Dixon arrived at the colonies on November 1763 and worked until 1766 on a formal line known now as the Mason and Dixon line. Stones were erected every five miles between those colonies One side of the stone had the engraved coat of arms of Pennsylvania, and the other that of Lord Baltimore. At each intermediate mile, a smaller stone was placed, with one side engraved with a P and one with an M.

McDowell's Mill Fort during Pontiac's Rebellion

Everyone believed the Easton Treaty of 1758 with the American Indians would hold but things between the British and American Indians began to slowly unravel which would affect Armstrong once again. On the British side, General Amherst ordered a reduction in the number of presents given to American Indians on February 22, 1761. There seemed to be a general contempt towards the natives and cost saving measures were being introduced. Trade was restricted and the British violated the treaty by constructing taverns between Bedford and Pittsburg.

Discontent within the Western tribes had never been fully resolved, which propelled the Seneca to meet secretly with the Shawnee in July, proposing an attack on the Forts at Detroit, LeBoeuf, Pitt, Sandusky and Venango, along with frontier settlements. Present at that conference were the Chippewa, Ottawa, Potawatomi and Wyandot. The Wyandot, however, persuaded the other tribes not to join in the venture at that time. Nevertheless, attacks in the Conococheague had begun again in mid-August of 1762, but they were at first looked at as random.

Things had also changed for the settlers who were more determined to stay. Harvest time had always been the most desirable time for Indians to attack settlers as they focused on their produce. The Indians reasoned that destroyed crops would result in famine. The cut in food supplies would surely drive settlers away. Those in the fields were easy prey as was the isolated traveler. James Walker of Fannettsburg was on his way home from Fort Loudoun when he was fired on by Indians. His horse was killed. Unfortunately he was trapped under it and subsequently captured. The natives fastened his saddle onto him to carry it west but he had the good fortune to escape to Fort Littleton.[9]

Great Britain declared war on Spain early in 1762. It was a short war with peace reached by November but it resulted in both Spain and France relinquishing to England the territory east of the Mississippi. The French, while losing Canada to the British, were able to keep two small islands in the Gulf of the Saint Lawrence. Spain traded Florida to England for Cuba and gained Louisiana. The Mississippi was now open for navigation by British vessels.

Western Indians feared this sudden expansion of the British colonies. Those tribes that had mixed well with the French were confused and still held grudges against the English. They desired the return of their allies. The signing of The Treaty of Paris in February of 1763 formally ended the Seven Year's War, of which the French and Indian War was a part, but did little to address Indian affairs. The treaty would not offer newly installed Pennsylvania Governor John Penn, grandson of the founder, the peace expected. In fact, all the colonies would soon feel backlash from American Indians. Coordinated attacks would soon begin in what is now Pennsylvania, New York, Maryland, West Virginia, Ohio, Indiana, Michigan, and Wisconsin.

Pontiac, chief of the Ottawa on Lake Michigan, believed that if Indian forces could drive the English out, the French would surely return to recover French lands. Indian life could be restored with their help. He had sent messengers to many tribes, urging them to join in a rebellion against the English to preserve the Indian way of life. He assembled tribes from the Mississippi and Allegheny Rivers together on April 27, 1763, and presented his plan. A secret league was formed to attack both British forts and frontier settlements.[10] What is called Pontiac's War or Pontiac's Rebellion began May 9th with an American Indian attack and siege at Fort Detroit which lasted until October 30th. Pontiac led this assault himself. On May 10, 1763, Pontiac's forces also attacked the British forts at Sandusky, Michilimackinac, and Presqu'Isle. Forts in the Ohio Country fell one by one.

Forts Pitt, Ligonier and Bedford also came under attack as on May 29th Indians began the siege of Fort Pitt. To make matters worse, in June the commander of Fort Pitt, Swiss Captain Simeon Ecuyer, wrote to Henry Bouquet in Philadelphia telling him of an outbreak of small pox at the crowded fort. Two Delaware, Turtle's Heart and Mamaltee, stood outside the fort and demanded a conference on June 24th to urge the abandonment of the fort. The conference was held but abandonment was refused.

The Indians delivering the news also asked for gifts of provisions and liquor before departing. They were given two blankets, silk handkerchiefs and linen from the small pox hospital. Those distributing the items knew full well that they were infected with the virus. It was recorded as given intentionally "to convey the small pox to the Indians."[11] This use of biological warfare resulted in many Indians catching the virus and dying. General Jeffery Amherst is usually blamed for the first use of biological warfare against the Indians because he wrote to Henry Bouquet about the possible use of this method to get rid of them but this clearly was used prior to Amherst's letter.

There were actually multiple infections of tribes through contact with and the capture of British settlers who were infected. There had been an outbreak among settlers along the Juniata River as well. An estimated 400,000 to 500,000 American Indians would ultimately die of the disease during these years and the years that followed. This new use of biological warfare would later be applied by the British during the Revolutionary War. They would lay people infected with small pox in the path of the advancing Continental Army.

The Forts at Presqu'Isle, Le Boeuf, Venango, La Ray, St. Joseph's, Miamis, Onaethtanon, Sandusky and Michilimackinack had all fallen into Indian hands between May and June of 1763. Forts Pitt, Niagara and Detroit were able to hold their garrisons, but they were under great stress.[12] General Amherst assembled the 42nd and 77th Highland Regiments on Staten Island to address the attacks. He send 360 Highlanders to Carlisle under Henry Bouquet in June and on July 8th, the Pennsylvania Assembly authorized the recruitment of 700 men to guard the territory east of the Allegheny Mountains.

The Upper Cumberland Valley was soon overrun by Indian scalping parties who burned houses, barns and crops. Some inhabitants to the west of the valley had escaped to Fort Bedford and some escaped to Shippensburg and Carlisle. Others fled to Lancaster County and York, and some set up shelters in the woods. The military road was filled with families fleeing without provisions as the 700 militiamen raised tried to save the wheat and rye crops. Attacks on Pennsylvania setters were great with 2,000 killed, and numerous animals slain. In Virginia, Shawnees annihilated a settlement on Greenbrier River and massacred many at Kerr's Creek. Settlers were understandably terrified.[13]

Colonel Bouquet looked at the distress in Cumberland Valley and saw that they were unable to defend themselves without arms and ammunition, and plantations were widely scattered and not clustered for easier defense. The harvest was being burned by bands of Indians. He knew that if the country became deserted, it would prove fatal to the entire province because he would not be able to supply the western forts.

Bouquet informed Governor James Hamilton on July 2, 1763, that he had a plan. He realized that certain portions of the county would inevitably be lost, but if the settlers were encouraged to stockade seven to eight places which included water and a mill, then they would at least have bread and water. Grain and provisions could be moved into these strongholds with all settlers sharing in the provisions and helping each other. A law would need to be passed, however, to prevent privateers.

He suggested securing the following properties: Carlisle would use Callendar's Mill and Lochlin's Mill by Big Spring; Shippensburg would use Richard Chamber's Mill; Ben Chamber's Mill was already in place in what would be Chambersburg; J. "McDowall's" (McDowell) Mill was already in place; Maxwell's Fort could use the mill of Caspard Walters; and Sheerman's Valley would use Rodger's Mill.[14] Each would hold food stores for their region. Many of these were then garrisoned with detachments of soldiers. A detachment of the Black Watch Scottish Highlanders Regiment was housed at McDowell's Mill Fort during this time.[15]

Bouquet was in command of the 1st Battalion of Royal Americans, with part of the Black Watch Royal Highlanders and part of Montgomery's Highlanders with them. On July 3, 1763, he mentioned that he felt York County could be covered by Cumberland County and that they should join in building posts and trying to save the harvest. He wrote the governor again on July 19, mentioning the emotional climate in the Cumberland Valley. "The Inhabitants of this Country have been in a great Ferment imagining the Government was insensible of their Distresses & the Measures taken for their Protection insufficient."[16] This combination of fear, anger and outrage would only grow over the next ten years.

The roads were still filled with families looking for shelter in Shippensburg, Carlisle, Littleton and Bedford. Bouquet had to open some of his military provisions to help the distressed in his path and then came the news of 200 women and children coming from Fort Pitt to Carlisle. Churches tried to help. Members of Christ Church and St. Peter's in Philadelphia sent flour, rice and medicine with two chests of arms, 200 pounds of swan shot and 1000 flints.[17]

Armstrong wrote that he needed horses and wagons to launch his trip west, but had to send for those from back east. There were none available. He would then travel with 500 men to Fort Ligonier and farther west.

A detachment of thirty men under Colonel Bouquet was then ordered to relieve Fort Pitt. Bouquet left Carlisle on July 18th using the Forbes Road and reached Bedford. Once there, he recruited scouts and woodsmen. He then proceeded to Fort Ligonier on August 2nd where he transferred his goods from wagons onto 340 packhorses. The Indians were in the midst of attacking Fort Pitt but then learned of Bouquet's arrival. They left Fort Pitt to fight Bouquet's forces one mile east of Bushy Run on August 5th and 6th in what would later be called the Battle of Bushy Run.

Bouquet's relief column was attacked by Delaware, Mingo, Shawnee and Wyandot in Westmoreland County, Pennsylvania. He resisted by using a Roman-style method in fending off the hostiles. He created a circular formation on a mound with his pack-horses and supplies in the center and used bundles, barrels, saddles, tree trunks and rocks for protection while firing down on the Indians who were widely spread out. It was successful and he would later repeat this tactic in engagements with repeated success. The Indians were defeated on the second day and Fort Pitt was relieved, which was a turning point in the Pontiac War.[18] Bouquet, victorious, reached Fort Pitt on August 10th with the much needed supplies. This resulted in Indians on the upper Ohio leaving their villages and crossing the Tuscarawas. Colonel Armstrong had also advanced on the Indian towns at Muncy and Great Island. They were destroyed by his forces.

The fleeing western settlers brought small pox and flux to Carlisle.[19] The people in Carlisle were already in mourning and filled with resentment towards their provisional government for not sufficiently protecting them and for not having settled the issues with the Indians. Poor Indian policy would be the continual conversation among them. Neglected by Britain with its botched Indian affairs, colonists were left to suffer. Many of the settlers in southcentral and western Pennsylvania who were filled with resentment were also the ones seeking more and more Indian land, but few colonists connected the Indian's actions with that fact. Trouble was brewing in places like Donegal and Paxton in Lancaster County with many colonists gathering, expressing anger.

While Bouquet had been battling Indians, attacks had continued on the settlers behind him. William White's house on the Juniata, with four men and a boy inside, was attacked by Indians on July 10th. The house was burned and only William Riddle escaped. Another man arriving at the house was shot but escaped. The same day, 1 ½ miles from that house, Robert Campbell with six men was at home. Three to four Indians attacked with one killed. George Dodd was the only settler to escape. Later in the day, six to seven miles up the Tuscarora, William Anderson, and a boy and girl were murdered.[20]

Twenty-four men set out to check on the upper part of Shearman's Valley on July 11th. Colonel John Armstrong with Thomas Wilson, Esq. and 30 to 40 men from Carlisle also gathered to bury the dead there. The second group, while passing through Tuscarora, reported seeing houses in flames or burned to the ground. The grain which was bundled had also been torched. Hogs were already eating the dead but it was unsafe to bury anyone there, so they had to leave bodies as they lay. Returning over the Tuscarora Mountain, the group were fired upon by about 30 Indians. William Robinson and John Graham were killed and four others went missing. Armstrong returned with his party on the 12th and reported that Indians were traveling throughout the valley burning farms. Six more were killed on the 13th, and Armstrong reported that from Sunday morning to the 13th, 25 people total had been killed with forty-five wounded.[21]

McDowell's Mill Fort during Pontiac's Rebellion

Another party of thirty men was sent out from Carlisle under Sheriff Dunning, and William Lyon with 80–90 volunteers also were sent to scout the woods. The inhabitants of Shearman's Valley, and Tuscarora were clustered in Carlisle along with the masses. Everyone complained about needing arms and ammunition but they had no money to buy powder. The growing attitude among the settlers seemed to be: kill the first Indian you see. This sentiment would place friendly Indians in a dangerous position.

Carlisle was now the barrier, with no families staying to the west except those in forts. Both sides of the Susquehanna River were filled with people and their cattle camping in the woods next to small bonfires as Armstrong busily tried to raise another party to meet up with the sheriff's group.

The sheriff's party met fifteen Indians by Alexander Logan's home in Shearman's Valley. Logan had been killed along with his son and another man with a fourth man dying later from wounds. The house had been robbed and cattle shot. An engagement occurred with natives resulting in four to five Indians killed. The sheriff's party was able to bring back the cattle to Carlisle, but the farmer's horses had been taken. A man named Pomeroy with his wife, and the wife of a man named Johnson, were killed between Shippensburg and North Mountain on the 21st. One scalped woman lived for a short time with a broken arm and fractured skull. Shippensburg was filled with 1,384 refugees on the 25th: 301 men, 345 women and 738 children who were living in barns, stables, cellars and sheds, since the inns were all full.[22]

Soldiers accompanied settlers from Shearman's Valley on July 30th as they tried to save some of their home goods. Twenty to thirty volunteers traveled near the Tuscarora Mountains to scout for Indians and to bury the dead who had been left by the prior raid. They also helped those salvaging what they could. They were able to bury the remains of three dead persons, but they heard war cries in the distance which let them know that warriors were still in the area. Gun shots were also fired but no encounter occurred. On the 31st men from the Tuscarora valley, under guard of soldiers, tried to save their crops.

In the midst of the struggles, the inhabitants of Great Cove and the Conococheague sent a letter to the House in Philadelphia requesting financial aid. They had been privately paying thirty men under Colonel James Smith to protect them and to scout the area since the middle of the year. It was the only way the settlers could remain at their plantations. Smith's men had been chosen because they were accustomed to hunting and had special skills for the dangerous work but local money was drying up. The letter was read before the Assembly.[23]

Most of the membership of the Upper West Conococheague Presbyterian Church were broken apart. William Maxwell, Esq., William Smith, Esq., John McDowell, William McDowell, Esq., John Welsh, Alexander White, John McClelland, Jonathan Smith, William Campbell, Robert Fleming and Samuel Templeton served as elders on the session trying to watch over those who were left, but they were all busy defending the area or serving in the administration of legal duties. The congregants had largely fled east or were also serving as rangers and militia. It was a time of war and the simple functions of regular services were disbanded. Indians had burned Steel's fort with its log meeting-house. The house used as a school was also burned and teacher John King was forced from the area. He returned to Lancaster County to further his education and entered the ministry only to return later and serve the congregation by the school as pastor.[24]

Indians were spotted in Shearman's Valley again in August, and attacks near Carlisle were reported. Jonas Seely, Esq., from Reading wrote in the fall, "We are all in a state of alarm. Indians have destroyed dwellings, and murdered with savage barbarity their helpless inmates." He didn't know who was friendly and who not. He pleaded for "an armed force to aid our Rangers of Lancaster and Berks."[25] He mentioned later that month to the governor that, "The Rangers sent in word, that these savages must consist of fifty, who travel in companies from five to twenty, visiting Wyalusing, Wichetunk, Nain, Big Island, and Conestogue, under the mark of friendly Indians. Our people have become almost infuriated to madness. These Indians were not even suspected of treachery, such had been the general confidence in their fidelity." He requested a force with money. He blamed the Seneca for tampering with "our Indians."[26]

This ownership of Indian tribes was one of the large problems in the European approach. They did not take into account the independent needs or fears of Indians in alliance with them. The expectation of total loyalty and service to the crown was bewildering to Indians who were used to a different form of self-government. Lumping all Indians together also did not take into account those who did actually see themselves as true loyal friends to the British, enjoying trade and interaction and those who did not. American Indians also regularly practiced hospitality with visiting Indians and never understood the European idea of barring Western Indians from their campfires. Hospitality to strangers insured their own safety should they range far from home.

Settlers who tried to take a pacifistic approach to the western Indians also ran into trouble. Eight Indians approached John Fincher, a Quaker, living on the north side of Blue Mountain in Berks County early in September. His wife and two sons and daughter asked them if they would like something to eat but both parents and sons were murdered and the daughter taken and assumed killed later. They had tried to establish friendship but the patterns of warfare were already too deep. A boy living with the Fincher family escaped and notified Ensign Scheffer who was part of Captain Kern's Company of rangers. Six members of that company pursued the Indians to the house of Mr. Millar where they found four children murdered and two others taken. Millar and wife had been working in a field and fled. Mr. Millar was chased a mile by an Indian. Scheffer's company overtook the Indians and the two children abducted were ultimately rescued.[27]

Frantz Hubler in Bern Township eighteen miles from Reading was attacked a few days later. He was wounded, his wife and three children taken. Three other children were scalped alive and two of those died. Then on September 10th in Berks five Indians were at the house of Philip Martloff's at the base of Blue Mountain. His wife was murdered and scalped along with two sons and two daughters. The house, barn and crops were burned. Martloff was not there at the time and one daughter escaped.[28]

The Susquehanna campaign under General Armstrong against Indians was in full swing in the fall of 1763. His forces burned Delaware and Monsey towns on the West branch of the Susquehanna and destroyed their corn. Colonel James Smith was part of this action.[29] King George III also tried to help reduce some of the Indian's fears by signing the October 7, 1763, Proclamation Line, reserving the land west of the Appalachian Mountains for the American Indians. It was hoped that that barrier line would help to stabilize the area, however it proved to be impossible to enforce.

While the efforts were being made to try to address Indian issues through raids and setting boundary lines, Sir William Johnson had written to General Jeffery Amherst earlier in October with reports delivered to him from friendly Indians. The Indians had seen war hatchet, bows and arrows delivered to the Delaware by the Ottawa Confederacy. They were to be used in attacks against places like Forts Pitt and Augusta. Johnson had been told that other parties of Ottawa, Twightwee, Huron with others would go to demolish Detroit and Niagara.[30] Friendly Indians were delivering good intelligence to the British. There were many who tried to keep treaties in place.

The Pontiac rebellion would last from 1763 to 1764. General Jeffery Amherst sent a pointed letter to Governor James Hamilton in Philadelphia on October 16th. It was hard for the British General to understand the passive nature of the Pennsylvania Assembly with attacks running rampant in the Provence.

> Sir:
> "I herewith inclose you a Paragraph of a letter which I received last Night from Sir William Johnson, containing some intelligence of the bad intentions of the savages on the Frontiers of Pennsylvania, & ca., and I acquaint Colonel Boquet thereof, that he may be on his Guard; but I cannot help repeating my surprise at the infatuation of the People in your Province, who tamely

look on while their Brethren are butchered by the Savages, when, without doubt, it is in their Power by exerting a proper Spirit, not only to protect the Settlements, but to punish any Indians that are hardy enough to disturb them. I am with great Regard, Sir,
  Your most Obedient humble Servant,
  Jeff Amherst[31]

James Hamilton at Council held on October 22nd was able to pass an act prohibiting the selling of "Guns, Powder or War-stores to the Indians."[32]

In Paxton and Donegal, rough men gathered to deal with the Indians in their own way. They were given the name the Paxton Boys. Most of the rabble were recent squatters from Ireland. They had asked the government to remove the tribes near them at Conestoga because they were believed to be harboring Western Indians. Western Indians were seen recruiting there and some Conestoga Indians had been recognized in raiding parties.[33]

Mennonite gunsmith Abraham Newcomer was also cited by the Paxton Boys as having been threatened with scalping by Indians Bill Soc and Indian John from Conestoga for not being willing to mend their tomahawks. Others in that community had also been threatened by Bill Soc. Area clergy, including Rev. John Elder pastor of Paxtang (Paxton) and Derry, had tried unsuccessfully to dissuade violence.

The Pennsylvania government ignored the requests. Conestoga Indians were considered friendly by the government, having settled there under a treaty issued by William Penn in 1690. Many of the Conestoga were Christians. The Paxton Boys took matters into their own hands on December 14, 1763 and attacked the Indian village, killing and scalping six persons of varied ages, including Chief Shaheas (She-e-hays) who had maintained treaties. Most of the villagers were out of the Indian camp at the time but their huts were burned.[34] The Indians who were killed in this action were listed by one Chee-na-wan and recorded by John Hay in Provincial records as Chief Sheehays, George (Wa-a-shen), Harry (Tee-kau-ley), Son of Sheehays (Ess-canesh), Sally an old woman (Tea-wonsh-i-ong), and a woman (Kannenquas).[35]

The Pennsylvania government issued warrants for the arrest of the Paxton Boys and gathered the Conestoga Indians in Lancaster with great care, first into the work house for safety and then into the jail because it was a stronger structure, but on December 17th fifty to sixty residents of Paxton and others gathered in Lancaster and marched to the prison, forcing the doors open. They butchered fifteen to twenty Indians inside.

The Governor of Pennsylvania then issued a reward for the capture of the Paxton Boys. Some were apprehended but there were no convictions. The Government also removed nervous Moravian Indians to Province Island but the natives still felt unsafe and requested passage to England. They were sent to New York where the Governor of New York refused them land as did the Governor of New Jersey. The Indians were returned to Philadelphia and were put under protective guard.[36]

The Paxton Boys then marched towards Philadelphia with about 250 men and gathered in German Town/ Germantown. The government set up six companies of foot, one artillery and two troops of horse to oppose them.[37] The governor fled the city to Benjamin Franklin's house who was able to conclude the conflict peacefully with representatives of the Paxton Boys, Matthew Smith and James Gibson. Most of the residents of the colony deplored the actions of the Paxton Boys but understood it. The hostility also made an impression on the Indians, both friendly and unfriendly.

The frontier was still in turmoil. Colonel John Armstrong in Carlisle wrote to the Governor on December 14, 1763, that his soldiers were daily changing their courses when ranging. People had been driven off of the Northside of the Mountain which formed his perimeter. They were then mixed into the settlement on the south side, leaving their personal effects behind. Ranging took place in that southern area but the people who lived there needed a guard to follow them back to their homes to retrieve their goods which were "stack'd in the field thro' the different Valleys, at a considerable distance beyond the Mountains . . ."[38] Armstrong complained that he needed blankets, kettles and ammunition as he served as both civil and military officer. He needed provisions and the sick needed coverage. He tried to keep 30 men to a company and was continually recruiting.

Indian raids continued and on March 19, 1764, Indians took five people within nine miles of Shippensburg and shot one man. They were pursued by 100 provincials, but the houses of John Stewart, William Baird, James Kelly, Stephen Caldwell and John Boyd had been burned.[39] Everyone tried to endure the last weeks of the winter and prepare for the warm weather attacks.

Colonel Armstrong wrote to Governor Penn on June 6th about an assault which took place four miles south of Fort Loudon which would have been two miles south of Fort McDowell.

> But yesterday I wrote yr Honr of the sundry mischiefs very lately committed in this County, and have this moment received a Letter from Capt Murray, of the Royal Highlanders, that yesterday Morning thirteen persons are kill'd and Several Houses Burn'd to the ground about four Miles South of Fort Loudon. Capt Murray has not mention'd the number of the Enemy, nor who the persons are who are kill'd, he sent out a Party who are already returned, a sufficient number of the Inhabitants and Provincials are attempting to make out the Tracks of the Enemy, and are yet in pursuit, but at this season of the year have but a small Chance of Success; the ground Hard, the Cover close, and the Enemy may well Lodge without Fire, which otherwise would tend to discover them. The Indians now appear to bend their force agst the Frontier, & by burning the Houses intend to lay as much of the Country waste as they can. The Summer opens with a dismal aspect to us. I shall be oblig'd to bring the Troops entirely on this side the Mountains, and for some time give up those Settlements on the other side, as we are not able to cover one half of the people; and how this country will make a stand, or their Crops be Sav'd, is not easy to devise; they are running upon me from every Quarter for what they call help, that is, for a few men to every

three or four Families living the most convenient. I hope there is Ammunition on ye Road; no doubt Capt Murry has wrote to Coll. Bouquet.[40]

Suppplies were sent to the troops in the form of tools, flints, powder horns, pouches for balls, cartridge boxes, wooden canteens, hatchets, blankets, shoes, orderly books, paper, quills, ink and pay for soldiers.

Captain Robert Callender also sent a letter to Col. Bouquet on March 27, 1764 in which he described the situation at both Fort Loudon and McDowell's Mill Fort. There were 2,000 casks of flour at Fort Loudon and about 600 at McDowell's Mill. There were no regular soldiers at McDowell's at that time and there were only a handful at Fort Loudon. He stated that Mr. McDowell and others asked him to request regulars to be sent to Fort Loudon. They also needed more stores. Callender mentioned people fearful and fleeing to places of refuge.[41]

The Pennsylvania government then set a bounty on the heads of hostile Indians on July 6, 1764. Settlers who brought male prisoners over the age of ten to a fort or jail would receive 150 Spanish pieces of eight; a female or male under ten would earn 130 pieces of eight; a scalp of a male over ten would bring 134 pieces of eight and the scalp of a female over age ten would bring 50 pieces of eight. The peaceful colony of pastoral settlers interacting equally with American Indians was no more.

Meanwhile in the Conococheague on Sunday July 22, 1764, two to three Indians were seen near Fort Loudon and on the 25th they met a pregnant Mrs. Susan King Cunningham, wife of Hugh. The Cunningham farm was ½ mile from McDowell's Mill Fort. The house had been burnt and so Susan was staying at that fort with her children. In fact, Susan's brothers, John and George King, would later marry John McDowell's daughters, so they knew each other well.

Things had been relatively quiet in the area and she was going home to get milk for her children. As she returned from her barn heading towards the fort, she was met by three Indians. Susan was attacked, killed and scalped. The fetus in her womb was ripped out and laid next to her.[42] It was meant to intimidate and shock the community and it did. Her

McDowell's Mill Fort during Pontiac's Rebellion

brother John, who had furthered his education back east, would later return and purchase her farm, living there until his death in 1812 with his wife, a McDowell. Hugh and Susan Cunningham's daughter, kept safely in the fort, would become the second wife of John McCullough who had been taken by Indians when he was a child.[43]

The next day, July 26, 1764, school master Enoch Brown was conducting lessons at the log school house three miles north of Greencastle in Antrim Township, southeast of Fort McDowell. Enoch, born in Northern Ireland had originally settled over the border in Virginia. He was married with at least one child. Brown also had family members in Mercersburg.

Enoch was the thirteenth child in his family and given the name Enoch, after the Bible character, for good luck. Brown was noted as being "respected for his truthfulness, integrity and Christian character, in short, he was an exemplary teacher of his day." The same Indians who had killed Susan King Cunningham approached the school, which is referred to as "Guitner's school house," situated on the "brow of the hill." Remnants of it were still standing in 1845. The log school was most likely a rustic cabin with an open chimney, slab benches and desks along the walls. It probably was a Latin-based education which was popular with the Ulster Scots.

A number of children did not attend school that day with some playing hooky and some doing summer chores. Sarah "Sally" Brown, daughter of George Brown who built Brown's Mill, was one of those absent. She was helping the family as they pulled flax in the fields. She would later marry Benjamin Chambers, son of the founder of Chambersburg. Elenore Cochran, living with the George Brown family, also missed school that day for the same reason. Elenore Pawling, daughter of the owner of Pawling's Tavern, missed school and Mary Ramsey stayed home with a premonition something might happen. James Poe played hooky and received a licking for it. Isabella Potter and Catharine "Kitty" Hamilton probably attended the school but are not recorded. Two who did attend school mentioned to the teacher that they thought they might have seen Indians in the bushes. The teacher felt they might be rumors and ignored the warning. Eleven children total were present.[44]

After the morning Bible session, a noise was heard at the door. Opening the door with Bible still in hand, the teacher was confronted by three/four Indians.[45] Some accounts mention two old and one young Indians but John McCullough who was held captive by Indians from which the war party came said that he knew the Indians and that there were three who were under age 20.[46]

Enoch Brown reportedly begged for the lives of the children and offered himself in their place, but he was hit on the head with a maul, killed and then scalped.[47] The teacher's hands had also been broken in self-defense.[48] The Indians proceeded to strike each child on the head with tomahawks, killing them and then scalping them. Little Archie McCullough initially was hiding by the wood near the fireplace but was found by the Indians and scalped. Of the children Ruth Hart, Ruth Hale, Eben Taylor (15), George Dunstan (younger than 15) and Archie McCullough (the youngest of the children)[49] are identified with the rest unknown.

Archie was cousin to John McCullough being held prisoner. According to Glen L. Cump in his account of the event, two children survived scalping and four were taken prisoner. Archie, though scalped, survived but the physical and emotional trauma encountered resulted in him never regaining mental health.[50] Hours after the event, the children's blood-soaked bodies were found by local farmers and little Archie was found crawling among them. Neighbors buried the mutilated bodies of the children and school teacher in a large box, alternating head to foot in a common grave.[51] This traumatized not only the local community but the entire colony with reprisals following in memory of the lost children.

John McCullough, present at the Indian camp as a prisoner when the warriors returned with the scalps, later wrote that the killing and scalping of the children was denounced by the half-king of the Delawares, Neeppaugh-Weese or Night Walker, and by other elders. The young warriors were called cowards by their leaders.[52] There was no honor in the murder of children. In a time of violence, the victims are often the defenseless.

Years later on August 4, 1842, citizens of Greencastle launched a search for the quickly buried bodies of the teacher and children, and located them. In the decaying box with skeletal remains, they found a number of items; "Metal buttons, part of a tobacco box, teeth, etc., were

McDowell's Mill Fort during Pontiac's Rebellion

The Enoch Brown Monument and common grave commemorate the Enoch Brown school massacre on July 26, 1764. During the Pontiac Wars, school teacher Enoch Brown and his eleven students were attacked, scalped and killed by Indians while they were in class session, with young Archie McCullough the only survivor. They were quickly buried in a common box. The grave was later found and the bodies re-interred here in the 1800s. The monument contains inscriptions describing the events. Enoch Brown Park with a playground for children is located three miles northwest of the town of Greencastle, Pennsylvania.

picked up as relics by those present . . ."⁵³ The bodies were re-interred in what is now known as Enough Brown State Park. Near the common grave is a monument which was unveiled August 4, 1885, erected with money collected by 5,257 school children, Sunday schools, churches and individuals. Twenty acres were initially purchased and now the remaining three-acre park with playground pays tribute to the event.

Shortly after the incident happened, the same band of warriors were seen at McDowell's Mill Fort, pursuing two men. Indians also killed the daughter of James Dysart. Lieutenant James Potter, son of John Potter the first sheriff of Cumberland County, served in Colonel John Armstrong's battalion. James commanded a company of settlers who pursued the Indians who had committed the massacre of Enoch Brown and the children.⁵⁴ His family members had attended the school.

James Potter would go on to serve in the Continental Army and be Vice President of the state in 1781. James Poe who played hooky that day from school would later marry Potter's daughter, Elizabeth. The search party did not apprehend the Indians, and it was believed that the same Indians who murdered the children wounded John Kennedy who had a settlement in the southwestern portion of Antrim Township. The Indian Chief Cornplanter was the original owner of his property and they were friends.⁵⁵

John had been hunting for his horse by the creek when Indians attacked him. His horse was killed and he was wounded in his right thigh and shoulder. He hid and then crept on to Cross' Fort. Cornplanter came to him there and pursued the Indians into the mountains.⁵⁶

The Governor gave orders to the two Battalions at Carlisle for an expedition to chastise the Indians but he also received a letter from the Duke of Halifax on August 11th stating that the House of Commons had passed a resolution to defray the cost of defending and protecting the colonies. Stamp Duties would be enacted. Penn was to transmit to him a list of all

> Instruments made use of in publick transactions, Law Proceedings, Grants, Conveyances, Securities of Land or Money, within

your Government, with proper and sufficient Descriptions of the same, in order that if Parliament should think proper to pursue the Intention of the aforesaid Resolution, they may thereby be enabled to carry it into Execution in the most effectual and least burthensome manner.

If you should be unable it yourself to prepare a List of this kind with sufficient accuracy, you will in such case require the Assistance of the Principal Officer of the Law within your Government, who is the proper Person to be consulted towards procuring the said information in the manner required.[57]

It was followed in another letter with the demand "it cannot be doubted but the Legislatures of the several Colonies will readily & cheerfully contribute to the success of a Plan . . ."[58]

To the west on August 12, 1764, a preliminary treaty was signed with the Delaware and Shawnee by Colonel Bradstreet at Presqu'Isle. He reported that the issue was solved but engagements continued as Bouquet coordinated his area of responsibility. The preliminary treaty did little to stop the bands on the frontier.

In August Indians were seen almost daily. Two men were pursued by four Indians near Justice William McDowell's home and James Dysart and his daughter were murdered and scalped at Big Spring. On August 30th Indians were seen at Bedford and thirty to forty of them killed Isaac Stimble of Ligonier. More were killed twelve miles from Winchester, VA.[59]

Colonel Henry Bouquet prepared for an Expedition into the Ohio Country during the summer of 1764 to address the problem. Fort Loudon would be a gathering place once again for militia who would join British soldiers from August to September. His troops reached the Tuscarawas River on October 13th where he met with representatives of the Shawnees, Senecas and Delawares who sued for peace.

Bouquet moved his army to the Muskingum River at present day Coshocton, Ohio, and established a partial treaty with a formal one to be done in New York under Indian agent Sir Johnston. All white captives were to be exchanged with promises in return not to destroy Indian villages or to seize Indian land. Over 200 prisoners were released by the Indians initially with more followed at Fort Pitt as word spread to distant tribes. The Pontiac War was formally ended December 5th.

Tears of joy were shed by many as they found their way to freedom, but some of those taken captive did not want to re-unite with their families. Many had been taken as children and no longer remembered English or western customs. Some youths had married Indians and had children with their spouses. Some women did not feel their European families would accept them with these children. In one case a German woman could not identify her child taken captive but was encouraged to sing a familiar German hymn. The little girl remembered the song and found her way to her mother.[60] Bouquet, for his part in this successful venture, would later be promoted to Brigadier-General of all British forces in the southern colonies.

Many American Indians found themselves held to strict treaties following the Pontiac War which would result in them being pushed to attack settlers in British military campaigns during the Revolutionary War. Pictured here are actors depicting the dress worn by settlers and American Indians in the Cumberland Valley during the mid 1700s. Photo courtesy of the Fort Loudon Society.

CHAPTER EIGHT

1765—1769

McDowell Interaction with the Black Boys

Indian attacks in the Conococheague Settlement finally stopped and Fort Loudon's garrison was reduced with a half-company of 42nd Highland Regiment under Lieutenant Charles Grant. Problems again surfaced for the community when in November George Croghan and Robert Callender, working with Philadelphia merchants, set out with trade goods for the western Indians which were in excess of those allowed by General Thomas Gage, who had recently loosened the trade laws with Indians as a sign of peace. The Pennsylvania Governor, however, still outlawed trade with Indians.

Colonel Bouquet instructed post commanders in January of 1765 to assist Croghan in the shipment of "presents" to the Indians. Croghan would deliver 65 packhorse loads of goods to Fort Pitt. He stored his load of goods at Pawlings Tavern and various other places in the Conococheague Settlement for future shipment.

Local settlers in the community learned of the trade goods stored at Pawling's Tavern in March. They were believed to include gunpowder, lead and scalping knives. After launching an investigation, they found scalping knives and sent out an alarm. Material bound for the west usually passed through the check point at Smith's Town (Mercersburg) where

Justice William Smith, Esq., and his brother-in-law James Smith regularly inspected goods carried west. They were charged by the Governor to issue vouchers verifying the goods and the reputation of the traders. All Justices in each township within that region had the same charge.

Two long trains of packhorses with goods headed towards Smith's Town on March 5th. One train was led by Robert Allison of Antrim and one was led by Elias Davison. Elias and his brother would later marry two of the daughters of the miller John McDowell. Thirty to 50 armed men stopped the caravans several times asking them to store the items until they could be inspected. The region had struggled under Indian attacks and the fear of resupplying the enemy was great. The drivers were threatened with gun fire.

Davison showed his pass from George Croghan which stated that Col. Bouquet had given permission for the goods and went on to Fort Loudon to show it to the commander. Alisson continued on with the combined train into the Great Cove. The drivers of the goods would not listen to repeated requests from locals to stop for an inspection.[1]

James Smith then gathered ten of his old rangers, later called Black Boys because they blackened their faces and dressed as Indians in disguise, and planned an ambush near Sideling Hill. As the packhorses reached within a mile or two of Sideling Hill on March 6th, Smith's men attacked. They shot and killed two to four horses. The traders were told to take their own personal property but the rest was to be burned. Rifles, war items and rum intended for the western tribes were discovered in the bundles. The drivers fled to Fort Loudoun to complain to the Post commander, Lieutenant Charles Grant. Grant sent Sergeant Leonard McGlashan with a squad of eleven out to apprehend the Black Boys.

Local settlers were then harassed by the military men and some arrested between March 6th and 7th, many of whom were innocent of the activities. They were placed in the fort's jail. Guns taken from settlers along with recovered goods were also taken to the fort. Smith continued to organize two to three hundred area riflemen between March 8th and 9th and proceeded to march to the fort. The garrison at the fort was small.

McDowell Interaction with the Black Boys

This was the first armed assault on a British fort by colonials, long before the events in Massachusetts. The prisoners were released but the guns were still held. The Black Boys blew up eight barrels of gunpowder from the train found at Justice William Maxwell's home. They continue to patrol the area for any other western goods passing through. George Croghan was later chastised by General Gage for having shipped goods in excess of those allowed. The Grand Jury did not find enough evidence to prosecute anyone for the event.

Joseph Spear attempted to send a large train of packhorses to Fort Pitt on May 5th. His goods were unloaded at Fort Loudoun for safe keeping. The next day drivers who were pasturing horses were attacked by the Black Boys. Horses were killed and wounded with saddles and blankets burned. Lieutenant Grant was informed at Fort Loudon and ordered Seargenat McGlashan with twelve men to rescue the drivers. An engagement occurred at Widow Barr's house against 50 to 80 Black Boys.

McGlashan and his troops were allowed to leave the area after they released one prisoner. James Smith with Justices William Smith, Allison and Reyonald arrived at Fort Loudoun on May 10th with 150 to 200 armed men. They demanded to inspect Spear's goods. They were refused and the Justices complained that military passes did not trump magistrate authority. All trade goods needed a pass from a Justice of the Peace according to State law.[2] The fort, they continued, was a Provincial fort and not a King's fort. That meant that they came under the authority of the governor of Pennsylvania. The road upon which the fort was seated was a Provincial road and not a King's road.

Things continued to escalate when Captain Grant was out riding by the fort with two men on May 28th. They were captured by James Smith and four of his men. Grant was held in the woods overnight and later agreed to release the settler's rifles which were still being held. He was let go, but did not release the weapons. Justice William Smith also issued a warrant for the arrest of Sergeant McGlashan for shooting James Brown on the Widow Barr's property.

Governor Penn repealed his restrictions on Indian goods on June 4, 1765 (effective June 20) after being chastised by General Gage for the behavior of those in the Cumberland County. The magistrates were also accused and Justice William Smith was summoned to Philadelphia on July 30th where he successfully defended his actions but the Justices were then ordered to suppress rioters in the future.

Lieutenant Grant defended his own actions and the question of what to do with the rifles was mentioned without resolve. The garrison at Fort Loudon was ordered in November to move to Fort Pitt. The Black Boys feared the weapons would be taken with the troops. They rallied people. One hundred to two hundred armed men surrounded Fort Loudoun between November 16th and 18th and demanded the return of the nine guns. They laid siege to the fort for two days and nights, firing hundreds of rounds at the fort.

Lieutenant Grant agreed to give the nine guns to Justice William McDowell on the 18th under bond until the ownership of each could be verified. It does not appear that McDowell was part of the disruption. He seemed to be respected by both parties. The receipt for the guns read:

> Received of Lieutenant Charles Grant, of the 42 Regiment, the number of Five Rifles and Four Smooth Guns, which was taken off the Country People, & I promise that the above mentioned Arms shall remain in my possession till the Governor's Pleasure is known to Dispose of them as he shall see fit, either to the Respective owners or otherways.
> Given under my Hand at Fort Loudoun, 10th November, 1765 (signed,) WM. M'Dowell[3]

William McDowell also collected a bond from Smith and his company.

> Know all men by these Presents, that we, Jonathan Smith, WM. Marshall, Thoms Orbison, and John Welsh, all of Peters Township, in Cumberland County, are holden, and firmly bound to WM. M'Dowell of Sd Township and County, in the just and full sum of Two Hundred Pounds, Pennsylvania Currency, to be paid to said WM. M'Dowell, his Heirs or his Assigns, for the payment

where of we bind ourselves, our Heirs, Execut'rs and Adm'rs, firmly by these Presents, sealed with our Seal, and Dated this 18th Day of Novr, 1765.

The Condition of this Obligation is such, that if the above bound Jonathan Smith, WM. Marshall, Thom's Orbison, and John Welsh, shall keep the said WM. M'Dowell indemnified from any Assault, Arrest, Attachment, or Suit at Law, either for themselves or any other for them, or any other for them present, or Person or Persons whatsoever, on the account of Five Rifles and Four Smooth Bored Gunds, deposited with Sd William M'Dowell, by Lieut. Charles Grant, Commanding at Fort Loudoun, until the Governor's pleasure be known concerning the said Guns, to remain in full force and virtue.[4]

Lieutenant Charles Grant then wrote to the governor that he felt that the arms were "as safe with Mr. M'Dowell, as if I had taken them to Fort Pitt,"[5] and he forwarded the documents. Copies of the passes issued by William and James Smith were also sent to the governor. Each pass had "Permit shall not Extend to Carry any Warlike Stores, or any Article not herein mentioned"[6] printed on it with the date, a seal and signature. An inquiry was made with depositions taken. By January of 1766 the Governor removed William Smith from the office of magistrate. He sent a writ for the arrest of James Smith, but James was not arrested, leaving later to explore Tennessee and Kentucky.

The actions of the settlers sent people like Sir William Johnson into a rage. He wrote to the Governor on April 12th calling the behavior of the inhabitants "Extraordinary" in the bad sense. He felt that it would "produce dangerous consequences to the Province." The military was there to protect them. "All I fear is, that these Rash people may do something still more outrageous if opportunity offers."[7] He was correct in a sense, more was coming.[8]

The Stamp Act which had been issued by Parliament was levied on stamped paper used by the colonies and meant to help Britain recover from its large war-debt. It had gone into effect on November 1st.

McDOWELL'S MILL FORT

Justice William McDowell built Woodland about 1762 after two of his prior homes had been burned. The house stands in current St. Thomas Township on the Old Mercersburg Road between Markes and Route 30. It is on the National Register of Historic Places. The confiscated rifles during the Black Boys incident were stored here. Photo by author.

Philadelphia newspaper buildings were already draped in mourning colors beginning the end of October, refusing to print on stamped paper. The people also dressed in homespun and resolved not to use imported goods, but rather to encourage the production of colonial products. It must be remembered that many in the colony had just lost loved ones and personal property during the forays with the French and Western Indians with little assistance by the British government and the tax was seen as a lack of sensitivity to their suffering as they tried to recover.

British manufacturers in England felt the boycott financially and put pressure on Parliament to repeal the law, which it did on March 18, 1766. After the failed Stamp Tax, England still looked for revenue from the colonies to pay for the war debt. A duty tax would be levied in 1767 on tea, paper, printer's colors and glass.[9] Once again settlers rebelled and after sending petitions from the colonies, the tax rate was reduced in

1769 and then abolished in 1770, except 3 pence a pound on tea. It didn't seem to matter how much the tax was, it was the principle that bothered colonists.

John McDowell at McDowell's Mill Fort was in morning during the discussions on Parliamentary taxes. He lost his wife, Agnes Craig on August 8, 1766. She was only forty-nine when she died, and he fifty. They had been through so much together and now with the Western Indians addressed, the promise of peaceful times was once again a possibility but John would go forward without her. Her grave is the oldest recorded grave in the cemetery, though older ones most likely exist. The dead were often buried at night without tombstones during the conflicts to avoid the desecration of the bodies by scalping. We do not know the cause of Agnes' death, but it must have been difficult for her to live in a fort for years with repeated Indian intrusions, most likely tending the injured and sick. John continued to run a general store and mill out of the fort, and the fort became the center of both civic and military events with homes clustered around it. A small village developed which was known as McDowell's Mill during this period.

The Indian peace was disrupted once again with the threat of a reprisal. A massacre of Indians happened at Penn's Creek on January 10, 1768. Indians from Big Island on the West Branch of the Susquehanna had settled on Middle Creek in the spring of 1767, building cabins. They were identified as White Mingo, Cornelius, John Campbell, Jones, three Indian women, two girls and one child. They were friendly to the settlers and had come to hunt.

Six of that group approached the house of William Blyth at the mouth of the Middle Creek where they were treated well. They then approached the house of Frederick Stump, who had lost his wife and children during Indian raids. Stump, with his servant Ironcutter (Eisenhauser), murdered the Indians and dumped the bodies into the cold creek through an ice hole. Stump and Ironcutter continued four miles from Stumps' house and found an Indian woman, two Indian girls and a child and murdered them all, setting two cabins on fire with the bodies in them to cover their deeds. It seemed like a perfect crime but the body of one of the Indians placed in the creek floated to the Harrisburg Bridge on the Susquehanna River and soon the murder was uncovered.

Governor John Penn issued a proclamation seeking the apprehension of both men while two strings of wampum were sent to the Indians on the Susquehanna, asking them not to retaliate. Sir William Johnson, Indian agent, invited chiefs of the Six Nations and other tribes living on the Susquehanna and Ohio to a convention.

When apprehended and taken to the Carlisle jail to await trial, Stump claimed the six Indians were drunk and disorderly. He told them to leave, they wouldn't and he feared they would kill him. After killing them, he burned two cabins, covering the killing of one woman, two girls and a child. He was never brought to trial because an angry mob released him and he was never recaptured. The crime is now known as the Stump's Run Massacre. The Indians, to their credit, kept the peace.

The colony of Connecticut tried to lay claim to Pennsylvania territory in the middle of these conflicts based on the Massachusetts's Bay Charter which gave limitless extensions west, even to the Pacific Ocean, and south to the Northern limits of Lord Baltimore's Territory. Connecticut speculators purchased land from the Indians through a company known as the Susquehanna Company and promoted settlement in the area. Pennsylvania had purchased the same land from the Indians and had the Charters of King Charles and James giving the area to the colony. The new land was called by the New Englanders Northumberland. Arbitration was established. Later in September of 1775 a Pro-Connecticut committee of the Continental Congress granted Connecticut the central area of Pennsylvania equal to the size of Connecticut but the Pennsylvania Assembly rejected it. A final decision would not be reached until 1802 when Congress voted in favor of Pennsylvania's rights.[10]

While this land dispute were going on, the Conococheague farmers petitioned the Court of Quarter Sessions, Cumberland County, for another public road. The road was to run "from James Campbell's near Loudon through Chambersburg to the County line in Black's Gap." The road was finally granted in January of 1772 and Nathan McDowell, John's brother, was one of the appointed "viewers."[11]

McDowell Interaction with the Black Boys

The Rev. Dr. John King, who had served as a school master for three years from 1760–1763 in the log Latin-school near Steele's Meetinghouse at Church Hill and left after the murder of his sister, came back to the community after furthering his theological education. He continued the Latin school at Church Hill.[12]

King was installed as pastor of the "White Church" or Upper West Conococheague Presbyterian Church on August 23, 1769. He would remain there for 43 years.[13] Miller John McDowell became the Ruling Elder over District 7 of the Upper West Conococheague Church the same year.[14] With King on Session were William Maxwell, William Smith, Jonathan Smith, William McDowell, John Welsh, Alexander White, John McClelland, William Campbell, Robert Fleming and Samuel Templeton. Rev. King undoubtable spent much time at McDowell's Mill Fort for he later marry John's daughter, Elizabeth, on April 2, 1771. His brother, George, would marry Elizabeth's sister, Margaret called Peggy, on June 6, 1786. John King had Justice William McDowell's son, John, once again in his classes and he encouraged him to further his education in law and helped him attend college.

Things by McDowell's Mill Fort were returning to normal but the Western Indians again made assaults on the frontiers in 1769 as Bedford was plundered and a man named Reed in Cumberland County killed the only son of Seneca George, Gen-gu-ant. Reed was arrested and taken to jail and a conference was called at Shamokin, Fort Augusta, near Shenago with Seneca George and fifty-three Nanticoke and Conoy Indians. Seneca George called himself a Captain of the Six Nations. He received the tributes of sorrow from the government and a major conflict was avoided but traders once again tried to supply contraband to western Indians.[15]

A new group of Black Boys, not led by James Smith, waylaid traders near Bedford and destroyed their material in 1769 which was believed to have been destined for the Western Indians. The Commander of the fort arrested some men on suspicion of their participation in the acts who were then taken to Fort Bedford's jail. Among those arrested in Bedford was Constable James McDowell, brother of John, who was there on business, having a horse shod. He also was a surveyor-farmer and was surveying land in the area. His crime seemed to be that he had married Jean "Jane" Smith, James' sister which made him suspicious by association. James McDowell was also accused of having had a flyer posted near the road by his farm in support of the Black Boys, though only a copy was brought forth. James McDowell was not involved in any of the Black Boys' raids.

James Smith then gathered 18 of his old Black Boys to march to Fort Bedford in protest to the arbitrary manner in which settlers had been arrested. He surprised the garrison and captured the fort on September 12th. This was the second assault on a British fort by armed colonials and the first fort formally taken by American colonists.

A local blacksmith removed the irons from the prisoners and they were set free. A man was shot in the process and killed. Smith was later arrested and charged with second degree murder for that death, though innocent.[16] He was taken to Carlisle for trial but then 600 of his friends assembled with his Black Boys and marched to Carlisle to demand his release. Smith refused to leave the jail and made a speech telling the mob to disperse which they did.

After four months in prison, he was tried before the Supreme Court at Carlisle and acquitted of murder. He was then elected and served for three years as a County Commissioner in Bedford County. Sir William Johnson, the King's agent for Indian affairs, who made a treaty with the Western Indian, had purchased Indian land west of the Appalachian Mountains between Ohio and the Cherokee Rivers for himself.[17] Smith explored some of that land, moving to Westmoreland County. He served three years as County Commissioner there and in 1774 he was commissioned as a Captain of a company of men operating against the Indians. In 1776 he commanded a company of rangers in New Jersey during the Revolutionary War. With thirty-six men he defeated a detachment of 200 Hessians. He would hold more offices after his service to the new country.

CHAPTER NINE

1770–1784

McDowell's Mill Fort during the Revolution

Parliament was still seeking a way to find revenue to cover the debt from the French and Indian War. It had passed the failed *Stamp Act* on March 22, 1765, which was repealed. This was followed by the *Quartering Act* which required colonies to provide housing and food for British troops stationed there. *The Declaratory Act* or *The American Colonies Act of 1766* reinforced Parliament's authority over the colonies which pushed colonists in New England and New York towards more colonial manufacturing.

The Townsend Acts of June 29, 1767, required colonists to pay an import duty of paper, paint, glass, oil, lead and tea. Many of these items were needed in construction. The series of laws also sought revenue for the salaries of governors and judges, and to punish New York for failing to comply with the *1765 Quartering Act*. Protests on the part of colonist included boycotts of British goods. The British response was the occupation of Boston in October of 1768. The issue of taxation without representation had been circulating among colonist in the east with delegates from nine colonies meeting in New York to organize a united resistance called the "Sons of Liberty."

Things continued to deteriorate when on March 5, 1770, British troops fired on a crowd of men and boys who were throwing snowballs and chunks of ice. Three men died right away and two others died later from their wounds resulting in the event being called the Boston Massacre. John Adams with Josiah Quincy were involved in the trial which followed in which two British soldiers were found guilty of manslaughter, branded on the thumb and dismissed from the army. It seemed like things might stabilize as on April 12, 1770, Parliament repealed all of the *Townsend* duties except the one on tea.

These things were watched closely on the frontier of Pennsylvania, but the main focus was on the failed colonial Indian policies and on securing land. Most of the colonists in the Cumberland Valley expressed faithfulness to the King and any issues they might have had were usually targeted at Parliament and its taxation measures. The Lieutenant-Governor of Pennsylvania, John Penn (1763–1771 first administration), returned to England during this time and was succeeded by his brother Richard who held office from 1771–1773. John would later returned to Philadelphia as Governor and Proprietor from 1773–1776.

The colony had addressed the issues with the southern boundary but not the west. The Governor of Virginia, Lord Dunmore, laid claim to territory in the Monongalia Valley around 1773, including the area around Pittsburgh. Dunmore directed Dr. John Connolly, a Captain in the local militia, to organize the territory and to form a militia. Justice Arthur St. Clair of Westmoreland Court, acting on an order from Governor Penn, had Connolly arrested for taking the British garrison in the name of Virginia. Connolly was later released.

Dunmore refused to listen to commissioners from Pennsylvania on the matter and wanted to use force to keep the land in his colony, however his own provincial council did not vote money for him to do this.[1] Nevertheless, he had Justices Mackay, Smith and McFarlane arrested and imprisoned in Virginia, they were later released and then in 1775 the Virginia Governor had Robert Hanna and James Caveat jailed at Fort Dunmore in Pittsburg. They too were released after a posse surrounded the jail and re-arrested Connolly. The two colonies did not resolve the issue of that western boundary until 1779 by extending the Mason and Dixon line by 5 degrees longitude in a westerly direction.

Parliament tried again to bolster the sagging British economy. The *Tea Act* was passed on May 10, 1773. The East Indian Company was near bankruptcy and had a large surplus of tea which needed to be quickly unloaded. They were authorized to sell it directly to the public at discounted prices. This undermined tea merchants in the colonies who could not compete with those lower prices. Pennsylvania had turned away ships carrying tea but in Boston the protestors took to action. Colonists dressed as Mohawk Indians boarded three tea ships in Boston harbor on December 16th and emptied 342 chests of tea, worth 18,000 pounds sterling, into the water. This became known as the Boston Tea Party which resulted in Parliamentary forming a counter attack on March 31, 1774.

A law known as the *Intolerable Acts* was passed. Parliament closed the Boston harbor to all shipping until payment of the destroyed tea was paid. The public were then forbidden to meet in Massachusetts unless permission was given by the royal Governor, and any British official accused of a capital offense would be sent to England or another colony for trial, by-passing the colonies judicial process.

The provincial Governor of Massachusetts was removed. General Thomas Gage, Commander-in-Chief of the British troops in North America, became the Governor with four regiments of 4,000 men to back up his authority. He arrived in Boston on May 13, 1774. Gage fortified Boston with regular British troops and seized the arsenal at Charleston and took stores of military equipment at Salem and Concord. *The Boston Port Bill* discontinued the landing and shipping of goods at Boston. The custom house was removed.

The Quartering Act of June 2nd required Massachusetts residents to house and feed the British troops in private homes. Another law passed north of the colonies caused concern as well. The June 22, 1774, *Quebec Act* extended the boundary of Quebec to the Ohio River, granting rights to Catholics and Indians in that region. The northern frontier was now immense.

McDOWELL'S MILL FORT

The blockade of the Boston port by the British troops was of great concern to Pennsylvania, as was the revoking of a colonial charter. The colonists saw themselves as loyal British citizens and the actions appeared to infringe upon their rights as well. Groups began meeting to discuss the potential of those actions being pointed towards Penn's Woods. The colony sent provisions to those suffering in Boston, and they wrote letters urging for the repeal of the acts of Parliament.[2]

The leading men of Cumberland County, Pennsylvania, met at Carlisle on July 12, 1774, with John Montgomery, Esq., presiding to discuss the incidents at Boston.[3] The group at Carlisle unanimously signed a resolution condemning Parliament for closing the Boston port. They recommended a General Congress of the colonies, boycotting British goods and appointed deputies to set a meeting for the General Congress. They did not have a separation focus at that point, seeing themselves still as loyal to the king. On September 5, 1774, the First Continental Congress met in Philadelphia with all 13 colonies represented except Georgia. They approved the *Suffolk Resolve* to oppose the *Intolerable Acts*. At that meeting Congress resolved to not import or export goods from or to England. A declaration of rights was adopted and sent humbly to the King, but events were escalating in New England.

The Battle of Lexington and Concord in April of 1775 was the result of a British attempt to seize the military stores and leaders at Concord. Local militia responded and an engagement ensued resulting in 73 British troops killed and 200 wounded or missing in action. Forty-nine locals were killed with 46 wounded or missing. Skirmishes also happened near Boston and in coastal areas. A second Continental Congress met in Philadelphia and on May 10, 1775, to give updates to the colonial activities.

The Continental units laying siege to Boston against the British needed munitions and canons. They saw an opportunity at Fort Ticonderoga on Lake Champlain in New York. The fort gave the British control of the Canadian waterways and if it could be taken, the arms could be sent to Boston. Continental forces laid siege to the fort and the British were forced to surrender it, which assisted the colonial cause.

McDowell's Mill Fort during the Revolution

Michael C. Beidleman models the dress of a Pennsylvanian frontier rifleman in the Pennsylvania Continental Line at a re-enactment of the Battle of Monmouth in June of 2015. The original battle took place on June 28, 1778. Photo by author used by permission, the Division of Parks and Forestry, Trenton, New Jersey.

George Washington was called by congress to be the Commander-in-Chief of the new Continental Army on June 15, 1775, while a draft of the Declaration of Independence was created by John Adams, Benjamin Franklin, Thomas Jefferson, Robert Livingston, and Roger Sherman which would be accepted and signed on July 4th. George Washington organized and gathered his troops at Breed's Hill in Charlestown, Massachusetts. Patriot militia surrounded Boston laying siege to the city on June 17th. It was called the Battle of Breed's/Bunker Hill where British forces would lose half of their troops.

When the news of the battles at Lexington and Concord on April 19, 1775, reached central Pennsylvania, the Cumberland Valley organized to defend the rights of the colonies. On May 5th, men representing nineteen townships met at Carlisle. Three-thousand men had already associated into volunteer companies, Associators, and they had collected about fifteen hundred arms. Most of those associated troops were from regional groupings which had served during the French and Indian War. They were often made of men with familial and religious ties.

At the county meeting, the committee voted to raise five hundred paid and trained men to be ready to march when called. Their salaries would come from property and personal taxes.[4] The next day the number of men was raised to 1,500, or 2,000 if needed. Pennsylvania had been unique in not having military organizations in the early days of the colony. Most of the associated groups had spent time in voluntary service. Locals organized the associations with men from ages 16–60, which were more like civilian reserves who were to repel invasion in local areas. Most of these were based in townships serving larger neighborhoods as battalions.

These companies marched to join George Washington by the end of that summer at the siege of Boston, however the Pennsylvania Provincial Assembly, meeting as late as November 1775, did not want their representatives to vote for separation from Britain. The Cumberland Valley, almost to a man, did. A number of men from that area recommended an entirely new form of government.[5]

The Rev. Dr. John King had been installed pastor of the Upper West Conococheague Presbyterian Church in 1769. He had very strong feelings about the war. King had married John McDowell's daughter Elizabeth, called Betsy, on April 2, 1771. King's brother George would marry her sister Margaret, called Peggy. With the conflict brewing between the colonies and Great Britain, The Rev. Dr. King volunteered his services as chaplain to the battalion formed from his area to support Boston in a fight against the British. In his address to Captain Huston's Company he said,

> The case is plain, life must be hazarded, or all is gone. You must go and fight, or send your humble submission, and bow as a beast to it's burden, or as an ox to the slaughter. The king of Great Britain has declared us rebels-a capital crime. Submission, therefore, consents to the rope or the axe. Liberty is doubtless gone; none

could imagine a tyrant king should be more favourable to conquered rebels than he was to loyal, humble, petitioning subjects. No! no! If ever a people lay in chains, we must, if our enemies carry their point against us, and oblige us to unconditional submission. This is not all. Our tory neighbors will be our proud and tormenting enemies.[6]

Alfred Nevin mentions in his book on the Cumberland Valley during the Revolutionary War that the Presbyterian Church Session at Falling Spring (Chambersburg) actually brought charges against a member they felt needed church discipline for being "strongly suspected of not being sincere in his profession of attachment to the cause of the Revolution." Most of the Valley was fervently patriotic to the colonial cause and there were no Tories noted.[7] It is to be remembered that they were largely Ulster-Scots who had been mistreated in Northern Ireland by the British and neglected during the wars with the French and Indians. The Whig party had supported free religious expression for Protestants outside the Anglican faith.

A number of counties in Pennsylvania were organizing militia by the spring of 1775. Most of these voluntary independent groups, Associators, signed up to assist colonists at the siege of Boston for only one year. Associators from the Cumberland Valley were not paid during their training period but were paid once they were in the field. Many of the Pennsylvania Associators would roll into the militia system when it was enacted. Some would remain as independent troops.

Four hundred men in companies under Captain James Chambers, the eldest son of pioneer Benjamin Chambers, left the Cumberland Valley on August 26, 1775, and marched to Prospect and Ploughed Hill near Boston to support the patriots and protect the construction of redoubts. Justice William McDowell's son, William, would join them later, serving under James Chambers beginning on July 1, 1776 in the 1st Pennsylvania Regiment, 2nd Infantry. William worked his way up from 3rd Lieutenant to 1st Lieutenant and then Captain of a company over a long and difficult seven year enlistment.

The 2nd Pennsylvania Regiment was formed first under Colonel John Bull and then under Colonel John Philip De Haas in December of 1775. Colonel Irvine's 6th Regiment was formed shortly after with eight companies. The miller John McDowell of McDowell's Mill Fort would join Irvine's 6th Regiment in January as a 1st Lieutenant and become a surgeon and then Captain of a company in 1777. Three of the companies in Irvine's 6th Regiment were from the area around fort: 3rd Company led by Captain Abraham Smith with the miller's son-in-law Elias Davidson serving as a Captain of a flying camp in 1776 and a private James McDowell who most likely was Justice William McDowell's son; 4th Company under Captain William Rippey; and 8th Company under Captain Jeremiah Talbott.

At the outset of the war, Colonel Irvine reported to John Hancock, the President of Congress on March 22nd that he was ready to march to New York.

> Sir: I am honored with your orders to March my battalion to New York, which shall be complied with all possible expedition . . .Many of the arms are old, and want bayonets and other repairs. However, I shall not wait for bayonets, as I hope to be supplied at Philadelphia or New York. I have been obliged to purchase many rifles, but they, I presume, may be changed for muskets, should the service require it; knapsacks, haversacks, canteens, and many other necessaries the commissioners promised to forward for my battalion, are not yet come to hand. Though I do not mean to wait for them, yet I think it proper to acquaint you, as perhaps your further orders may be necessary.[8]

A plan had also been devised in the early stage of the war to entice the French Canadians into the patriot cause but the time chosen for an assault there on December 31, 1775, was poor and the intelligence was faulty. The Battle of Quebec in Quebec City, Provence of Quebec, Canada, resulted in a terrible loss for the patriots. The French Canadians had recently been offered the right to govern themselves in French with religious liberty to remain Roman Catholic. Churches were able to keep their holdings and they seemed content under British rule. They did not support the Patriots and any hope of gaining Canada to the united colonies was lost.

The campaign at Canada lasted from the spring of 1776 through the summer. Brigadier-General William Thompson commanded part of the Pennsylvania brigade with the 2nd Battalion of Colonel St. Clair, the 6th Battalion of Colonel William Irvine and the 4th Battalion of Colonel Anthony Wayne. They were sent first to reinforce the army under Generals Montgomery and Arnold which were poised to lay siege of Quebec. As part of the Quebec campaign they were ordered to attack the British at Three Rivers which would be Pennsylvania's first solo battle.[9] The Battle of Trois-Rivières on June 8, 1776, resulted in a win for the British Army under Quebec Governor Guy Carleton. The continental forces were not able to stop a British advance up the Saint-Lawrence River valley. Isolated in a swamp, they were forced to retreat with many prisoners taken including General Thompson and his staff, and Colonel Irvine. The remainder retreated under John Sullivan to Fort Saint-Jean and then to Fort Ticonderoga. Many men were wounded including Colonel Wayne.

Wayne was credited with saving the rest of the army by rallying them in a difficult retreat and he was placed in command at Ticonderoga and began addressing the continual issue of trying to clothe and feed his men. By the end of the winter many had died of disease or famine at the fort and they needed relief. There was no bedding for the sick and no medicine. The hospital had been moved to Albany which was too difficult to reach in the winter.[10]

Colonel Johnston had written to Richard Peters in Philadelphia, the Secretary of War in the fall of 1776. "It appears to me that the Pennsylvanians were originally designed for soldiers, their vigilance, assiduity & resignation to bad Usage, fatigue & ye strictest Discipline convinces me-their bravery too & enthusiasm in the Service are equally remarkable,"[11] even the sick were willing to serve.

As a result of the capture of Colonel William Irvine, the 6th Regiment with then Associate Surgeon 1st Lieutenant John McDowell was led by Captains David Grier and William Alexander. John McDowell was a surgeon's mate initially but soon was promoted to full surgeon in 1779.[12] Captain Abraham Smith's Company with Justice William McDowell's son John as a private was also in Irvine's Group. Captain Samuel Hay's Company was led by 1st Lieutenant John Grier. Captain Jeremiah Talbot's Company; Captain William Rippey's Company; Captain Moses McClean's Company; Captain James A. Wilson's Company; and Captain Robert Adam's Company all had familiar family names from the Cumberland Valley.

The Major-Generals in the Pennsylvania Line from July 1776 to November 1783 included Thomas Mifflin, Arthur St. Clair, Anthony Wayne and Edward Hand. Those listed within that time period as Brigadier-Generals were John Armstrong, William Thompson, Thomas Mifflin, Arthur St. Clair, Anthony Wayne, John Philip DeHaas, Edward Hand, William Irvine, Richard Humpton and Stephen Moylan.

The Cumberland Valley had three companies: Captain Noah Abraham's Company from Path Valley; Captain Patrick Jack's Company from Hamilton Township; and Captain Charles Maclay's Company from Lurgan Township. 2nd Battalion formed under Colonel John Davis with Captain Charles Leeper's Company in it from Lurgan Township. 4th Battalion had Captain James McConnell from Letterkenny Township. 6th Battalion was made of men who would later be in Franklin County. It was commanded by Colonel Samuel Culbertson with Lieutenant-Colonel John Work and Major James McCammont/McCalmont. Dr. Richard Brownson, son-in-law to John McDowell, married to Mary McDowell, served that Battalion as surgeon. In the Battalion were Captain Patrick Jack's 2nd Company from Hamilton Township; Captain Samuel Patton's 3rd Company from Letterkenny Township; Captain James Patton's 4th Company from Peters Township with 1st Lieutenant Thomas McDowell; Captain Joseph Culbertson's 5th Company from Lurgan Township; and Captain William Huston's 6th Company made of Montgomery, Peters, and Hamilton to whom Rev. King ministered; Captain Robert McCoy's 7th Company from Peters and Captain John McConnell's 8th Company from Letterkenny Township. The 8th Battalion was commanded by Colonel Abraham Smith with Lieutenant-Colonel James Johnston (married to Annabelle McDowell, daughter of pioneer William McDowell) with Major John Johnston (married to Annabelle, daughter of Constable James McDowell) and Adjutant Thomas Johnston.

This Battalion had four companies from the valley. 1st Company from Waynesboro was commanded by Captain Samuel Royer; 2nd Company from Lurgan Township was commanded to Captain John Jack; 3rd Company from Antrim Township was commanded by Captain James Poe and 8th Company from Lurgan Township was commanded by Captain John Rea. In addition to these were separate organization from the community who sent squads and rangers for terms of service. Colonel James Smith of Peters Township raised a Battalion of Rifle rangers to serve in New Jersey.

In the Continental Line of the 1st Pennsylvania Regiment from July 1, 1776 to November 3, 1783 under Field and staff officers Colonels Edward Hand and James Chambers was 1st Lieutenant William McDowell. Captain James Chambers would later be promoted to Colonel and then Brigadier-General. His company served almost the entire seven years of the war. On August 26, 1775, four hundred men from Cumberland County serving under him were sent to Prospect and Ploughed Hill near Boston, Massachusetts. His Company joined the Pennsylvania 1st Rifle Regiment under Colonel William Thompson also of Cumberland County. "This group was particularly noted for accuracy in their aim."[13]

Chambers was ordered to Long Island on March of 1776 where he participated in the Battle of Flat Bush and at King's Bridge. In August Pennsylvania troops, mostly from Franklin County, were in reserve to cover the retreat of the Colonial army from Long Island. William McDowell would later be promoted to Captain under Colonel Daniel Brodhead.[14] William's Lieutenant's book of the southern campaign (1781–1782) is in the Pennsylvania State archives and records the difficulty under which the Pennsylvania troops often served. He often noted having only rice for dinner and sleeping without tent coverage because the baggage wagons were not able to reach the men. Every time he received a normal meal it was noted with great delight.[15] William did hard service as did his brothers: John (LL.D) was a private for a short time under Captain Samuel Patton; Nathan served under Captains James Patton and Samuel Patton; Alexander served under Captains James Patton, Thomas McDowell and William Huston; Andrew served under Captains Robert Dickey and Conrad Snider; and sister Mary's husband Dr. William Magaw served as a surgeon.

Constable James McDowell served as a Sub-Lieutenant for Cumberland County under Captain Robert McCoy who was later killed at Crooked Billet. By March enlistment was compulsory under constables and he was busy enlisting men at Carlisle, holding election of officers, purchasing supplies and arms, and collecting fines. His children participated in the war effort as well: daughter Mary was married to Captain Thomas Campbell who was captured at Fort Washington; and son Robert was a private under Captains James Patton and Robert Dickey.

Pioneer William McDowell's son Thomas served as a 1st Lieutenant under Colonel Samuel Culbertson's Battalion of Cumberland County Associators for the length of the war. He had many of his nephews in his company which must have been harrowing.

The miller John McDowell was now serving in Wayne's Division as a lieutenant and surgeon to the 6th Regiment under Captains Robert Magaw, and Richard Humpton in Colonel Samuel Culberston's Battalion. The 6th would later be rolled into the 7th and John would become a Captain of a company. John's son-in-law Elias Davidson was a Captain of a flying Camp in the 8th Battalion under Abraham Smith; and son-in-law Hugh Davidson was a Lieutenant-Colonel in the 2nd Battalion of Bedford County Militia. Son-in-law Reverent King was a chaplain.

John McDowell's work as a surgeon would have been done under extremely difficult conditions, and he was in his 60s. He had to tend to soldiers wounded by musket balls and canon shards with little understanding of infection and sanitation, using archaic tools. In some cases limbs needed to be removed without anesthesia, while the patient simply bit on a stick. Blood-letting was still believed to balance the four humors in the body, usually about 10 ounces were taken every other day.

Soldiers who suffered from exposure and starvation also contracted things like yellow fever, flux, diarrhea, small pox and viruses. There was little understanding of bacteria and germs, however George Washington insisted on his men being inoculated from small pox because it was being used as a biological weapon by the British, as they left the sick in the path of the advancing Colonial Army. John would have lanced a sore from a sick man and run a thread through the wound and then make a small cut in a healthy man and run the thread through the open wound of that man to carry out that order. Some contracted the disease in milder form and this saved many lives.[16]

He also would have served as his own pharmacy, making tonics of minerals, herbs and barks. Some medications contained alcohol, mercury, silver, sulfur, opium and arsenic. Doctors also served as dentists, removing teeth and dealing with oral infections. His brother wrote in his journal about an infected tooth, and about "taking the vomit" something which was used to help balance out the system from fevers. John would have used what he felt worked and what he had learned from trained doctors serving at his fort.

John would have also been responsible for the condition of the camp, overseeing its cleanliness. He would have been traveling between flying camps and battlefields throughout the length of the war which must have been exhausting, with extremes in temperature and often without supplies. He became a Captain, most likely of a corps of invalids who were capable of doing light garrison service. He would have assigned them to tasks like guard duty.

It is not known how skilled John was in the practice of medicine, however Hugh Mercer and William Irvine, noted surgeons turned military leaders, had been assigned to command companies garrisoned at McDowell's Mill Fort for a block of time during the wars with French and Western Indians. Some general knowledge of medicine might have been learned when John was at the fort as families fled there for safety.

John initially served under Irvine, until Irvine was captured. It is doubtful that the commander of the regiment who was a trained physician would have placed an inept person in care of his troops. He must have had some type of confidence in John's potential. John also had family members with professional training. His son-in-law Dr. Richard Brownson was a surgeon in this Regiment. Justice William McDowell's son-in-law Dr. William Magaw also served during the war, and his son Dr. Andrew McDowell served in Captain Robert Dickey and Conrad Snider's Companies. There were resources within the family to assist John. There was also some type of ongoing training offered for those in the field which was led by professional physicians, using what they believed to be the latest in medical science.[17]

The daughters of the pioneer William also sent their men off to war. Annabell McDowell was married to Lieutenant-Colonel John Johnson, an officer in the 8th Battalion under Abraham Smith. Jean was married to Archibald Irwin, a Quartermaster in Colonel Samuel Culbertson's Battalion, and their son James served as a private. Sarah's husband was Captain William Piper, Commissioner of Excise for Cumberland County during the war. The family, like their neighbors were well represented in the ranks of the Pennsylvania Line and most of their community would know the sorrows of war.

The British next moved the center of their operations in the mid-atlantics from Boston to New York City. Their plan was to cut off communication between New England and the southern colonies by dominating the route from New York to Quebec. In response, George Washington moved his troops from Boston to New York to meet them. Those serving under Captain James Chambers were ordered to Long Island on March of 1776. His forces participated in the Battle of Flat Bush on August 27, 1776, with Captain John Steel's Company, and then served as a reserve to cover the retreat of George Washington's forces from Long Island but during that engagement, George Washington lost one-fourth of his command.

Congress in Philadelphia formally adopted the Declaration of Independence on July 4, 1776, as they reflected on the structure of the Continental Army. General Washington had pushed Congress to form a standing army instead of a cluster of one-year volunteer organizations

Joe Roth models the uniform worn by a Continental soldier during the Revolutionary War at a re-enactment of the Battle of Monmouth in June of 2015. He is carrying a reproduction musket. Photo by author used by permission, the Division of Parks and Forestry, Trenton, New Jersey.

but Congress was afraid of having all of that power under one command, so Washington watched the British from the heights of Harlem in Manhattan, and tried to prepare for another engagement with his rag-tag organization. The Battle of White Plains, New York, on October 28, 1776, was fought by the Patriots against British and Hessian troops which were three times the size of Washington's forces. It resulted in another retreat with local skirmishes.

This is a typical Revolutionary War camp fire. This one was set up for a re-enactment of the Battle of Monmouth. The Pennsylvania troops were often without food, proper clothing, and tents. Photo by author used by permission, the Division of Parks and Forestry, Trenton, New Jersey.

The colonials tried to take Fort Washington at Washington Heights on Manhattan Island from the British on November 16, 1776, in what was called The Battle of Fort Washington. The fort overlooked ships on the Hudson River but the Patriots lost which resulted in Manhattan and Fort Lee being abandoned by colonial forces. Constable James McDowell's daughter Mary was married to Captain Thomas Campbell who was the Captain of a Flying Camp. He was captured by the British that day but later released on December 26th on parole. He would serve the patriots again.

George Washington then moved his forces towards Philadelphia, Pennsylvania, to protect the colonial capital. His troops were lacking proper clothing, with many sick and with numbers deserting due to expired terms. They surprised a Hessian picket guard outside Trenton, New

Jersey, on December 26, 1776, in what was called The Battle of Trenton. This win after so many losses in New York boosted the moral of the colonial troops for a short time. It was followed by The Battle of Princeton on January 3, 1777, where the troops met Cornwallis' forces. The British were then forced to abandon New Jersey, except for the corridor from Perth Amboy to New Brunswick. It was a second win for the Patriots.

Following the victories at Trenton and Princeton, 5,000 members of the Continental Army entered winter quarters at Morristown, New Jersey, early in January of 1777. Many of the men who had enlisted had expiring terms. Washington needed the time to rebuild his army but smallpox was a perpetual problem depleting them. Washington again ordered inoculations be done. By spring the army marched toward Middlebrook, Somerset County, New Jersey, hoping to engage the British forces in New Brunswick, but the British had returned to New York.

Reverent John Steele, who had served as a Captain in Armstrong's expedition against Kittanning in the fall of 1756 and had been garrisoned at McDowell's Mill Fort, served as the Captain of the 10th Pennsylvania Regulars and later of the 1st Pennsylvania Regulars, leading men from Franklin County in military actions. His regiment served during the encampment at Morristown in 1777, the New Jersey Campaign of 1777, engagements at Bound Brook, Brandywine, Valley Forge Encampment, and Monmouth, the Middlebrook Encampment, the New Jersey Campaign of 1779, the Morristown Encampment of 1779, the New Jersey Summer Campaign, the Blockhouse-Bergen Heights, the Morristown Encampment of 1780, the Southern Campaign, Yorktown, and the Carolina Campaign. [18] The Reverent was vigilant and maintained his vigor throughout.

Those remaining in the Cumberland Valley were also busy as they waited for letters from their loved ones on the front which often took six months to reach them. On January 9, 1777, the Council of Safety in Philadelphia had given orders to the counties to supply grain for horse feed for the army. Each township was to send a percentage to the County Committees. The McDowell farms would have participated in this. Wagons were also collected in Lancaster County.[19]

McDowell's Mill would have been busy grinding wheat, mainly in the summer and fall, for the community. Bringing in crops would be difficult with many of the able bodied men in the valley mustered in the Pennsylvania Line. That left older men, women and children to do the work as well as those who had served brief terms in private forces. Some women who were without means simply followed the army and received half rations for doing wash, cooking and tending to the ill so that they would not starve. Many of the Ulster-Scot women from the valley were equally good with a rifle as their men.

Colonel James Smith raised a battalion of riflemen on February 10, 1777,[20] and that year Company 4 was formed from men in Peters Township. It was commanded by Captain James Patton with 1st Lieutenant Thomas McDowell, 2nd Lieutenant John Welsh and Ensign John Dickey. Alexander and Nathan McDowell, Justice William McDowell's younger sons, were privates in this company.

Company 6 also was formed with men from both Peters and Montgomery townships. It was commanded by Captain William Huston, 1st Lieutenant William Elliott, 2nd Lieutenant James McFarland, and Ensign Robert Kyle. William Smith, Jr., the founder of the town of Mercersburg, was a Lieutenant in this company and he later served as a Captain in 1780. Some of the soldiers in the company included Captain John Marshall, Joseph Mitchell, James Morrison, Walter McKinney, James Smith, James Herod, William McDowell (Justice McDowell's son) folded into this unit, Sir Robert McCoy, Samuel Patton, William Waddell, Robert McFarland, and Jonathan Smith. [21]All these men were from founding families in the valley while Justice William McDowell, Esq., called a Patriot, served as a Judge along with brother James who also served as a county Sub-Lieutenant.[22]

Anthony Wayne (1/1/1745–12/15/1796) was commissioned a Brigadier-General in February of 1777 and placed in command of the Pennsylvania Line. He was given the nicknamed "Mad Anthony" due to his quick execution of military duties in the face of personal danger. He often showed extreme courage and caution against formidable odds using surveying, mathematical and military gifts. Wayne, a protestant of Irish and English descent, was somewhat different than his troops

2/3rds of which were Presbyterian Ulster-Scots with the other third made largely of Germans. Most of the Ulster-Scots in this line were from the 1717–1730 migration like the McDowells.[23] Most of the Philadelphia troops were more recent arrivals. His troops dearly loved him through terrible years of deprivation under a Pennsylvanian government which was often unresponsive to their needs.

The political infighting in Philadelphia between Conservative Whigs, Loyalists, Tories and Quakers would result in many excuses for not properly providing for the Line. Wayne expected his troops to be well groomed and the lack of clothing and ammunition continually vexed him. He ordered a barber for each company to make sure the men were at least shaved and had their hair cut. Those with long beards were punished.[24]

He ran into trouble with those who had joined the army as Associators. Associator companies had terms which had expired and they expected release, after all they had volunteered for a set period of time. He would have a few mutinies during his service with men feeling promises made to them were not kept. Being held beyond expired terms, lacking proper clothing, food and pay would all contribute to an undercurrent of unhappiness in some of the men. Their love for their commander never wavered and often rallied them in times of difficult service.

Wayne had to rebuild a new army in 1777 from scratch as many of those in Associations formally joined the Continental Army with terms of three years or the "duration of the war," a term which would later cause trouble as the war dragged on. Line troops from Pennsylvania could serve at the battles along the eastern seacoast from north to south or to the west on the frontier fighting Indians in alliance with the British who made continual raids on settlements.

Militia was formally organized into compulsory enrollment issued through local constables in March of 1777. The Continental Line received their orders directly from Congress. They had longer enlistment terms than the Associators, and the discipline was often quite severe. All white males age 18–53 were expected to fight with limited exemptions. Some had already done short duty and if they did not sign up with the compulsory enrollment they paid a fine.

A complaint was raised to Major-General John Armstrong in Carlisle by Nathan McDowell, Sr., Thomas Maxwell and John McDowell, son of William, who had served in Associators Companies in Cumberland County from Peter's Township. They were now facing a fine for not following the compulsory draft. No credit was being given for their tour of duty. Major-General John Armstrong conveyed the concern to President Warton. He felt that if they had served by contract and obeyed their Captain, they should not be fined.[25]

Cousin Alexander McDowell also informed Vice President Bryan about the difficulty for those who were Mennonite or Quaker. The obligation to fight countered their pacifistic understanding of scripture. He reported that he believed they would faithfully serve the state of Pennsylvania and would do not harm, but they saw the order to bear arms as religious persecution. Alexander recommended a larger tax for them since others were protecting them, but not a fine.[26] Taking the oath of allegiance required of white males over age 18 in Pennsylvania by 1779 would also be troublesome for those in the same groups who, based on what they saw as Biblical prohibitions in the book of Mathew, would not take oaths.

Wayne was ordered with his newly formed troops to join Washington at Camp Morristown, New Jersey, on April 12th. As commander of the Pennsylvania Line, he oversaw the needs of his regiments of infantry plus small Pennsylvania cavalry and artillery companies in the Continental Army. This line made up a large portion of George Washington's army. Wayne remained cheerful and loyal to the cause.

Eight regiments formed a division of two brigades in the spring. 1st Brigade was composed of 1st Regiment under Colonel Chambers; 2nd Regiment under Colonel Walter Stewart; 7th Regiment under Lieutenant-Colonel Connor and 10th Regiment under Lieutenant-Colonel Hubley. 2nd Brigade was composed of 4th Regiment under Lieutenant-Colonel William Butler; 5th Regiment under Lieutenant-Colonel Johnston; 8th Regiment under Colonel Broadhead and 11th Regiment under Colonel Humpton. 1,700 men were in this division.

Their pay was often delayed, and Continental currencies devalued. Certificates of the Funded, or Militia debt, were issued and redeemed at face value and many were sold at discount. At the end of the war, Pierce's Certificates granted Donation Lands in the Western Counties which would be free of taxation as long as the soldier lived on the property and retained ownership of it.

Justice William McDowell's son Alexander would later serve as the Deputy Surveyor of the Donated Lands in Pennsylvania after the war. Lots would be carefully surveyed to include features like water sources and the men would draw tickets with acreage according to rank. Alexander would later work for the Holland Land Company doing much of the same. Pennsylvania was short on cash. Many land speculators in Holland bought tracts of land in the western part of Pennsylvania to give much needed currency to the colony. These tracts were later sold to settlers.

Indians were still a concern in central and western Pennsylvania. The British had held the Indians to their treaties. They were to fight with the British against the colonials. Many of those tribes felt the war was an argument between brothers but they quickly found themselves forced to take sides in the white man's war. Those in alliance with the British again stalked settlers. In 1777 the Tull family, living six miles west of Bedford with nine daughters and one son, were attacked by Indians. The son was absent at the time but the aged parents with the sisters were home. A number of area settlers fled. The house was found burning by a man named Williams and his son. Mr. Tull was dying and the Williams fled to the fort. The next day a group from Fort Bedford found the mother with an infant in her arms, both scalped. The girls were discovered dead one by one.[27]

Problems surfaced again in December when a number of families fled to the fort from the Johnstown area. One of the men was named Samuel Adams and the other men had the last names of Thornton and Bridges. They were attacked when returning to gather belongings from their home. Samuel was killed and the Indian who killed him also died. A number of men serving under Captain Dorsey also later were killed at "The Harbor" by Ray's hill. John Lane a scout under Captain Philips was out scouting and upon return to the fort found Captain Philips and 15 men killed and scalped.[28] The frightening news of western Indian attacks circulated in the Cumberland Valley while their men were back east in New Jersey.

Major-General George Washington moved to the Middlebrook encampment in June of 1777. The British had wanted to engage his army on the plains because they knew they would win there but Washington wisely chose to protect his forces in the heights. Meanwhile British soldiers were moved by sea with a plan to take Philadelphia which opened the Philadelphia Campaign of the war. General Wayne with his division was sent to protect the capital, marching through the city to Wilmington, Delaware under the belief that the British would attack the city from that direction. He prepared for an engagement which would be remembered as The Battle of Brandywine.

While the armies shifted their positions, the Continental Congress authorized the creation of a new flag on June 14, 1777. It was to have 13 red and white stripes and 13 white stars on a field of blue to represent the North American colonies. This would be the first time the Patriots would have a flag to rally around which became the symbol for a new nation yet to be established.

Wayne was complaining to the Board of War in June that his troops never received any uniforms, only hunting shirts which were now worn out. He called the units "a body of fine men," but in "rags and badly armed."[29] Wayne would continually try to clothe his army, meeting excuses from his own provincial government, and faulty fabrics from disreputable contractors. He even used his own money to get provisions which were often too little too late. Without pay for long periods of time and then receiving devalued certificates, the men could no longer provide for themselves or their loved ones.

While elements of Washington's army were engaged in battles in the New York area in August, trying to break the British hold over the Hudson Valley, Major-General John Armstrong complained to the powers that be in Philadelphia that the Pennsylvania Line was suffering from "shameful neglect and abuse." He told President Wharton that they were in great need of arms. Some of the arms they had needed repair and he sent them back to Philadelphia. He would also have the unhappy news in December that the treasury was drained and a fateful letter from The Council in February of 1778 stating that "Pennsylvania must suffer. It is not to be avoided. It only remains to make the suffering as light as possible."[30] Lieutenant William McDowell later wrote that the army could have done better if the soldiers had been given money for their own clothing. They could buy their supplies cheaper and of better quality than what the army was receiving.[31]

The Philadelphia Campaign had the new objective for the British of controlling the seat of the 2nd Continental Congress and the Delaware River. The British moved into position to take the city. The Colonial Government quickly moved to Lancaster County in anticipation. George Washington attempted unsuccessfully to defend the city. The Battle of Brandywine, near Chadd's Ford, Pennsylvania, took place on September 11, 1777, along a road leading towards Philadelphia where the British under Sir William Howe with General Knyphausen were gathered with 15,500 men. Washington had 14,600 men. Things had gone badly for the colonials in battles in New York and morale was low. General Knyphausen attack Washington's troops and they were forced to retreat. Colonel James Chambers was wounded in the side at Brandywine and a "Lieutenant Holliday/Holiday" was reported killed. Mary McDowell, daughter of Nathan, was married to Lieutenant John Holiday. Captains Grier and Craig were wounded as well.[32]

Washington planned another attack on the 16th at Whitehorse Tavern, near Malvern. It was aborted due to torrential rain and thereafter titled The Battle of the Clouds. Washington was forced to retreat and the British could not follow due to their own bogged down equipment.

A force under General Wayne had been left behind on the 20th to try to harass the British as they moved toward Philadelphia while Washington concentrated on moving his troops. Wayne with the 1st, 2nd, 4th, 5th, 7th, 8th, 10th, and 11th Regiments, Hartley's Regiment of Artillery and a small dragoon force camped close to British lines. Wayne's forces were surprised at about 10 P.M. by the British led by Major-General Charles Grey. This action was called The Battle of Paoli Tavern or the Paoli Massacre. The British decided to take no prisoners and brutally hacked and bayonetted fallen men on the enemy line.

Colonial troops attempted a surprise attack on British regiments in Germantown on October 4, 1777, called The Battle of Germantown. The Continental Army was again defeated and suffered two times the losses as the British. Washington finally chose to enter winter quarters with his men at Valley Forge which was a day's march from the city.

The troops quickly constructed about 1,500 log huts and two miles of fortifications. The site was chosen because it had natural barriers on two sides: the Schuylkill River to the north and Mount Joy to the west. The 1st and 2nd Battalions of the Pennsylvania Line were placed at the southern outer defensive line under Generals Wayne and Scott. The men suffered from hunger and the cold that winter with lack of clothing and provisions. Surgeon John McDowell would have been busy moving through-out the encampment and at flying camps treating men suffering from wounds, influenza, typhoid, small pox and exposure. Close to 2,000 men died from disease alone in this location. His nephews William and John were also at camp.

This is the exterior of a re-constructed hut which demonstrates the style of dwelling used by the troops at Valley Forge. They were constructed in haste and as a result, drafty. 1st Lieutenant John McDowell was a surgeon at Valley Forge. His nephews 1st Lieutenant William McDowell and Private John McDowell were also there. Photo taken by the author.

McDowell's Mill Fort during the Revolution

This is the interior of a re-constructed hut at Valley Forge. Photo taken by the author.

This is an ornamental reproduction canon at Valley Forge in cast iron instead of an authentic one which would have been made of the cast bronze. The 3–4 pound mobile cannon used at Valley Forge shot solid or grape shot and had a flat trajectory of between 1,000 to 2,000 yards. This one is located where General Wayne's Pennsylvania Line were camped along the southern defensive area. Photo by author.

Half of the men at Valley Forge were without shoes, stockings or proper clothing, resulting in many having bloody feet. Wayne purchased things for the Pennsylvania Line using his own money only to have vendors unable to deliver items to him. He sent a force into New Jersey out of desperation to try to acquire cattle between Bordentown and Salem, an act which earned him the nickname "Drover Wayne."[33]

Baron Von Steuben, a professional Prussian soldier who now served the colonials as Inspector-General, instituted strict military discipline on the cold, exhausted and hungry troops. They steadily drilled and learned the correct use of the bayonet. Friendly Oneida Indians also camped at Valley Forge with the troops.

The Cumberland Valley was busy trying to supply flour to the soldiers. The seed had been hand-planted in fields and the crop harvested and bundled, with chaff removed, before being hauled to a mill where it was grounded into flour and bagged. It was a labor intensive way to make a living, but people rallied to the cause. Congress had authorized Pennsylvania commissioners on February 17, 1778, to purchase stores of flour on the east side of the Susquehanna with set prices.[34]

The settlers still lived in fear of Indian raids. The back settlements in Pennsylvania suffered attacks with murders, scalping and capture of those left behind in May of 1778. Families were evacuated and clustered into small concentrated locations. The two branches of the Susquehanna were cleared of settlers who flew into forts for protection. Repeated pleas were sent for regiments to come to address the problem but most of the able bodied men were in the Pennsylvania Line to the east with Washington.[35]

General Armstrong reported to Congress that incursions had occurred on both sides of the Allegheny River and on the East side to the Center of the state. Many were in great distress beyond the Kittany Mountains and in need of a chain of patrols, but there were none to spare. People were once again moving from Paxton as Indians sent scalping parties on the West Branch of the Susquehanna on June 14th.[36] This added pressure on the Cumberland Valley as those who remained there feared they would revisit the actions of the Indian Wars and become the frontier for the state. The local farms were still necessary to produce food for both settlers and for the army. The British knew that and took full advantage of it as had the French before them.

Hope seemed possible for the struggling nation when the Americans signed *The Treaty of Alliance* with the French on February 6, 1778. Having the French fully committed to the war effort meant that America would have the financial and military backing they desperately needed. This alliance provided the possibility of the French blockading the Delaware River against British stationed in Philadelphia.

The British made plans to evacuate the city in early June. The French had supplied the colonials with ammunition and guns prior to this but would now be sending standing troops. The Spanish were allied with the French and would recognize the United States as independent the following year. They had also supplied the colonials from their stores kept in New Orleans and Havana. The Dutch had assisted the colonials

This is a re-enactment of the 6th Pennsylvania's camp at the Battle of Monmouth taken in June of 2015. Photo by author used by permission, the Division of Parks and Forestry, Trenton, New Jersey.

financially beginning in 1776 and would finally declare war on Great Britain the end of 1780. Bringing these European countries into the American conflict greatly affected the outcome of the war. England was now fighting on too many fronts.

Sir Henry Clinton succeeded Sir William Howe as Commander-in-chief of the British forces in North America on June 8th and when Clinton arrived, he ordered the formal evacuation of Philadelphia. George Washington saw this as an opportunity. He ordered a harassing rear attack on the exiting British forces. The half-starved colonial army prepared for an engagement with new vigor in the midst of the awful heat of summer.

General Sir Henry Clinton abandoned Philadelphia with Loyalists and a 12 mile-long baggage train on June 18, 1778. They began their march towards New York City. The British had decided to protect both New York and Florida from a formal French naval attack. The next day the Continental Army under General George Washington left Valley Forge. A harassment of the retreating British was led by General Charles Lee and resulted in the last major battle of the northern campaign on June 28, 1778, The Battle of Monmouth Court House or The Battle of Monmouth, Monmouth County, New Jersey.

This battle was the largest field artillery battle of the American Revolution. It ended in a tie but Washington's forces held the field while the British continued on towards New York, and it was seen as a political win for the colonists. General Anthony Wayne led Pennsylvania forces in this hot and difficult struggle. Much of the loss of life that day was due to the extreme in temperature.

General Wayne was again complaining to Pennsylvania officials in October about the lack of clothing for his forces. Pennsylvania appeared to be slower that other colonies in raising money and recruiting for its militia. At this point, unfortunately, leaders in Philadelphia believed that with the French now engaged in the conflict, the war must be near its end and further support would not be needed, which was clearly not the case. The colony was struggling financially for various reasons. Massachusetts had an abundant harvest and seaports available for imports and exports.

Virginia had many shores and rivers with a large store of tobacco for sale. Pennsylvania had been cut off from the rest of the world by the British. Its principle city, Philadelphia, had been under occupation and those now returning to the city to govern seemed to be involved in in-fighting.[37]

Washington and his troops spent the winter of 1778/1779 camped at Middlebrook in New Jersey. The Pennsylvania line was in desperate need of clothing, supplies and pay. Dirty and near-naked, there were disputes even among ranking officers. General Wayne sent Colonel Walter Stewart and Colonel William Irvine to the Assembly to alert them of the conditions at camp and to tell them that the men were demoralized, but Philadelphia was in deep debt with depreciated money and lacked credit.

The Assembly, in March of 1779, extended the term allowed by Congress for ½ pay during seven years, to be for the duration of the life of the soldier. They also fixed prices for articles used for soldiers. They agreed to provide uniforms and exempted taxation on lands granted to soldiers for their life.[38] As the troops tried to prepare for the winter cold, on December 29, the British moved to capture Savanah, Georgia. Colonial forces had tried to protect the city, but it would be held by the British until July 11, 1782.

Indian attacks in the western sections of Pennsylvania continued. A company of men were raised in Path Valley under Captain Noah Abraham to quell the Indian disturbances. Letterkenny Township also sent a company of men.

The Cumberland Valley struggled during the fall of 1779 from insufficient crops. An insufficient amount of flour had been collected due to a combination of frost and mildew, and what flour was available for the army was delayed because the roads were in bad physical condition.[39] Lancaster and York were the storage points for feeding the troops. This scarcity of crops would add to the difficulty for the men in the Pennsylvania Line who spent the winter of 1779–1780 at Morristown, New Jersey, sharing 1,000 huts at Jockey Hollow with twelve men to a hut. The Pennsylvania Line was encamped south of Sugar Loaf Road to the northwest of route 287 and Route 202 North. December added to the difficulty by introducing the worst winter of the century at Morristown with over 20 snowstorms. The men occupied themselves with activities like guard duty, inspections, drills, training and work details. Food sources dwindled and the men were extremely cold.

Lieutenant Moses Van Campen, an ensign under Captain Thomas Robinson of the Pennsylvania Continental Line, was placed in charge of recruiting and organizing for the defense of the frontier during the summer of 1780. George Washington had wanted the Six Nations to remain neutral during the war, but the British had coerced the tribes to abide by their treaties and to lead attacks on frontier settlements.

Abraham Smith of Cumberland County wrote to Joseph Reid, Esq., on August 7, 1780, with orders for volunteers to join the army and militia. One company was to go to the frontiers of Northumberland County and another to the frontiers of Bedford. Bedford had been in distress three weeks prior due to attacks. A captain with twelve men had been killed. Abraham Smith's group had to cover them. His hope was that the new companies at the frontier would improve the moral of the settlers in those parts. He requested ammunition and wagons to supply the newly called militia. The recruits seemed to all want bayonets, but all they had were muskets. They also were waiting for state funds promised to buy additional supplies.[40]

An Indian attack occurred on two sisters named Sarah and Jane Renfrew. They were at the farm of A.J. Fahnestock near Waynesboro and were washing clothes by the banks of the Little Antietam when two Indians killed and scalped them. An infant was also killed, having its head bashed against a tree.[41] The Indians were pursued by two local hunters and overtaken at the Great/Big Cove. The Indians were then killed and scalped by the whites. Those scalps combined with the retrieved scalps of the girls were buried in the girls' coffins. Van Campen mentioned in his narrative on this matter that Captain Robinson was "no woodsman nor marksman," but Van Campen was and Van Campen was considered a very good scout. He went on to relate about a formation of a "constant chain of scouts around the frontier settlements, from the north to the west branch of the Susquehanna, by the way of the head waters of Little Fishing Creek, Chillisquaka, and Muncy . . ."[42]

The settlers were once again forming a defensive line. It would seem likely that McDowell's Mill Fort would have participated in this line of defense, especially with natives stalking in the Great/Big Cove. It was a structure which was still standing which had barracks. Even with this diligence, two to three families at Penn's Creek were killed and scalped by a party of 20 to 30 Indians. The Western Indians continued attacks on settlers living on the western frontiers of Ohio, Washington, Youghagany and Westmoreland Counties in Pennsylvania. Many of those living in Franklin County had relatives living in those new counties. Men with a horse and gun and one month's provisions were enlisted to protect them. They marched on June 4th to the Sandusky area where Colonels Williamson and Marshall led engagements against Wyandot towns. Settlers west of the Appalachian Mountains struggled as war broke out with Indians in the Ohio and Illinois territory.

Things were also heating up within the Continental troops which would result in mutinies. The first one in May of 1780 was made by two regiments of the 1st Connecticut Brigade. The second would take place in January of 1781, made by Pennsylvania troops who marched toward Philadelphia to demand provisions and back pay. Those giving years of service to the Pennsylvania Continental Line had several challenges. They often enlisted for a given time, but were not released. They were under fed, ill clothed and often without shelter in the field. They either went without pay for long periods of time or were given notes that devalued. This left many families on the frontier farms in dire financial straits while fearing Indian raids from the west. Complaints were continually sent to the government about their economic condition with little attention given.[43]

Soldiers also worried about the function of their farms during their long absence. How would the work be accomplished while they were marching up and down the Atlantic seacoast for years without end? The answer for some was to turn to slaves.

There had been about 4,000 slaves in Pennsylvania in 1730, mostly centered around Philadelphia, and by 1790 that number had increased to 10,000, with 6,500 African-Americans free.[44] The large number of

Ulster-Scots in the Cumberland Valley before the Revolutionary War tended not to have enough money for the purchase of slaves. They had suffered economically during the Indian forays which left their resources depleted.

Things began to shift as the men were away for an extended period of time. The tax records for 1779 show troubling things about the McDowells who were busy with others serving in far off colonies. John McDowell's gristmill was taxable with 248 acres of land, three horses and four cows. His brothers' acreage and animals are also recorded with some owning more land and some less. John, William, James and Nathan McDowell all had stills to convert some of their grain into alcohol which was easier to transport, and for the first time one "negro" shows on Lieutenant John McDowell's tax record. The Franklin County Unbound Project which is preserving the names of some of the slaves from the 1780 gradual abolition of slavery act lists the African American man working at McDowell's Mill Fort and the surrounding fields as Poll, age 35. This person does not show on prior tax records and would be listed for only a few years.

Sub-Lieutenant Nathan McDowell had two children listed in the 1780 list, Jack age 14 and Fann age 9. An African American man named John is listed in the 1786 role of Communing Member of the Upper West Conococheague Presbyterian Church who worked for Nathan, perhaps these were his children.[45] The fact that he received communion points towards at least some level of inclusion within the congregation, though he was still in slave status which is dehumanizing. He would be baptized years later which opened him to full church membership. It is unclear how slaves were viewed by this particular congregation during this time or by their owners.

Justice William McDowell had one slave and we know her name was Dina/Dinna/Dinah from his probated will. She was only nine in 1780. She and two mulatto boys came from William Maxwell's house, presumably to serve Mary Maxwell McDowell. The boys were never listed as slaves or bound boys in William's tax record. Their parents are never listed. The boys would later be placed in the custody of William's son Thomas, though not listed as slaves. Dina was later set free by William McDowell at the end of his life.[46] We do not have a record of her experiences during this period but she may have served in the home, helping Mary.

Others in Franklin County were also recorded as having one or two slaves. People like the Maxwells and Davidsons had a few more. Slavery never materialized in the county in the form practiced on isolated plantations in the south. The fact that it existed at all shows a level of disconnection between fighting for one's own independence and freedom while restricting it from others. The issue of slavery did weigh heavily on the minds of many in Pennsylvania. The Pennsylvania Assembly had passed the *1780 An Act for the Gradual Abolition of Slavery*, shortly after the McDowell's joined in the practice, which may be why some in Franklin County stopped the practice all together, and why some later moved south to continue it.

The Act stated that those born in Pennsylvania after that date were declared free, but would be in an "indentured status" until age twenty eight. Adults enslaved prior to that date spent the rest of their lives as slaves. This awkward language kept persons of color in a type of limbo for many years. Slavery would be outlawed in Franklin County on September 9, 1784, so it seems that the moral issue was being discussed within the community during this period with some seeking a permanent solution.

The Mason and Dixon Line at the base of the county, would later mark freedom for those crossing into the Valley from the south on their way north to Canada. The Underground Railroad would then run through Casey's Knob in the south, Heister's Mill and north to Mount Parnell.[47] Those traveling to Canada could also just follow the Appalachian Mountains north. Franklin County would eventually have a large population of free blacks, called Little Africa,[48] and a steady stream of fugitive slaves with aggressive bounty hunters following using the mountain trials and the same roads the founding families had requested to bring products to the ports. The Underground Railroad would run through the Cumberland Valley with some members of the community supporting it and others returning runaway slaves to bounty hunters, according to United States law.

While the demographics of the valley were changing, to the east the war continued. The next campaign began in May of 1780. The Continental army was at Morristown. Sir Henry Clinton, leading a superior force of British, returning from the south with Tory refugees, had a plan to capture the military stores at Morristown. George Washington, however, moved his men towards the highlands.

Washington's troops were at half-strength by September, so he had the army march back and forth between Morristown and West Point to avoid the British. During the summer, they were able to capture the block-house behind Bergen Heights which had a deposit of stolen horses and property plundered from the area but the real object for the colonials was preparation for battle.

The focus of the war turned to the south. The southern campaign had as its agenda to drive the British out of their strongholds there. It began with the Seige of Charleston, South Carolina. British Admiral Mariot Arbuthnot and Sir Henry Clinton with a force of 13,500 were pitted against Benjamin Lincoln's forces of 5,466 on March 29, 1780. It went badly for the Continentals when they were abandoned by the French fleet who sailed to the West Indies for the winter. Continental forces were taken as prisoners of war on diseased prison ships. This left no Continental forces in the South and Charleston was held by the British.

The Battle of Camden, South Carolina, also was a British victory on August 16th. The British would hold the Carolinas for a few years. The *Journal of Lieutenant William McDowell of the First Pennsylvania Regiment, in the Southern Campaign, 1781–1782* gives one man's account of the exhausting activities during that period as the men in his unit covered 2,755 miles on foot often without cover and with sparse quantities of food.[49]

The campaign of 1780, however, was overshadowed by the September treason of Benedict Arnold who exchanged West Point for 20,000 pounds and a commission as Major General in the British army. The mutiny of men in the Pennsylvania Line who felt that their contracts had been violated by the Pennsylvania government was another undercurrent. At issue had been the non-payment or depreciated pay, insufficient supply of clothing and provisions, the fact that men with expired terms were not able to leave, and sheer exhaustion. William, as an officer, recorded a number of Court Martials and that he could understand some of the discontent within the line. Their distress in service had been prolonged and often severe. They had fought while nearly starving and suffering from the elements without proper clothing. This resulted in the January 2, 1781 discharge of those due to go.

A committee was established to settle the term "three years or the war," a bounty of $100 was offered for any wishing to re-enlist (and many did), auditors were sent to settle pay issues, clothing was given to the men discharged and a general amnesty was established for those involved in the mutiny.[50] A revolt in the New Jersey Line followed for the same reasons and was addressed. The Pennsylvania revolt had been a more serious problem. They made up a larger portion of George Washington's army. There was a very real fear that they might defect to the British, though that was never the intention of the men. The British fully expected a defection and made plans to receive them.

Seventeen eighty-one signaled the last phase of the war while the Articles of Confederation were adopted on January 30th. James Chambers was succeeded by Colonel Daniel Broadhead in May. His forces joined General Marie Joseph Paul Yves Roch Gilbert du Motier Marquis de La Fayette (Lafayette) at Raccoon Ford on the Rappahannock on June 10th and were at Green Spring by July 6th. His troops opened the second parallel at Yorktown, Virginia, under General Wayne which was the last battle of the war.

Lieutenant William McDowell had a light-hearted entry in his journal about a gathering of his company in a local orchard while in the south. He "refreshed himself with fruit" as did the "Marquis," Colonel Robinson and General Wayne. This entry was a brief message of hope, most of the time he wrote about being "destitute of every necessary of life." He often had to take the rain without a tent, building a bower in the woods, and when he ate meat instead of just rice, every detail was recalled. He was sent at one point on a mission to try to secure liquor for the men. After returning with 708 gallons he was personally thanked by General Wayne.[51]

The Battle of Yorktown, or the Virginia Campaign took place on October 9. 1781. The British forces numbered 8,980 under Lord Charles Cornwallis. Washington's forces with the French fleet numbered 20,600. General George Washington with the French Lieutenant-General Jean-Baptiste Donatien de Vimeur, comte de Rochambeau (1725–1807) laid siege to the town. The superior forces resulted in a British surrender and the beginning of peace negotiations.

William McDowell recorded his impressions of the surrender on October 19th: "Major Hamilton with a detachment marched into town and took possession of the Batteries, and hoisted the American Flag- the British Army marched out and grounded their arms in front of our Line. Our whole army drew up for them to march through. The French Army on their right and the Americans on their left. The British Prisoners appeared to be much in liquor. After they grounded their arms, they returned to town again."[52] He wrote that "the General" {Washington} congratulated the Army later for their part in the victory and that the General had been inspired by the Fleet, thanking Rochambeau for his counsel and assistance and giving warm wishes to the other French officers as well as to Major-General Lincoln and Steuben.

It is also clear that William had been writing home to his father in the "Conogig," to his brothers in other units and to his uncle Lieutenant John McDowell during the long struggle for independence. In those letters they may have commented on the fact that friends living in what is now known as Washington County, Pennsylvania, were still in conflict with Virginia over boundary issues. Men in that area found themselves bound in military service to the two competing states. It was often confusing. They tried to elect Justices but the issue still had kinks in it.[53]

A detachment of Colonel Butler, Colonel Walter Stewart and Colonel Craig's Battalion with Colonel Gist's Maryland battalion were ordered on November 1st to leave Williamsburg, Virginia, to reinforce General Greene's army in South Carolina. That group was commanded by Brigadier-General Wayne and Major-General St Clair. They joined Greene at Round O in South Carolina on January 4, 1782.

Wayne was sent on to Georgia with a small force to re-establish American authority there. The people of Georgia were grateful for his assistance. Those who had supported the Tories were offered pardon if they submitted to the new government by a certain date.[54] Wayne was able to isolate the British in Savannah, Georgia, from their Indian allies in the interior. Savannah was evacuated by the British. Charleston, South Carolina, was also evacuated. Wayne had left Georgia with his forces on August 1782 for South Carolina.

The Pennsylvania Line suffered in South Carolina as many soldiers fell to disease. New casualties resulted in their truncation down to one battalion equaling 600 men with a small group of one-hundred and fifty 18–month men. The colony of Pennsylvania was not helpful during this time either in terms of enlarging the numbers. They believed that recruiting was no longer necessary. They would send no more men or pay.

The exhausted men later returned to Philadelphia but then, in March of 1782, Pennsylvania militiamen were sent to neutralize American Indians in Gnadenhutten resulting in a large Indian massacre. This forced General Wayne to spend the winter negotiating peace with the Creeks and Cherokees at Augusta, Georgia.

Lieutenant William McDowell was listed in January of 1783 as being in the 2nd Regiment under Colonel Richard Humpton with his uncle Captain John McDowell, owner of the Mill Fort. It was the first time we see the two serving in the same regiment, though they had served at similar engagements during the war. John was now about 67 and William was about 34. They had both served during the entire length of the war from the northern colonies to the southern.

One hundred thousand British Loyalists fled from the newly formed United States, mainly to Nova Scotia, in 1783. Congress then had to hammer out some form of government for the new confederation of states. Those who had served in the Continental Army as officers wanted to memorialize their struggle for independence, and on May 13th they formed The Society of Cincinnati.

George Washington was to be the symbolic head of the new organization, though he was warry of it. General Irvine was eventually against it. Lieutenant William McDowell, Jr., was one of the founding members of this organization but he did not renew his membership. Some feared the organization would set themselves up as a hereditary organization which might try to function like the aristocratic orders in Europe, perhaps installing a king. General Wayne would be elected president of the Georgia State Society of the Cincinnati on July 5, 1790.[55]

Wayne, reflecting on the war, stated: "The revolution of America is an event that will fill the brightest page of history to the end of time. The conduct of her officers and soldiers will be handed down to the latest ages as a model of virtue, perseverance & bravery."[56] He was right and he went on to serve his new country in civilian life.

Wayne and John McDowell each served a term for their individual counties in the newly created Council of Censors which met jointly every seven years but had no legislative powers. Two censors were elected from each county to inquire as to whether or not the Constitution of the United States had been violated, whether taxes had been properly collected and to insure that the laws of the State were faithfully executed. They had the power to censure an offender and recommend to the Assembly any repeals of law that fell contrary to the Constitution which in turn required a 2/3rds vote from the governing body. Wayne would also go on to serve the Assembly and then in 1792 Wayne was appointed Commander-in-Chief of the United States Army by President George Washington.

The Paris Peace Treaty of September 3, 1783, formally ended the Revolutionary War and gave the United States the land east of the Mississippi River, south of Canada and north of the "Floridas." The issue of the Oath or Test Act of 1777/1778 in which residents of Pennsylvania needed to renounce the King of Great Britain and swear their fidelity to the State of Pennsylvania, was raised. Quakers had refused to do it as had Tories and those who declared themselves Neutrals, waiting to see the outcome of the struggle. They were now unable to vote, hold office, serve in government, serve on juries, or keep schools, except in private homes.

General Wayne was one of those pleading to abolish the act in the 1780s which was finally repealed in 1789.

John McDowell returned to the Mill Fort in the Cumberland Valley for a short visit. He had served in the Pennsylvania Line as a surgeon for the entire length of the struggle for freedom, but now would serve as a US Infantry surgeon from August 12, 1784 to July 24, 1788 after which he finally resigned at age 72.

The sons of the patriarch William McDowell had acquired much land by 1781, some in the new territory to the west and some still in the area around Mt. Parnell. In Peters Township John had 462 acres by his mill with more land in surrounding counties, Justice William had 304, William, Jr., had 300, Nathan 448, James 448, Thomas 196, John 462 and Robert 196.[57]

Petitions for the formation of a new Franklin County in the Cumberland Valley had been sent to the Assembly in 1780 and one of those who signed the petition was Nathan McDowell.[58] The population of the county at the time was about 13,000 and Chambersburg would be set as the Franklin County seat when it was formally established on September 9, 1784. William McDowell, Esq., of Peters was one of the first Judges serving in the new county. He served as a Justice of the Peace in the new Franklin County from September 9, 1784, to September 2, 1791.

CHAPTER TEN

1784—1840

The Fort is Dismantled

Franklin County was separated from Cumberland County on April 9, 1784. The new county established its seat of government in Chambersburg. Justice William McDowell became a Judge in the new county and presided over the 2nd Court Grand Jury on December 2, 1784. One of the other legal duties he would hold was working with his son Alexander. Those who had fought during the Revolutionary War and had been promised "donated lands" in the west following their service. Alexander McDowell, who had served as a private from 1780 to 1781 under Captains James Patton, Thomas McDowell and William Huston, was promoted and appointed Deputy Surveyor of the Donated Lands on the west side of the Allegheny River within the Commonwealth of Pennsylvania according to an Act of the General Assembly. He directed the distribution of the donated lands to veterans.

Alexander also became an agent for the Holland Land Company at Franklin on June 15, 1785 as settlers gradually began to populate the western part of the state. The Holland Land Company was a Dutch land speculation company. Dutch businessmen had lent money to the colonial government and were given tracts of land in exchange. After the war they carved up their territories and began selling lots. Alexander would

The Fort is Dismantled

live the remainder of his life in Venango County.¹ His home in the town of Franklin originally was a log cabin without windows and a door. Later he constructed a weather-board house which was completed in 1802. It stood on a bluff overlooking French Creek. The house was demolished in 1874. Alexander worked with friendly Indians and became a friend to Chief Cornplanter's people who often warned him about hostel bands in the area. He spent much of his time surveying in the dense woods alone.

The legislative founding heroes of the new country were clustered in Philadelphia as capital. Benjamin Franklin, now 80 years old, asked to be relieved as minister to the court of France in 1785. He returned to the United States and was elected the President of the Council.

The convention to frame the United States Constitution was held in May of 1787 in Philadelphia and it was adopted on December 12th with people split between being Constitutionalists and non-Constitutionalists. The debate was often quite heated in Pennsylvania. George Washington became the first President of the United States of America on April 30, 1789 and worked with leaders to try to define the new country.

Even though the Revolutionary War was over, new fears crept up to the west. The Indians in the Northwest were still working under English influence attacking settlers on the frontier. The English had not fully complied with all of the articles of the 1783 treaty. They still held the forts in the Northwest Ohio Country. They also impressed seamen and confiscated cargo sent by the United States to the French West Indies. A military campaign was launched to deal with the Indians with a real fear of beginning another war with the English. European settlers under the British treaties were not to settle west of the Ohio River but the Indians were dealing with a new nation now. Many of the Indians in the Northwest were Shawnees and Delawares, called Miamis, driven from Pennsylvania after the capture of Fort Duquesne by Bouquet in 1763.

General Josiah Harmar (1753–1813) was ordered by General St. Clair, Governor of the Northwest Territory, to put an end to Indian atrocities against settlers with a compliment of 1,400 men in 1790. Harmer's combined forces totaled 1,453 men who invaded Miami towns in the Fort Wayne, Indiana, region and burned structures but the population of natives had been evacuated prior to their arrival. The army was forced to retreat and lost at The Battle of Kekionga. Ensign Nathan McDowell, Esq., son of Justice William McDowell, served in Josiah Harmer's Federal Militia Regiment of the Western Frontier (10/21/1784–1785). He was stationed at Fort McIntosh and distinguished himself in a 1785 Indian conflict. He commanded a detachment which was attacked by Tawawa and the Chipewa Indians. His unit repulsed the attack with many losses.

Nathan had also spent his childhood in McDowell's Mill Fort and may have learned many skills during the French and Indian War, the Pontiac War and as a private in Captain James Patton's Marching Company with 1st Lieutenant Thomas McDowell, and in Samuel Patton's company during the Revolutionary War.

Lieutenant John McDowell was a United States Infantry Surgeon from August 12, 1784, to July 24, 1788.[2] There is a letter from Lieutenant-Colonel Josiah Harmar dated June 30, 1788, in the Pennsylvania Archives which reads; "Doctor John M'Dowell has resigned his commission on the 1st instant. The surgeon's mate, Richard Allison, is fully qualified, I believe, to succeed him."[3] John appears to have had enough fighting, after all he was seventy-two.

Harmar's army had been ill-armed and undiscipline. They were forced to retreat from the present site of Fort Wayne, Indiana, to Fort Washington, Cincinnati. This action only irritated the savages. To complete Harmar's expedition, St. Clair led an expedition in 1791. His goal was to establish a chain of forts from Cincinnati to the Maumee River with 2,300 troops, many of whom became ill or deserted. They were attacked by a large force of Indians and defeated.

The failure of both Harmar and St. Clair resulted in a reorganization of the army under General Wayne which was called the Legion of the United States.[4] General Wayne returned in 1794 and construct a fort which would be named after him, Fort Wayne. Wayne confronted the English held garrisons and the Indians were then willing to negotiate for peace. The Indians were subjugated and forced into an August 1795 treaty at Greeneville. The territory west of Ohio and North of Detroit was ceded. The Indian lines were now to be from Lake Erie along the

The Fort is Dismantled

Cuyahoga River to the Portage, West to Maumee, down river to the lake and back.[5] On October 1784 the last treaty with the Indians in the state of Pennsylvania had been signed at Fort Stanwix.[6] The Erie Triangle had been purchase in 1792.

The troubled conflicts between the colonists and the Indians in the 1700s would lay the seeds for the Indian Removal Act of 1830. There are now no federally recognized reservations in the state of Pennsylvania. Most of the tribes were re-located to Oklahoma, though individual Indians still reside within the state. The Pennsylvania government gained territory, power and money from land sales to settlers.

Relations with England were re-negotiated in the *Jay's Treaty*, though there were still difficulties. The British formally evacuated Detroit, Oswego and Niagara, during the winter of 1796 but opposition to the *Jay's Treaty* were often violent. The Senate had ratified the treaty but the House of Representatives did not make provisions to support it. The English tried to renew their relations with the Indians during the period of instability but finally dropped it when the *Jay's Treaty* was finally fully enacted. In addition to the finishing work with the English treaty, in 1794 new fears centered on the Mississippi River. A possible war with Spain presented itself. Their posts on the river from New Madrid to New Orleans made it difficult for western people to navigate. Wayne had military jurisdiction there. He tried to keep settlers from descending down the river. During all of this the mill at Fort McDowell continued to grind wheat into flour.

The new Congress then looked for sources of revenue and on March 3, 1791, set a tax on distilled spirits of four pence per gallon. George Washington was a large whiskey producer. The McDowell family members and others in the Cumberland Valley had stills on their farms and there was one at McDowell's Mill Fort but Franklin County largely accepted this tax but problems began in Washington, Westmoreland, Allegheny and Fayette Counties to their west. Those counties produced large amounts of grain but because their farms were far from the eastern markets, it was easier for them to convert their grain into whiskey for transportation. Some of the citizens in those counties rebelled against the tax collectors, seeing it as an economic intrusion, after all the colonists had rebelled against the British over the same issue. Most of those who were causing the major disruptions, however, were reportedly not large land owners. The rebels had little or no property to loose and were generally considered an unruly group sprinkled in area towns.[7]

The tax was reduced on May 8, 1792, but it was still an issue with those complaining that it was crippling local economy. This proved a threat to the newly established government of George Washington and he told the rebellious counties to submit to the tax in September of 1792. The enforcement of this was temporarily blocked by the 1793 yellow fever epidemic in Philadelphia. Nearly 5,000 people died from the disease and the government of the United States was temporarily moved from Philadelphia to Germantown, Pennsylvania. The Cumberland Valley tried to quarantine those coming from Philadelphia, setting guards at the important passes and check persons for infection, but it also hit that area. The valley was hit again in March by another disease called "March miasmata" which was believed to be centered at the Le Tort's spring near Carlisle, by a tannery and mill. The spring was cleaned and the tan yards were razed.[8]

George Washington finally was able to leave from Philadelphia to quell the Whiskey Insurrection on the Pennsylvania frontier in the fall of 1794. Letters had been sent to all of the Judges, Justices, Sheriffs and Brigade Inspectors in the Western Counties, especially in Washington and Allegheny Counties, alerting them of the President's coming. Washington had called for 12,950 troops from Virginia, Maryland, New Jersey and Pennsylvania to accompany him. Pennsylvania sent 5,196 men and of that Franklin County sent 281.[9]

One Division was under Major-General William Irvine. The three Brigades were led by General Thomas Proctor, Brigadier-General Francis Murray and Brigadier-General James Chambers. Chambers' brigade was from Franklin County. President Washington, Secretary of War General Henry Knox, Secretary of the Treasury Alexander Hamilton and United States District Court representative Richard Peters set out for Western Pennsylvania on October 1st. They reached Chambersburg on October 11th where they enjoyed the support of Franklin County.

The Fort is Dismantled

This is the grave of John McDowell at Spring Grove Cemetery in Lemasters, Pennsylvania. John lived from 1716 to June 6, 1794, dying in Chambersburg. His tomb reads, "John McDowell, s/o William & Mary (Irvine) McDowell, was married to Agnes (Craig) McDowell with whom he had 5 daughters, Agnes, Elizabeth, Mary, Catherine and Margaret McDowell. Built McDowell Grist Mill/Fort and 2 story log house (both with a liberal supply of port holes) in 1754 near Bridgeport, Franklin County, Pennsylvania." Agnes' grave is the oldest recorded grave in the cemetery, though older ones probably exist. Agnes had lived from 1717 to August 8, 1766, dying in McDowell's Mill fort. Setters who died during that period were often buried at night and their graves disguised to prevent Indians from desecrating the bodies and collecting scalps from the departed. John outlived his wife by twenty-eight years.

McDOWELL'S MILL FORT

Washington stayed in the Greencastle town square at the tavern run by Robert McCullough in Franklin County, this was four miles south of McDowell's Mill Fort, and then dined with Benjamin Chambers, lodging at the Morrow's Tavern in Chambersburg. The troops then passed through the county on the western military road carved out first by Burd and then by Forbes, reaching Pittsburg in November. Those living by McDowell's Mill Fort would have had no trouble watching the procession which would have passed by them to their north. It would be unlikely for men like the McDowells, who had served under George Washington, to have missed their commander's passage by the road near them. Washington must have also reflected on his own campaigns against the French while passing through the small towns and forts along the way. The tax issue was resolved quickly and Washington's authority was re-established.

John McDowell, however, missed Washington's powerful entry into Franklin County, though he would have known about the whiskey tax law. He died in Chambersburg on June 6, 1794, at age 78. Coming to America as a small child, he had lived through the turbulent years as the colony struggled against extreme odds and he had witnessed the birth of a new nation while tending the men who gave so much to insure her safety. John was buried in the McDowell plot at Waddel's Cemetery which was later known as Etter's, and now Spring Grove Cemetery on Etter Avenue in Lemasters, Pennsylvania. The cemetery's location is down the road from McDowell's Mill Fort.

The McDowell section within the cemetery would grow row upon row through the centuries. John's grave has a large horizontal stone marker with the inscription, "John McDowell, s/o William & Mary (Irvine) McDowell, was married to Agnes (Craig) McDowell with whom he had 5 daughters, Agnes, Elizabeth, Mary, Catherine and Margaret McDowell. Built McDowell Grist Mill/Fort and 2 story log house (both with a liberal supply of port holes) in 1754 near Bridgeport, Franklin County, Pennsylvania." The same year of John's death and Washington's march through the valley, a new church was erected in Mercersburg serving the Upper West Concocheague Church congregation. Something new had emerged in the valley as the nation moved into the next chapter of its life.

The Fort is Dismantled

The McDowell family still held many acres in Franklin County, Pennsylvania in the 1795 tax table. Their properties combined amounted to about 2,154 acres at that point. The enclosed fort was still in an area known as "McDowell's Mill" within Peter's Township in Franklin County. After the death of John McDowell, according to Eugene Etter in *History of Lemasters, Pennsylvania*,[10] the mill and fort were sold to Christian Beam in 1794, his neighbor. Beam's daughter Barbara then married Christian "Christy" Hoover who took over the mill until 1831 when he died.

There was a report of a massive flood on November 13, 1810, of the West Conococheague Creek in *The Centinel* (Gettysburg, November 21, 1810 edition). It seemed to have centered "at Buckwalter's Mill, Beam's Mill and Loudontown" where bridges were swept away and property damaged.[11] The Bridge on the East Conococheague near Greancastle was also taken and the mouth of the joining East and West suffered damage. "Scarce a mill or improvement of any kind on the whole extent of that stream has escaped damage . . ." This was the worst flood area residents had ever seen.

It seemed to point to yet another conflict to come. Peace with Great Britain had been short lived. A series of naval issues surfaced. The English had boarded American ships looking for suspected deserters from the British Navy and proceeded to drag American seamen off ships, impressing them into service for England. President Jefferson had ordered British vessels to leave American waters in 1807 and an embargo was laid down.

Men in the Mercersburg area had formed a regiment named the Mercersburg Rifles before the War of 1812 which included 72 officers and men. The regiment was commanded by Captain James McDowell. When President Madison declared war against Great Britain in 1812, the Mercersburg Rifles left the county and served under Captain Patrick Hays as part of the first detachment leaving Franklin County on September 5, 1812, commanded by Major William McClellan.[12]

After the burning of Washington, D.C., by the British on August 24, 1814, units from Franklin County were sent to Baltimore to protect it. The county would send eight companies. Captain Samuel Culbertson formed a company in Chambersburg with a William McDowell; Captain Purdy formed a company with Samuel McDowell. A cavalry group under Captain Matthew Patton left for Baltimore, however cavalry was not needed in that engagement, so they became an infantry unit and the company was placed under Captain Thomas Bard, leaving in September of that year.[13]

In Bard's company from Mercersburg were 1st Lieutenant James McDowell, Corporal William McDowell and privates with the last names of the first settlers like Campbell, Cox, Craig, Hamilton, McDowell (James, Thomas and William, Sr), Maxwell, Patton, Rankin and Waddle. Pennsylvania then organized two divisions. Companies from Franklin County included the Antrim Greens rifle company with sixty men; the Franklin County Light Dragoons with forty-one men under Captain Matthew Patton; the Mercersburg Rifles with seventy-two men under Captain James McDowell; the Concord Light Infantry with thirty men under Captain Michael Harper; and the Chambersburg Union Volunteers with fifty-one men under Captain Jeremiah Snider. These troops were sent to the northwestern frontier via Bedford, Pittsburgh and Meadville. They were re-organized and then marched to Buffalo, New York.

More men were drafted from the state of Pennsylvania in 1814, and another thousand men left from Franklin County. McDowell's Mill Fort stood through the enlistment process. Many of the McDowells and other settlers served in these additional companies, the sons and grandsons of the Revolutionary War heroes.

When the war ended in favor of the United States, life went on in the hamlet of McDowell's Mill but an 1821 fever epidemic with dysentery hit Franklin County in the summer and ran through the fall. It may have been a form of influenza but it claimed many lives. The harvest areas were hit the hardest which would have included the area around the mill fort. There was also a report in the *Franklin County, Pennsylvania News* dated January 9, 1824 of a December 31st grist mill and fulling mill fire of one Christian Hoover in Peters Township. The two mills near each other could not be saved and "friction" was suspected.

The hamlet of McDowell's Mill changed its name in 1825 when it was called Bridgeport/Bridge Port after a triple arched stone bridge built

The Fort is Dismantled

across the West Branch of the Conocheague. It was contiguous with one of Hoover's reconstructed mills used for flouring. A modern bridge has replaced the old stone bridge on Lemar Road. The name Bridgeport, however, would later be changed due to a larger town already existing by that name in Pennsylvania. The final name chosen for the area would be Markes, after a man living in the area by that name.[14] A small town had shaped around the fort ruins by 1828.[15] "The blockhouse which was part of the fort, stood on what is now part of the Loudon road and slightly westward" serving as a butcher shop in 1840.[16]

Hoover's son, Martin, ran the mill for flouring and lumber at the old fort site until 1848 when the mill burned but was rebuilt. The mill might have gone through updates during this period which would have moved from mostly hand work to more mechanized work with gears, conveyors, drills and pullies. Books like Oliver Evans' *Young Mill-Wright and Miller's Guide*, printed in 1795 demonstrate a greater understanding of mathematics and science in mill work which would have made the miller's life much easier.[17]

During Martin's ownership in 1840, the log walls of McDowell's Mill Fort were finally dismantled. The area was exposed for the first time in many years with clear views of the fields, roadway and Mt. Parnell. James B. Scott was also mentioned as running the mill prior to 1840.[18]

In 1846 the village had a saw, fulling[19] and grist mill, a store, and a house of worship by the stone bridge which crossed the Conocheague Creek. The stone bridge was said to be contiguous with Hoover's large mill.[20] The 1846 mill by the creek was used for lumbering and flouring. Jacob Wister bought that mill and also owned McDowell's Mill, according to Etter. He sold it to Hoke Hoffeditz and that mill caught on fire. The mill was rebuilt and the town grew between 1848 and 1878. A United States post office was run from the village from 1878–1882 which later was moved one mile south to Lemasters Station.[21]

By 1887 the town still had flour and lumber mills, dry goods store, plus a blacksmith, two carpenter shops, a shoe maker, and a coach maker. It was a center of industry. At one point, the area had a two-room grade

McDOWELL'S MILL FORT

A triple arch stone bridge was constructed across the Conococheague Creek in the 1800s which is no longer there. A new one has replaced it. When the first bridge was constructed, the village of McDowell's Mill was renamed Bridgeport, but due to another Pennsylvanian town having that name, the town was then renamed Markes. Pictured above is also an 1846 mill. The original McDowell's Mill would have been to the left of it up a bit on Mercersburg Road. It was set back from the road by the mill pond. The mill pictured was not part of the fort but was converted from flour production to electricity and used by the Mercersburg, Lemasters and Markes Electric Company, managed by Edgar B. Diel and Seth Lamaster. The company extended service to Fort Loudon, St. Thomas, Williamson and Upton. It was the third mill on this site but this mill later burned and was not replaced. Advertisements for the electric service were in the *Mercersburg Journal* in 1905. Photo curtesy of the Fendrick Public Library in Mercersburg, Pennsylvania.

school which was also used for church activities and the population soared to a whopping one hundred and forty persons.

Jay Gilfillan Weiser in his 1896 book on the frontier forts in Cumberland Valley stated that he had received information from elderly residents who had seen McDowell's Mill Fort. They gave the same descriptions of it being built of logs in a rectangular shape with many loop-holes. He repeated the fact that the fort stood until 1840. The area farms were still being tended by descendants of the original settlers, and a mill was

The Fort is Dismantled

These falls were used by the Mercersburg, Lemasters and Markes Electric Company in Markes to generate electric power. Photo curtesy of the Fendrick Public Library in Mercersburg, Pennsylvania.

still present at the fort's site in 1896. Weiser went on to write, "There is a store house erected on or near the site of this fort, which stands northeast of the store about ten feet."[22] The owner of the premises in 1896 according to him was William Branthaver. Branthaver may have been a descendant of the 1750s Branthavers who suffered greatly during the early Indian raids at Little Cove.

The other stone flour mill set by the creek and bridge originally used kerosene light. It was sold to Edgar B. Diehl and Seth Lamaster and was converted into a generating electric plant called The Mercersburg, Lemasters and Markes Electric Company, about 1904. It supplied electricity to those towns and the villages slowly adopted the new technology. Electric service was then extended to Fort Loudon, St. Thomas, Williamson, and Upton under the ownership of Harry E. Geiser. That mill eventually burned down and was not rebuilt, instead the electric system was sold to Baker, Young and Company of Boston, Massachusetts.[23]

With the fort long gone, the Pennsylvania Historical and Museum Commission, Enoch Brown Association, the descendants of John McDowell and the citizens of the area chose to memorialize the spot of

This colonial secretary dates to the 1700s. It was passed down to Elizabeth Robinson McDowell Rankin (3/17/1822–7/25/1893) who married Andrew N. Rankin, Esq. (10/9/1821–10/3/1890). Her family line went from the pioneer William (1682–1759) to Justice William (1722–1812) to Nathan (1759–1830) to her father William, Esq. (1793–1825) who is buried at Browns Mill Cemetery in Franklin County. Her furniture traveled with her to New York after the burning of Chambersburg and is now in the possession of Ruth Rankin Leaper in Massachusetts, the author's mother.

The Fort is Dismantled

This is a photo of Elizabeth Robinson McDowell Rankin.

McDowell's Mill Fort on October 5, 1916. They erected their stone marker which is now the only witness to those tragic events.[24] Years later in 1947 a historical marker was erected near the stone by the Pennsylvania Historical and Museum Commission. The monument and sign stand quietly on a lonely country road.

Though time has passed, the ground still holds occasional scars from the violent history with its many struggles occurring between settlers, Indians, militia and European troops during the birth of the United States of America. Area historical societies are now the keepers of the stories and offer re-enactments and historical education about the violence which once ran rampant in the sleepy farming valley. Peace had a price and it was initially paid by those who held onto their vision to forge out a new life in a new land. They gave those following an opportunity to live within a democratic structure, securing rights for anyone coming to these shores with a dream.

McDOWELL'S MILL FORT

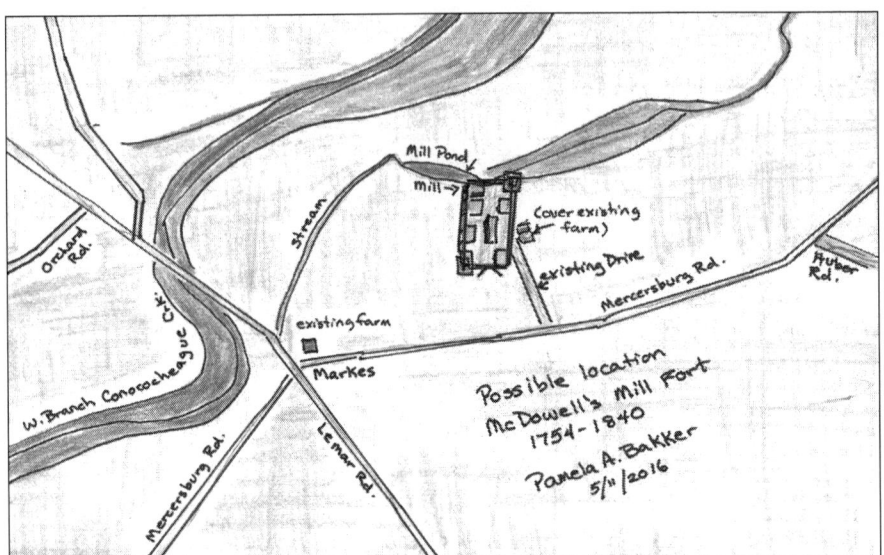

The drawing above by the author is a possible modern location for McDowell Mill Fort based upon the 1700s survey.

APPENDIX A

A Partial Genealogy of Pioneer William McDowell to His Grandchildren

Pioneer **William McDowell**[1] was born in Antrim County, Northern Ireland about 1682, perhaps in Raloo Parish, Gleno. William's father, according to one family genealogist, was **Thomas McDowell** who had married **Anne Locke** of Antrim. The McDowell forefathers may have originally been Danes who settled in Galloway, Scotland. Some genealogies tie them to the Lords of Galloway. William's ancestors then moved to Ulster, Northern Ireland, in the 1550s as part of the plantations designed to establish a protestant presence there and to suppress Irish Catholics. William married **Mary "May" Irvine** (1684–2/17/1782) in Ulster. He sailed with brothers and their families to the American continent in 1717, settling first in the extended Chester County, Pennsylvania, near New London. William appears to have then moved west to the Donegal settlement in Lancaster County, PA., about 1720. He moved his family farther west to the frontier of the colony in south-central Pennsylvania about 1730 to settle by the Northwestern branch of the Conococheague Creek at the foot of Mount Parnell in what is now Peter's Township, Franklin County, Pennsylvania. William obtained a Blunston License in December of 1736 for the land after it was officially purchased from the Indians. His sons began acquiring land in 1737. William fled to Wrights Ferry/Wrightsville on the Susquehanna in 1755 when his plantation and home were burned by American Indians working with the French during the French and Indian War. He died August 12, 1759, and was buried in the Old Donegal Presbyterian Church graveyard in Lancaster County, Pennsylvania. Mary died on November 27, 1760.

Children of pioneer William and Mary Irvine McDowell:

1. **John McDowell** (born about 1716 in Antrim, Northern Ireland, and died June 6, 1794, Chambersburg, Franklin County, Pennsylvania) married **Agnes Craig** (born in the enlarged Chester County in 1717 and died August 8, 1766 at Markes, Franklin County). John built a one and one half story log gristmill with a two story log home next to it around 1740 in what is now Markes, Pennsylvania, along the east side of the West Conococheague Creek. The mill became a private fort in 1754 used by volunteer militia. It was made into a provincial fort by the governor and stockade in 1755 to serve as a chief fort for General Braddock's campaign against the French at Fort Duquesne. Paid militia were garrisoned there. It was later replaced as a provincial fort by Fort Loudon and returned to private fort status still housing militia. It stood as a private fort until 1840. John was a ruling elder of the Upper West Conococheague Presbyterian Church in Mercersburg from 12/19/1767 to 1/28/1785 and presiding elder of District 7. During the Revolutionary War he served in Anthony Wayne's Division of the Pennsylvania Line as a First Lieutenant and Surgeon in Colonel Samuel Culbertson's Battalion of Cumberland County Associators from 1770–1780. In 1777 he was in the 6th Regiment under Colonel Robert Magaw with Lieutenant-Colonel Josiah Harmar and Majors Jeremiah Talbot and Richard Humpton. In 1781 the 6th Division was led by Colonel Richard Humpton with Lieutenant Stephen Bayard and Major James Greer. Members of the 6th Regiment, including John, were then rolled into the 7th. He became a Captain of a Regiment, most likely invalids who did lighter service. After serving on the Pennsylvania Line he was a U.S. Infantry surgeon from 8/12/1784–7/24/1788, retiring at age 72. He and his wife are buried in Spring Grove Cemetery, Lemaster, Pennsylvania. Agnes' grave is the earliest recorded grave in the cemetery, however

earlier burials were most likely done in secret, without head stones, to keep Indians from scalping the dead for bounties offered by the French.

Children of miller John and Agnes Craig McDowell:

A. **Agnes McDowell** (9/9/1740–6/9/1790) married on 3/19/1771 **Elias Davidson** (1736–4/15/1806) of Antrim by Mr. Lang. During the Revolutionary War, he was a Captain of a flying Camp in 1776, in Col. Abraham Smith's Battalion, Cumberland County Associators 1777–1779. He was an extensive landowner and ruling elder of the Presbyterian Church in Greencastle.
   Children of Agnes and Elias Davidson:
   a. **Patrick Davidson**
   b. **Elias Davidson** who married **Nancy Allison** and then **Rebecca Allison**
   c. **John M. Davidson**
   d. **William Davidson**
   e. **Nancy Davidson** who married **Lazarus Brown**
   f. **Elizabeth Davidson** who married **Patrick McDowell**
   g. **Mary Davidson** who married Presbyterian pastor **Rev. Robert Kennedy**.

B. **Mary McDowell** (1743–4/22/1833), called "Polly," married before 1764 **Dr. Richard Brownson** (5/3/1737–3/23–25/1790) of Mercersburg. The spelling is sometimes Brounson. During the Revolutionary War, he was a Surgeon in the 6th Battalion under Colonel Samuel Culbertson's Cumberland County Assoicators 1776–1780.
   Children of Mary and Richard Brownson:
   a. **Nancy Brownson** who married **Col. John Findley**
   b. **John Brownson**
   c. **Timothy Brownson** (1771–8/1/1777)
   d. **Abigail Brownson** (1773 and died unmarried 5/12/1816)
   e. **Asa Brownson** (died unmarried in Cincinnati 9/10/1805)
   f. **Nathan Brownson** (10/2/1776–1/26/1856)

g. **Elizabeth Brownson** (1779–unmarried).

C. **Elizabeth McDowell** (died 12/12/1822), called "Betsy," married 4/2/1771 **The Rev. John King**, D.D. (12/5/1743–7/15/1813) pastor of the West Conococheague Presbyterian Church, Mercersburg. Rev. King served the church beginning 8/23/1769 for 42 years and is buried at Church Hill, Mercersburg. He was a chaplain during the Revolutionary War.

D. **Margaret "Peggy" McDowell** (died 1828) married 6/6/1786 **George King** (1758–3/24/1840), the pastor's brother. His brother performed the ceremony.
Children of Margaret and George King:
   a. **Robert King** (1792–8/29/1856) a Captain in the Mercersberg Light Infantry, postmaster Mercersburg 1827–1829 and married 1/1/1824 **Jane Skiles** (died 12/25/1857)
   b. **John McDowell King** (born 1791)
   c. **James King** (born 1799) married 4/24/1823 **Jane Morrison**
   d. **George McLaughlin King** (born 1800)
   e. **Agnes Craig King** married **Thomas Carson**.

E. **Catherine McDowell** (born 1753 Franklin County, died 2/10/1818 in Plum, Allegheny County, and buried in Laird Cemetery, Allegheny County) married 11/21/1774 **Judge Hugh Davidson, Esq.** (1745–1820) by Rev. John King, DD. During the Revolutionary War Hugh was a Lieutenant-Colonel in the 2nd Battalion of Bedford County Militia in 1781. He became a Justice of the Peace in 1784 and then he represented Huntington County in the State Legislature in 1787 and 1788 and was appointed Associate Judge in 1791.
Children of Catherine and Hugh Davidson:
   a. **John Davidson**
   b. **Elias Davidson**
   c. **Hugh Davidson**
   d. **Nancy Davidson**
   e. **Margaret Davidson**

Appendix A: A Partial Genealogy

    f. **Catherine Davidson**
    g. **Mary Elizabeth Davidson**
    h. **Arabella Davidson**

2. **Elizabeth McDowell** (born 1718/1721 in Chester County-1814) married first in 1739 **Lieutenant James Holliday** (born Ireland-6/9/1757), son of pioneer John Holliday of Peter's township. James served as a Lieutenant in Rev. Capt. John Steel's Company for the 1756 Kittaning Expedition. He was killed 6/9/1757 while commanding a detachment reconnoitering in the mountains west of Fort Loudon. They were surprised by Indians in the Big Cove and lost a number of men. In 1760 Elizabeth married **Daniel McAlister** of Carlisle.
Children of Elizabeth and James Holliday:
A. **John Holliday** (1740) who married **Mary McDowell,** daughter of Nathan and Cathrine Maxwell McDowell.
B. **William Holliday** (died before 1761).
C. **Samuel Holliday** (3/24/1745–11/10/1841) of Erie. He went to the Presque Isle Settlement in 1795. As a citizen of Erie he served in the War of 1812 and was married to **Janet Campbell** (7/1755–6/27/1851).
Children Elizabeth and Daniel McAlister:
D. **Mary McAllister** (born 1760) married **William McClure.**
E. **Jane McAllister** (born 1762)
F. **Elizabeth McAllister** who married **John Mitchel.**

3. **Judge William McDowell, Esq.** (1722 Chester County– 9/17/1812) was a Justice of the Peace. He married in 1749 **Mary Maxwell** (1727–4/9/1805), daughter of Major William and Susan Maxwell. He was a ruling elder, district 8, of the Upper West Conococheague Presbyterian Church from December 19, 1767 until his death. In 1765 he negotiated a treaty between Lieutenant Charles Grant, Commander of Fort Loudon and the Black Boys. McDowell was given custody of the arms collected from the residents during the

"Black Boys" assault of Fort Loudon. Patriot. He became a Judge in the newly formed Franklin County. His five sons were farmers.

Children of Justice William and Mary Maxwell McDowell:

A. **Captain William McDowell** (1749– 6/19/1835) married 2/8/1786 **Elizabeth Van Lear** (1759–6/11/1818). William served in the Revolutionary War for seven years working his way up the ranks to 1st Lieutenant and Captain in Waynes' Division. He served in 5/13/1777 under Colonels Edward Hand and James Chambers in the 1st PA Infantry and then under Captain John Holliday. By 1778 he served in Captain John McLellan's 6th Company with Lieutenant Ben Chambers. He fought in the 1st PA Line, 2nd Infantry, Company 6 under Captain William Huston, 3/22/78–11/3/1783. In 1781 the 1st Regiment came under Colonel Daniel Brodhead with Lieutenant –Colonel Thomas Robinson and Major James Moore. In 1783 Lieutenant William McDowell served under Colonel Richard Humpton, Lieutenant-Colonel Thomas Robinson and Major James Moore while his uncle John served as Surgeon, and brother John was a private. Captain William McDowell was an original member of the Society of the Cincinnati (1778–1783) but did not renew his membership. Reverend King, his cousin's husband, was chaplain to his unit. The Pennsylvania Archives has a copy of his Lieutenant's book for the southern campaign.

Children of Captain William and Elizabeth Van Lear:

a. **Mary Maxwell McDowell** (11/21/1786–5/5/1840 of cancer) unmarried
b. **Elizabeth McDowell** (1788–7/1803)
c. **Jane Van Lear McDowell** (1790–1878) married 3/8/1818 **Patrick Davidson**
d. **William McDowell** (1791–1862)
e. **Margaret McDowell** (1794–3/11/1853)
f. **John McDowell** (1796–10/11/1879) who moved to Delavan, Illinois and married 6/23/1843 **Agnes (Nancy)**

Appendix A: A Partial Genealogy

McDowell (1806–6/19/1845), daughter of Patrick and Elizabeth Davidson McDowell.
g. **Matthew Van Lear McDowell** (1798–1823)
h. **Nathan McDowell** (1802–9/1/1803)

B. **John McDowell,** LL. D. (2/11/1751–12/22/1820). John reported living at times within Fort McDowell age five to twelve. He was educated John King's school and then tutored from 1769–1782. John graduated from the College of Philadelphia in 1777. He was a private in Captain Samuel Patton's Company in 7/28/1777. 1783 he studied law in Maryland and became an attorney. From 1789–1801 he was Professor of Mathematics and Principal of St. John's College, Annapolis, MD, returning from 1815–1817. He corresponded with George Washington about the education of the latter's nephew at St. John's. 1806–1810 he was Professor of Natural Philosophy and third Provost of Pennsylvania University from 1807–1810.

C. **Susan/Susannah McDowell** (1752–5/17/1839) married 2/5/1778 **Dr. John Martin.** John was a physician from Talbot County, Maryland.
Children of Susan and John Martin:
a. **James Martin**
b. **William Martin**
c. **Mary Martin**
d. **Nancy Martin**
e. **Jane Martin**
f. **Margaret Martin**

D. **James McDowell** (1754–1754).

E. **Mary "Polly" McDowell** (1756–died 5/9/1799) married 10/1790 **Dr William Magaw** (1740–May 1, 1829) by Rev. King. William was a surgeon during the Revolutionary War. Mary was his second wife.
Child of Mary and William Magaw:
a. **Jesse Magaw** (1786–1823)

F. **Nathan McDowell, Esq.** (1759–2/1/1830) married in 1795 **Mary McLanahan** (1759–10/22/1818). Nathan enlisted in the Revolutionary War at age 19. He was a private 7/28/1777–78–80 under Captains James Patton Marching Company with 1st Lieutenant Thomas McDowell, and then under Samuel Patton, 7/28/1777–78–80. Josiah Harmer was an Ensign at that time in the regiment. Nathan was later an Ensign in Lieutenant-Colonel Josiah Harmar's Federal Militia Regiment of the Western Frontier (10/21/1784–1785). He was stationed at Fort McIntosh and he distinguished himself in a 1785 Indian conflict. He commanded a detachment and was attacked by Tawawa and the Chipewa Indians and repulsed the attack with many losses. He was also one of those who signed the proposition to form Franklin County in July of 1784. Nathan was part of the uniting of the East and lower West (Welsh Run) Conococheague Presbyterian congregations. (He may also have been in the war of 1812). He lived in Antrim and is buried at Brown Mills Cemetery.
Children of Nathan and Mary McLanahan McDowell:
a. **William McDowell, Esq.** (1/28/1793–5/9/1825) married in 1812 **Martha Greenwood Galaher** (born Baltimore-died 1818). William served during the War of 1812 and was in Captain John Flanagan's Company during the defense of Baltimore in 1814. (The author's family follows this line through their daughter Elizabeth McDowell Rankin, buried in Greenwood Cemetery in Brooklyn, New York. The family still has some of William and Martha's furniture and needle work.).
b. **Isaiah McDowell**
c. **Sarah Margaret McDowell** (1796–1856)
d. **Mary Maxwell McDowell** (1797–1843)
e. **Susanna Bella McDowell** (1799–1800)
f. **John McClanahan McDowell** (1801–1882)
g. **Nathan McDowell, Jr.** (1803–1860)
h. **Rebecca Margaret McDowell**

Appendix A: A Partial Genealogy

    i. **John Alexander McDowell** (died early)
    j. **Mary McLanahan McDowell** (died early)
    k. a second **Mary McDowell**.

G. **Colonel Alexander McDowell, Esq.** (1760–1/4/1816 Franklin, Venango County, PA) was a private during the Revolutionary War from 1780–1781 under Capts. James Patton, Thomas McDowell, and William Huston. He was later appointed the Deputy Surveyor of Donated Lands on the West side of the Allegheny within PA territory, district number seven in June of 1793. He directed the distribution of lands promised to Revolutionary War troops from the state. He moved to Frankstown, Venango County in 1794 and he became a friend to Indian Chief Cornplanter and his people, working on land to which they had given clearance. He later was an agent for the Holland Land Company at Franklin. Dutch land speculators had lent money to the colony and were given large tracks of land in exchange for the much needed currency. The company then sold the land to settlers through Alexander. Alexander's home in Franklin initially was log without windows or doors. He later built a weather-board house completed in 1802 on the bluff overlooking French Creek which was demolished in 1874. Many friendly Indians were there at the time, but there were also unfriendly Indians conducting raids. He was often alone in the woods and relied upon friendly Indian warnings and would seek refuge at Fort Franklin. He became a Justice of the Peace and general arbitrator for settlers. Alexander married on 2/24/1785 **Isabel McKinney** by Rev. King. When he died, he left a widow and children. His nephew John McDowell, LL.D., worked out the details for the family.
Children of Alexander and Isabel McKinney McDowell:
    a. **Elizabeth McDowell** (1796–1808)
    b. **Susan McDowell** (1798–1806)
    c. **Margaret McDowell** (1799–1/28/1825) who married 10/1819 **Archibald Tanner**

    d. **Sarah McDowell** (1801–7/21/1821) married **Alexander S. Hays**

    e. **Thomas Skelly McDowell**

    f. **William McDowell** (1/25/1805–4/21/1839) married **Elvina McNutt**

    g. **Josiah McDowell** (3/1/1787–10/23/1867) buried in Lemasters, PA.

H. **Dr. Andrew McDowell** (1761–1/13/1846) first married on 5/9/1793 **Nancy (Agnes) McPherson** (1765–11/9/1827) by Rev. King. His second wife was **Jane Porter**. Andrew served under Capts. Robert Dickey and Conrad Snider during the Revolutionary War. He graduated from the Medical department of the University of Pennsylvania in 1787. He briefly was a Professor of Latin and Greek but then served as a physician in Chambersburg for forty years. He oversaw the Poor-house's medical needs from 1815–1818 and 1829–1830 and was one of the founders in 1825 of the 1st Medical Societies in the County.

Children of Andrew and his wives:

    a. **William McDowell, Esq.** (1794–9/21/1825) studied law and was clerk of the county Commissioners 1811–1815 and then a prosecuting attorney 1815–1819. He served in Captain Samuel D. Culbertson's Company to defend Baltimore in 1814. He inherited John McDowell, L.L.D.'s law books.

    b. **Dr. John McDowell** of Mercersburg.

    c. **Ann M. McDowell** who married **Otho Williams** of Williamsport.

    d. **Dr. Robert M. McDowell** of Ohio.

    e. **Dr. Andrew Nathan McDowell** of Pittsburgh who married on 7/13/1824 **Jane Denny Porter**. Their daughter **Jane** married **Stephen Collins Foster** the song writer.

    f. **Patrick McDowell**

    g. **Mary Maxwell McDowell** who married **Samuel Bailey**

Appendix A: A Partial Genealogy

I. **Margaret "Peggy" McDowell** (1765–7/17/1853) married 5/6/1806 **Mathias Maris** (died 10/9/1811). He was born in Germantown Township. No children
J. **Nancy (Agnes) McDowell** (8/1767–1/2/1801)
K. **Patrick McDowell** (2/10/1770–4/24/1846) married 11/22/1803 **Elizabeth Davidson** (5/1780–8/2/1851) by Rev. King. He was a farmer and inn keeper at the "White House" near St. Thomas, PA. His wife was the daughter of Elias and Agnes McDowell Davidson.
Children of Patrick and Elizabeth Davidson McDowell:
   a. **Agnes "Nancy" McDowell** (1806–6/19, 1845 of consumption) married **John McDowell**
   b. **Mary Maxwell McDowell** (1807–11/1/1899)
   c. **William Andrew McDowell** (11/1/1811–11/17/1835 of consumption)
   d. **Elias Davidson McDowell** (born 1815) who kept a hotel near Mount Parnell and married **Mary Earl**.
   e. **Margaret McDowell** (1817–9/2/1866) married on 5/6/1806 **Dr. Mathias Maris**
   f. **Elizabeth "Lissie" King McDowell** (6/1/1843–1864) married 3/26/1835 **William Campbell** (6/15/1802–1/13/1884)
L. **Thomas McDowell, Esq.** (1772/1773–8/4/1851) married 3/12/1807 **Mary Craig Davidson** (1784–10/31/1854) by Rev. King. He was a ruling elder. At his father's death, he was given guardianship of two melato boys as a slave named Dinna/Dina, who originated with William Maxwell, was set free. It is not clear who the parents of these boys are and what their ages were at that point. They are not called slaves or bound boys in the paper work. Since they are listed with Dinna, it is assumed they belonged to her.
Children of Thomas and Mary Davidson McDowell:
   a. **Mary Maxwell McDowell** (1808–1874) who married on 3/7/1838 **Dr. William Humphreys** and then **Rev. A.K. Nelson** (1808–1874).

    b. **Catherine Davidson McDowell** (4/2/1811–8/4/1893) who married 11/1/1842 **Rev. Nathan Grier White** (4/11/1810–9/29/1895)
    c. **William Henry McDowell** (1813–1900)
    d. **Hugh Davidson McDowell** (9/1814–2/16/1840)
    e. **John Alexander McDowell** (born 1819)
    f. **Susan Agnes McDowell** (6/21/1822–6/18/1843)

4. **Nathan McDowell** (born 1722ca in Chester County-6/2/1801) was a farmer and land owner. He married in 1753 **Catherine Maxwell** (born 1722). She was the daughter of Susanne and Major William Maxwell, Esq.
Children of Nathan and Catherine Maxwell McDowell:
  A. **Mary McDowell** (4/16/1754–1/1828) married 1/31/1775 **John Holliday** (1740–1818) by Rev. King. John was the first Chief Burgess of Chambersburg. They had no children.
  B. **William McDowell** (5/9/1756–1/30/1782)
  C. **James McDowell** (8/14/1759–4/9/1789)
  D. **John McDowell** (8/5/1761–1/28/1785)
  E. **Susan/Susanna McDowell** (2/12/1764–3/29/1790)
  F. **Nathan McDowell** (12/19/1767–10/31/1820) married 3/14/1792 **Nancy Jean Irwin**.
    Children of Nathan and Nancy:
    a. **Catherine McDowell**
    b. **Mary J. McDowell** (8/16/1795–?)
    c. **James McDowell** (8/27/1797–1798)
    d. **Martha I. McDowell** (born 3/1/1799)
    e. **Nathan McDowell**
    f. **Matilda McDowell** (born 4/13/1804)
    g. **Joseph Irwin McDowell** (born 1/28/1806)
    h. **John H. McDowell** (born 4/18/1808)
  G. **Dr. Maxwell McDowell** (2/8/1771–1848) was a physician in York, Pennsylvania, and then in Baltimore, Maryland. He married **Ruth Bayley** (born 1773).

Appendix A: A Partial Genealogy

Children of Maxwell and Ruth Bayley McDowell:
a. **John McDowell**
b. **Mary McDowell**
c. **Susanna McDowell**

5. **Thomas McDowell** (1725ca-5/2/1806). Thomas was an officer of militia from 1747–1748. He later served as a 1st Lieutenant under Captain James Patton's Company in Colonel Samuel Culbertson's Battalion of the Cumberland County Associators from 1777–1780. He served with Lieutenant John Holiday (1777–78–80). His wife was **Annabelle** and he lived by Fort Loudon in 1769. No children. Some list her as pioneer William's Daughter but that Annabelle married someone else. Thomas' wife died prior to his death. Some sources list him as the first son born in 1715. Most material lists him as the fifth child. All agree that he had no children.

6. **Judge James McDowell, Esq**. (2/5/1728 in New London, Chester County-2/5/1811) was a farmer and surveyor by Mount Parnell and then a constable. He married on 6/17/1761 **Jean "Jane or Janet" Smith** (1743–8/28/1784), daughter of Robert and Jean Smith, sister of Captain James Smith of the Black Boys and sister of the wife of Justice William Smith, Sr. James had various properties, some were in Westmoreland County near Greensburg. James was falsely arrested in 1769 by Sheriff Holmes of Cumberland County under suspicion of participation with the Black Boys. He was brother-in-law to James Smith, leader of the group. On that particular date James McDowell had been surveying property with James Smith and Robert Smith. He went to Bedford to have a horse shod. James Smith's Black Boys had worked to stop traders from transporting war goods to the Indians in the past and in that work had assaulted both Fort Loudon and Bedford housing British troops. James McDowell was released by the Black boys and James Smith, not part of the events, turned himself in. Smith was never charged and was later released. During the Revolutionary War James McDowell served as a Sub-Lieutenant to Cumberland County from 11/29/1777 to 4/1780 under Captain

Robert McCoy (who was killed at Crooked Billet). After the war, he was Associate Judge in Franklin County from 1791–1811.

Children of James and Jean Smith McDowell:

A. **Mary McDowell** (4/5/1762–8/7/1821) married **Captain Thomas Campbell** (1751–4/5/1816), son of James and Rebecca Brown Campbell. He was a Captain in the "Flying Camp", and was captured at Fort Washington on November 16, 1776. In 1781 he was Captain of the 3rd Regiment. Thomas laid out the village of St. Thomas which had been formally called Campbellstown. Its new name is said to refer to Thomas Campbell's habit of using bad language.

   Children of Mary and Thomas Campbell:
   a. **Jean Campbell** married **Joseph McKean**
   b. **Elizabeth Campbell**
   c. **Rebecca Brown Campbell**

B. **Annabelle McDowell** (12/24/1763–12/22/1807) married 8/21/1782 **Major John Johnson**.

   Children of Annabelle and John Johnson:
   a. **Samuel Johnston**
   b. **John Johnston**
   c. **Thomas Johnston**
   d. **Jane Johnston** who married **Andrew Boggs**
   e. **Rebecca Johnston** who married **Andrew Work**
   f. **George W. Johnston**
   g. **Mary S. Johnston** who married **William Smith**

C. **Robert McDowell** (6/13/1766–10/10/1806) married 11/24/1789 **Elizabeth "Betsy" Irwin** (11/24/1789 – 1808) on 11/ 24/1789 by Rev. King. He was a private under Captain James Patton and Robert Dickey 1780–1781.

   Children of Robert and Elizabeth Irwin McDowell:
   a. **William McDowell**
   b. **Thomas Campbell McDowell**

D. **James McDowell** (1st one) (6/5/1768–11/4/1770)

Appendix A: A Partial Genealogy

E. **Jane McDowell** called "Jannet" (2/13/1771–1/23/1847) married first on 4/30/1789 **Isaac Bard** (February 8, 1762–July 28, 1806) on by Rev. King. He was in the PA militia and a farmer in Peter's Township. They had no children. Her second husband was **John Findlay** (3/31/1766–11/5/1838), married on 9/7/1807. He was the brother of Governor William Findley and General James Findlay of Ohio. William had served in the Senate the same time John and James served in the House.

F. **Sarah McDowell** (10/13/1773–5/18/1828) married on 6/2/1794 **Daniel McLene** (died 1809) by Rev. King.
Children of Sarah and Daniel McLene:
   a. **James McLene**
   b. **Robert McLene**
   c. **Jane McLene** who married **Joseph Dunlap**
   d. **Phanuel McLene** who married **John Graham**
   e. **Mary McLene**
   f. **Annabele McLene**
   g. **Sarah McLene**

G. **William Smith McDowell** (10/20/1776–1/23/1834) married **Mary Erwin** (1/8/1781–1/4/1860), daughter of Alexander and Mary Holmes Erwin. He was a member of the state legislature from 1833–1834 and a farmer.
Children of William and Mary Erwin McDowell:
   a. **Mary Holmes McDowell** (born 1806) married **James Campbell**
   b. **Alexander Erwin_McDowell** (2/2/1808–3/7/1881) married **Margaret Bard** (7/31/1806–9/29/1885 of paralysis) on 8/26/1834.
   c. **Robert McDowell** (born 1812) went west.
   d. **Jane Elizabeth McDowell** (born 1816) married **Jacob Shellenberger**
   e. **Annabelle J. McDowell** (born 3/25/1818–9/27/1871, married **Thomas Gillan**

f. **William Erwin McDowell** (8/8/1824–7/4/1892) was a farmer in St. Thomas, PA and ruling elder of Presbyterian Church. He was a Captain of Company I, 158th Regiment, PA Volunteers, 11/4/1862. His wife was **Rebecca Jane Gillan** 8/22/1826–8/4/1877, daughter of James and Margaret Reed Gillan. They had **Sarah Elizabeth McDowell** 4/2/1901–12/25/1878).

g. **James McDowell** (8/23/1826–9/4/1877)

H. **Margaret McDowell** (6/8/1779–11/18/1819, unmarried)

I. **James McDowell** (12/6/1782–4/8/1861) married 10/27/1813 **Mary Jo Dunlap** (1/20/1789–10/9/1876). James was a 1st Lieutenant and Adjutant under Captain Thomas Bard in the defense of Baltimore in 1814 during the War of 1812 and later a County Commissioner from 1815–1817. Farmer.

Children of James and Mary Jo Dunlap McDowell:

a. **Mary Bard McDowell** (8/14/1814–2/13/1871) unmarried

b. **James Dunlap McDowell** (3/16/1816–10/9/1887) unmarried surveyor, teacher, Whig politician, Associate Judge 1871–1876, postmaster Mt. Parnell 1878–1880, and member of State Legislature in 1880.

c. **Jane Smith McDowell** (9/4/1817–7/24/1887) married **Charles Gillan** (2/8/1819–3/24/1878) a hotelkeeper near St. Thomas.

d. **Sarah Margaret McDowell** (7/26/1819–10/11/1872) unmarried

e. **Elizabeth Olivia McDowell** (9/21/1821–12/16/1878) unmarried

f. **William Findlay McDowell** (6/23/1824–2/5/1890)

g. **Robert Holmes McDowell** (10/8/1826–8/28/1913) lived near St. Thomas

h. **Catherine Poe McDowell** (7/12/1828–10/19/1890) who married **Alexander Campbell Armstrong** (7/1/1828–8/13/1897) and moved to Auburn, Nebraska.

Appendix A: A Partial Genealogy

7. **Jean B. McDowell** (4/19/1736 Mt. Parnel-8/16/1814) married in 1757 **Archibald Irwin** (1734–1799). He was an Ensign in Captain John Steel's Company in 1756 at the Kittaning Expedition. He also served as quartermaster of Colonel Samuel Culbertson's battalion from 1777–80. They lived in Montgomery Township at Irwinton Mills, he had a flour and saw mill.
Children of Jean and Archibald Irwin:
   A. **James Irwin** (4/14/1758–11/9/1843) who married 12/5/1787 **Margaret Piper**. James served as a private during the Revolutionary War and then as Assistant Commissary in the Western Army.
   B. **Mary Jane Irwin** (2/14/1760–6/28/1828) married on 12/1782 **Matthew Van Lear**.
   C. **Margaret Irwin** (born 9/15/1761) who remained unmarried.
   D. **Nancy Irwin** (4/23/1763–7/27/1824) married on 12/7/1791 **William Findlay** (1768–1846) Governor of PA in 1817 and a U.S. Senator from 1821–1827.
   E. **William Irwin** (2/5/1766–7/16/1824) married on 12/5/1787 **Mary Smith** and moved to Cincinnati.
   F. **Elizabeth Irwin** (Irwinton Mills 8/24/1767–3/20/1814) married **Robert Smith** on 11/16/1790, brother of Justice William Smith, who later became a Pennsylvania Legislator from 1807–09, 1811–1814 and 1815; Speaker in 1813, State Senator 1819–23 and Associate Judge 1836–1843.
   G. **Jane Irwin** (born 6/22/1769) married on 6/15/1797 **James Findlay** (born Mercersburg 1770–died Cincinnati), brother of the Governor. They later moved to Ohio where he became a Brigadier-General in the War of 1812 and then member of Congress.
   H. **Archibald Irwin** (2/13/1772–5/3/1840) married **Mary Ramsey** and then a second woman
   I. **John Irwin** (4/3/1774–6/8/1779) married first **Mary M. Van Lear**.

Children of John and Mary Van Lear McDowell:
a. **Margaret Irwin** (9/10/1761–died unmarried)
b. **Nancy Irwin** who married **William Findlay**
c. **Elizabeth Irwin** who married **Robert Smith**

8. **Sarah McDowell** (11/30/1738–9/5/1805) married 12/29/1759 **Captain William Piper** of West Pennsboro Township (10/31/1735–1/7/1793) and moved to the West Branch of the Susquehanna River, Warrior's Run now in Northumberland County, after serving in the Bouquet expedition of 1768. Piper had been a Captain in Colonel Clayton's Regiment in 1763. The land was acquired as a result of service to the province. The Indian forays during the Revolutionary War drove him back to Peters Township where he became the Commissioner of Excise for Cumberland County 1778–1780.
Child of Sarah and William Piper:
A. **Margaret Piper** (4/3/1765–2/20/1852) married first, on 9/2/1783, to **William Smith** who laid out the town of Mercersburg and then second, on 12/5/1787, to her first cousin **James Irwin**, son of Archibald Irwin and Jean McDowell Irwin.

9. **Margaret McDowell** (1739ca–1/1803) married **Robert Newall** (died 3/6/1787).
Children of Margaret and Robert Newall:
A. **John Newell**
B. **Robert Newell**
C. **William Newell**
D. **Margaret Newell** who married **Duncan Campbell**

10. **Annabelle McDowell** (1741–4/11/1800) married in 1769 **Lieutenant-Colonel John Johnson** (1747–10/21/1826), her cousin and lived by Fort Loudon. She was his second wife. Johnston was an officer in the 8th Battalion of Cumberland County Associators (1777–1780) under Abraham Smith and then commanded the 1st

Battalion of the Associators in 1780. He was a member of the Pennsylvania Legislature in 1784–1785 and 1788–1793.

Children of Annabelle and John Johnson:
A. **Samuel Johnston**
B. **John Johnston**
C. **Thomas Johnston**
D. **Jane Johnston** who married **Andrew Boggs**
E. **Rebecca Johnston** who married **Andrew Work**
F. **George W. Johnston**
G. **Mary S. Johnston** who married **William Smith**

11. **Susan/Susanna McDowell** was born after 1741. Family tradition has her married to a **Mr. Reynolds** with a son named **Thomas**.

APPENDIX B

British Monarchs Ruling From 1558–1830 and Pennsylvania Governors

BRITISH MONARCHS

Name	Reign
HOUSE OF TUTOR	
Elizabeth I	1558–1603 (daughter of Henry VIII and Anne Boleyn) was the head of the Church of England-Anglican-like her father.
HOUSE OF STUART	
James I	1603–1625 (son Mary Queen of Scots and Henry Stewart/Stuart) was a Presbyterian.
Charles I	1625–1649 (son James I and Anne of Denmark) was married to a French Catholic and was later executed.
COMMONWEALTH	
Oliver Cromwell	1649–1658 (Commonwealth) was a Puritan protestant.
Richard Cromwell	1658–1659 (Commonwealth), son of Oliver.
HOUSE OF STUART	
Charles II	1660–1685 (son of Charles I and Henrietta Maria Bourbon Princess of France) established anti-Catholic repression.

Appendix B: British Monarchs and Pennsylvania Governors

James II	1685–1688 (son of Charles I and Henrietta Maria; brother of Charles II) converted to Catholicism and repealed anti-Catholic laws.
William III & Mary II	1689–1702 (first cousins: he son of the Prince of Orange and Mary Stuart; she was the daughter of James II with first wife Anne Hyde.) was a protestant. He established a Constitutional Monarchy and deposed James II. They had no children.
Anne	1702–1714 (daughter James II and Anne Hyde, sister to Mary II; married to the Prince of Denmark). Her husband was the Lord High Admiral of the Royal Navy. She was now Queen of England, Ireland and newly added Scotland in what was then called Great Britain. She was an Anglican. She died without issue.

HOUSE OF HANOVER

George I (1660–1727)	1714–1727 (son Ernest Augustus Elector of Hanover and Sophia of the Palatinate, granddaughter of James I). Sophia was Anne's closest relative. George was the Ruler of the Duchy and Electorate of Hanover and a protestant.
George II	1727–1760 (son of George I and Sophia Dorothea of Hanover).
George III	1760–1820 (grandson of George I; son of Frederick Prince of Wales and Augusta of Saxe-Gotha).
George IV	1820–1830 (son of George III).

Provincial Governors and Proprietaries serving from 1718 to the Revolutionary War

Proprietaries:

William Penn, 2d, 1718–1720
John, Thomas and Richard Penn 1727–1746
Thomas and Richard Penn 1746–1771
Thomas and John Penn 1771–1776

Royal Provincial Governors:

Sir William Keith 1717–1726
Patrick Gordon 1727–1736
James Logan 1736–1738
George Thomas 1738–1747
Anthony Palmer 1747–1748
James Hamilton 1748–1754 (1st administration)
Robert Hunter Morris 1754–1756
William Denny 1756–1759
James Hamilton 1759–1763, 1771 (2nd and 3rd Administrations)
John Penn 1763–1771 (1st Administration)
Richard Penn 1771–1773 (2nd Administration)

Pennsylvania State Governors serving from the Revolutionary War to 1840

Thomas Wharton, Jr. 1777–1778
George Bryan 1778
Joseph Reed 1778–1781
William Moore 1779–1782
James Potter 1781–1782
John Dickinson 1782–1785
Benjamin Franklin 1785–1788
Charles Biddle (Acting President) 1784–1787
Peter Muhlenberg 1787–1788

Appendix B: British Monarchs and Pennsylvania Governors

David Redick 1788
George Ross 1788–1790
Thomas Mifflin 1788–1790, 1790–1799 (after the constitution)
Thomas McKean 1799–1808
Simon Snyder 1808–1817

Notes

CHAPTER ONE

1. The historical marker is a trademark of the Pennsylvania Historical and Museum Commission and the marker text is copyright protected. This is used with permission. The entire dedicatory service of the Fort McDowell monument is printed in Cyrus Cort, ed., *Fort McDowell Monument Dedicatory Service* (Pilot Print: Union Bridge, Maryland, 1917).

2. The historical marker is a trademark of the Pennsylvania Historical and Museum Commission and the marker text is copyright protected. This is used with permission.

3. Americans use the term "Scotch-Irish" for those who moved from Scotland to Ireland, however "Scotch" is an alcoholic beverage and not an ethnic term. They call themselves either a Scot or Scottish. The British call the group who settled in Northern Ireland Ulster-Scots which is a more accurate term. This term will be used in the book.

4. Some references list his birth in 1680 but most point to 1682, including his burial record. To view the author's attempt at combining numerous conflicting genealogies into one for the patriarch William McDowell through to his grandchildren, see Appendix One.

5. King David of Scotland (1084–Mary 24, 1153) had the Scottish name Dabid Mac Mail Choluim. To view a list of the English monarchs and the Pennsylvania colonial governors who ruled during the period covered in the book, see Appendix two.

6. Conococheague Institute Blog: "Fort McDowell and the McDowells" at www.cimlg.org/ciblog/2014/03/21/fort-mcdowell-and-the-mcdowells.

7. James G. Leyburn, *The Scotch-Irish: A Social History* (Chapel Hill: The University of North Carolina Press, 1962), 25.

8. Ibid., 1–32.
9. Ibid., 17.
10. Ibid., 159.
11. Ibid., 164.
12. Ibid., 167.

Notes

CHAPTER TWO

1. Samuel Penniman Bates, Jacob Fraise and Warner Beers, *History of Franklin County, Pennsylvania, Containing a History of the County, its Townships* (Chicago: Warner, Beers and Company, 1887), 42.

2. Trade goods with the Indians included items like brass kettles, duffels, blankets, clothing, shoes, buckles, stockings, gun powder, lead, guns, flints, tomahawks, hatchets, knives, scissors, looking glass, ribbon, rum, tobacco, pipes and money.

3. The Lenape would eventually be moved to Oklahoma in the 1860s by the United States government where 11,000 currently live. About 5,000 Lenape live in New Jersey and Pennsylvania within white cultures though there are no federally recognized Indian tribes in Pennsylvania today. The Pennsylvania Lenape language currently has no fluent speakers though there is an interest in trying to recreate it. About 3,000 Munsee Delaware live in Ontario and Wisconsin. The Munsee dialect has a handful of Ontario elders who can speak it. The Susquehannnock Iroquoian language is extinct and so is the tribe with mixed-blood descendants merged into the Iroquois and Lenape tribes. See "Native American Tribes of Pennsylvania," www.native-laguages.org/ pennsylvania.htm; "Native Languages of the Americas: Lenape (Unami, Delaware, Lenni Lenape," www.native-languages.org/lenape.htm; "Native Languages of the Americas: Munsee Delaware (Minsi, Muncey, Minisink)," www.Native –languages.org/munsee.htm; and "Susquehannock Indian Languages (Conestoga)," www.native-languages.org/susquehannock.htm. Also see www.delawarenation.com for more information on the Delaware Nation.

4. Jacob Fraise Richard, and Thomas Henry, *History of Beaver County, Pennsylvania, Volume 1* (Pittsburgh: University of Pittsburgh, 1999 digital version of the 1888 edition), 13–14.

5. Bates, Fraise and Beers, 17–18.

6. Francis Parkman, *The Conspiracy of Pontiac and the Indian War After the Conquest of Canada, Volume I* (Boston: Harvard University Press, 1851), 254.

7. William A. Hunter, "First Line of Defense, 1755–56," *Pennsylvania History*, vol. 22, no. 3, July 1955, 231.

8. James G. Leyburn, *The Scotch-Irish: A Social History* (Chapel Hill: The University of North Carolina Press, 1962), 169.

9. Robert McCrum, William Cran, and Robert MacNeil, *The Story of the English* (New York: Viking Penguin Inc., 1986) also gives an overview of how the language has progressed with its various influences.

10. Leyburn, 276.

11. Leyburn, 187.

12. McDowell names are on the Chester County taxable list in the *Pennsylvania Archives*, Third Series, 11:33, 52, 127, 244, 330, 415, 556.

13. J. L. Ziegler, *An Authentic History of Donegal Presbyterian Church: Located in East Donegal Township, Lancaster County, Pa.*, (Philadelphia: F. McManus, Jr., and Company Printers and Publishers, 1902), 9. Also see "Donegal, Pennsylvania History" on www.doak.ws/donegal.htm. for more information on the settlement.

14. Israel Rupp lists the following present at Donegal before 1720: "Patterson, Sempel, Mitchell, Hendricks, Speer, Galbraith, Anderson, Scott, Pedan, Porter, Kerr, Sterritt, Kern, Work, Little, Whitehill, Campbell, Lowrey, McClelland, Stevenson, Wilson, Fulton, Allison, Howard, Brown, Dinsmore, Hughs, Robinson, Chambers, McMaken, McDowell, Foster, Crocket, Gilson, Woods, Spear, Bailey, McCracken, Cunningham, Lyon, Bratchey, Mason, Jameson, Hutchison, Cook, Moore, Ramsey, McClure, McFarlane, Brenard, Craig, Thomson, Carson, Connelly, Patton, Gallaher, Stewart, Boggs, Kelly, Ramsay." Many of these names would be found in the Cumberland Valley when it opened for settlement. Israel Daniel Rupp, *The History and Topography of Dauphin, Cumberland, Franklin, Bedford, Adams, and Perry Counties* [*Pennsylvania* (Lancaster, Pennsylvania: Gilbert Hills, Proprietor and Publisher, 1846), 35.

15. Another Donegal settlement would be established in 1762 in Somerset County west of Pittsburgh.

16. William A. Hunter, *Fort on the Pennsylvania Frontier, 1753–1758* (Harrisburg, Pennsylvania: The Pennsylvania Historical and Museum Commission, 1960), 10. For a more complete history of the Donegal community see www.donegalpresbyterianchurch.org. The Donegal Society and the church's historian team keep detailed records of the community.

17. C. A. Weslager, "Log Houses in Pennsylvania During the Seventeenth Century," *Pennsylvania History*, January 1955, vol. XXII, no. 1., 256; William W. Weaver "The Pennsylvania German House: European Antecedents and New World Forms," *Winterthur Portfolio* 21(4):243–64, 1986; and Fred Kniffen and Henry Glassie, "Building in Wood in the Eastern United States: a Time-Place Perspective," *Geological Review*, 56(1):40–66. Also see Sidney Nill, "Our Conococheague Settlement, 1732–1782 (Chambersburg: Franklin County Chapter of the Daughters of the American Revolution, 1971), 1–2.

18. Bates, 77–81.
19. *Pennsylvania Archives*, Fourth Series, 1:423.
20. Rupp, 52.
21. Rupp, 53.
22. Kris Hocker, "The Problem with Owning Land as a German in Colonial Pennsylvania," November 3, 2013, on www.krishocker.com/the-problem-with-owi=ning-land-as-a-german-in-colonial-pennsylvania/.
23. McCrum, 156–157.

CHAPTER THREE

1. Samuel Penniman Bates, Jacob Fraise, and Warner Beers, *History of Franklin County, Pennsylvania, Containing a History of the County, its Townships . . .* (Chicago: Warner, Beers and Company, 1887), 137.

2. Shirley B. Fenstermacher and Margaret L. McDonnell, *Franklin A Frontier Country* (Mercersburg, Pennsylvania: Mercersburg Printing Company, 1975), 4.

Notes

3. The Conococheague Institute is located at 12995 Bain Road, Mercersburg, PA, 17236. It provides educational programs related to the early Conococheague Settlement; see http://cimlg.org/.

4. Calvin E. Bricker, Jr., "Notes on the Early History along the Conococheague Creek in Antrim Township, Franklin County, Pennsylvania," March 25, 1998 (unpublished).

5. I. H. McCauley, *Historical Sketch of Franklin County, Pennsylvania* (Chambersburg: D. F. Pursel, 1878), 27.

6. The Chester County, Pennsylvania, deed book shows Will and John McDowell of New London selling land in the 1730s. www.pa-chestercounty.civicplus.com, 190.

7. Bates, 150.

8. Bates, 151, 573.

9. Bates, 151.

10. Israel Daniel Rupp, *The History and Topography of Dauphin, Cumberland, Franklin, Bedford, Adams, and Perry Counties* [*Pennsylvania* (Lancaster, Pennsylvania: Gilbert Hills, Proprietor and Publisher, 1846), 117.

11. Thomas Francis Gordon, *The History of Pennsylvania: From its Discovery by Europeans, to the Declaration of Independence in 1776* (Philadelphia: Jesper Harding, Printer, 1829), 50.

12. "Native Languages of the Americas: Lenape (Unami, Delaware, Lenni Lenape)," www. Native-languages.org/Lenape.htm.

13. For a partial genealogy of the McDowells, see Appendix 1.

14. Bates, 690–691.

15. Bates, 273.

16. Virginia Shannon Fendrick, *American Revolutionary Soldiers of Franklin County Pennsylvania* (Chambersburg: Daughters of the American Revolution, 175.

17. Eugene Etter, *History of Lemasters, Pennsylvania: Local History in and around Lemasters, Southern Franklin County on the Occasion of Their Centennial Celebration* (Chambersburg, Pennsylvania: Robson & Kaye, Inc., Printers, 1972), 5.

18. George O. Seilhamer, "Old Mother Cumberland," *The Pennsylvania Magazine of History and Biography*, vol. 24, no. 1, 1900, 19; Israel Daniel Rupp, *The History and Topography of Dauphin, Cumberland, Franklin, Bedford, Adams and Perry Counties* [Pennsylvania] (Lancaster, Pennsylvania: Gilbert Hills Proprietor and Publisher, 1846), 36; and Ellis, Franklin and Evans, Samuel, *History of Lancaster County, Pennsylvania with Biographical Sketches of Many of the Prominent Men* (Philadelphia: Everts and Peck, 1883, 548. There would later be a post office in the old ferry house in Columbia by 1797 which points to the importance of this crossing point.

19. As per Joseph Michael McDowell in "The McDowell Family History: Scotland to Franklin County, PA, 1680–2011" an unpublished paper dated 2001.

20. Bates, 151. Some reports have some of these men present in the township in the 1730s.

21. Thomas Creigh, *History of the Presbyterian Church of Upper West Conococheague: Now Mercersburg, Franklin County, Pennsylvania* (Chambersburg: Repository Printer, 1877), 7–8.

22. Creigh, 5–6.

23. John G. Orr, Esq., "The Three Mountain Road," *Papers, Read Before the Kittochtinny Historical Society from March 1905, to February 1908* (Chambersburg, Pennsylvania: The Kittochtinny Historical Society, 1908), 5–6.

24. Currently the Evangelical Lutheran Church, United Church of Christ (German Reformed), Presbyterian Church (U.S.A.), and the Reformed Church in American (Dutch Reformed) are in a *Formula Of Agreement* in the United States, working in joint projects and exchanging pastors. The international branches of the reformed family of faith, which makes up 1/3 of all Protestants, works through the World Alliance of Reformed Churches. They are also members of the World Council of Churches and the National Council of Churches.

25. *Pennsylvania Archives*, Fourth Series, 5:22; and William A. Hunter, *Fort on the Pennsylvania Frontier*, 1753–1758 (Harrisburg, Pennsylvania: The Pennsylvania Historical and Museum Commission, 1960), 7.

26. William A. Hunter, *Forts on the Pennsylvania Frontier*, 7–8.

27. Edward P. Hamilton, *The French and Indian Wars: The Story of Battles and Forts in the Wilderness* (Garden City, New York: Doubleday and Company, Inc., 1962), 70.

28. Hamilton, 126–128.

29. Bates, 82.

30. Bates, 83.

31. Bates, 573.

32. This was from an email to author in August of 2015 from John N. Lovett, Jr., Ph.D., owner of Falls Mill & Museum in Belvidere, Tennessee.

33. Email to author from Lovett, Jr.

34. Cyrus Cort, *Fort McDowell Monument Dedicatory Service* (Pilot Print: Union Bridge, Maryland, 1917), 1–26.

35. Etter, 13.

36. The Warrantees of Land for the McDowells in Lancaster County are contained within the *Pennsylvania Archives*, Third Series, 24:467–486, 713–732; and for the newly formed Franklin County in 1784 in *Pennsylvania Archives*, Third Series, 25:29–33.

37. Etter, 13.

38. John G. Orr, Esq., "The Tree Mountain Road," Papers Read Before the Society from March, 1905, to February, 1908, Chambersburg, The Kittochtinny Historical Society, 75.

39. Virginia Shannon Fendrick, *American Revolutionary Soldiers of Franklin County Pennsylvania* (Chambersburg: Daughters of the American Revolution, 1944), 174. This is also in the family genealogy provided by Mary Creigh McDowell through

Joseph Michael McDowell, *The McDowell Family History: Scotland to Franklin County, PA, 1680–2001* (2001), unpublished.

40. Catherine was born in 1753 and died 2/10/1818 in Allegheny County. She is buried in Laird Cemetery. Her husband's dates are 1745–1820.

41. Letter "George Thomas in Philadelphia to Thomas Lawrie, Secretary to the Assembly, January 23, 1739," in *Pennsylvania Archives*, Fourth Series, 1:702.

42. Bates, 82.

43. Letter "Conrad Weiser from Tulpehockin to Richard Peters, June 21, 1747," in *Pennsylvania Archives*, First Series, 1:751.

44. Ibid., 758.

45. *Pennsylvania Archives*, First Series, 2:14, lists those with Indian trader licenses from 1747 through 1748.

46. Woman's Club of Mercersburg, "Old Mercersburg, Pennsylvania", *The Journal of American History*, 1913 (reprint Saltville, Virginia, Jeffrey C. Weaver, 2005), 6–7.

47. James A. Roberts, *New York in the Revolution as Colony and State* (Albany: Brandow, 1898), 9–10.

48. Hunter, William A., *Forts on the Pennsylvania Frontier, 1753–1758* (Harrisburg, Pennsylvania: The Pennsylvania Historical and Museum Commission, 1960), 14.

49. Bates, 85.

CHAPTER FOUR

1. Bates, Samuel Penniman, Fraise, Jacob, and Beers, Warner, *History of Franklin County, Pennsylvania, Containing a History of the County, its Townships . . .* (Chicago: Warner, Beers and Company, 1887), 506.

2. Bates, 401.

3. Bates, 155; and I.H. McCauley, *Historical Sketch of Franklin County, Pennsylvania* (Chambersburg: D.F. Pursel, 1878), 127–128.

4. Bates, 155.

5. William A. Hunter, "First Line of Defense, 1755–56," *Pennsylvania History*, vol. 22, no. 3, July 1955, 232.

6. Hunter, *Forts on the Pennsylvania Frontier, 1753–1758* (Harrisburg, Pennsylvania: The Pennsylvania Historical and Museum Commission, 1960), 9.

7. William A. Hunter, *Forts on the Pennsylvania Frontier*, 15.

8. Hunter, *Forts on the Pennsylvania Frontier*, 18.

9. Lee McCardell, *Ill-Starred General: Braddock of the Coldstream Guards* (Pittsburg: University of Pittsburgh Press, 1986 edition), 120.

10. Bates, 88.

11. Joseph Coulon de Jumonville was also known as Joseph Coulon de Villiers, Sieur de Jumonville.

12. I.H. McCauley, *Historical Sketch of Franklin County, Pennsylvania*, 17.

13. Bates, 89.

14. McCardell, 123.

15. Bates, 89.

16. Votes of Assembly, iv. 319, Aug. 1754 as per Rupp, Israel Daniel, *The History and Topography of Dauphin, Cumberland, Franklin, Bedford, Adams, and Perry Counties [Pennsylvania]* (Lancaster, Pennsylvania: Gilbert Hills, Proprietor and Publisher, 1846), 70.

17. The "Plan for Defence of the Frontier of Cumberland Co. from Phillip Davies to Shippensburgh, 1754" was most likely written by John Armstrong and is in the *Pennsylvania Archives*, First Series, 2:239–241. Also see Votes of Assembly, iv. 319, Aug. 1754 as per Rupp, Israel Daniel, *The History and Topography of Dauphin, Cumberland, Franklin, Bedford, Adams, and Perry Counties [Pennsylvania]* (Lancaster, Pennsylvania: Gilbert Hills, Proprietor and Publisher, 1846), 70.

18. Letter "George Croghan at Aughwick dated September 27, 1754, to George Hamilton," as per *Pennsylvania Archives*, First Series, 2:173.

19. McCardell, 124.

20. *Pennsylvania Archives*, First Series, 2:206.

21. McCardell, 214.

22. McCardell, 136.

23. I. H. McCauley, *Historical Sketch of Franklin County, Pennsylvania* (Chambersburg: D. F. Pursel, 1878), 69.

24. Eugene Etter, *History of Lemasters, Pennsylvania: Local History in and around Lemasters, Southern Franklin County on the Occasion of Their Centennial Celebration* (Chambersburg, Pennsylvania: Robson & Kaye, Inc., Printers, 1972), 8.

25. McCardell, 133.

26. Hunter, *Forts on the Pennsylvania Frontier*, 31.

27. Archer Butler Hulbert, *Historic Highways of America, Volume V: The Old Glade (Forbes's) Road* (Cleveland, Ohio: The Arthur H. Clark Company, 1903), 9.

28. McCardell, 145–147.

29. Official Correspondence, 1683–1727 (Penn MSS, Historical Society of Pennsylvania), VII, 9, as per James G. Leyburn, *The Scotch-Irish: A Social History* (Chapel Hill: The University of North Carolina Press, 1962), 227.

30. Letter "Governor Morris in Philadelphia to General Braddock, March 12, 1755" in *Minutes of the Provincial Council of Pennsylvania*, vol. 6, 335–336.

31. Letter "Governor Morris in Philadelphia to Sir John St. Clair, February 10, 1755," in *Pennsylvania Archives*, Fourth Series, 2:356–360.

32. Governor Morris' "Order Survey Road from Shippensburg to Intercept Army Road from Will's Creek to Fort Duquesne to George Croghan, John Armstrong, James Bird, William Buchanan and Adam Hoops of Cumberland," in *Pennsylvania Archives*, Fourth Series, 2:361–362.

33. McCardell, 186.

34. Thomas Balch, ed., *Letters and Papers Relating Chiefly to the Provincial History of Pennsylvania, with some Notices of the Writers* (Philadelphia: Crissy and Markley, Printers, 1855), 35.

35. Benjamin Franklin, William Temple Franklin, and William Duane, *Memoirs of Benjamin Franklin* (Philadelphia: M'Carty and Davis, 1834), 54.

36. "Benjamin Franklin's ad for Wagons, April 26, 1755" in *Pennsylvania Archives*, First Series, 2:294–296.

37. Franklin, "Memoirs," 57.

38. Vaughan, Samuel, *Samuel Vaughan's Diary, 1787–1796* (Washington, D.C.: Manuscript Division, only copy) or see Edward G. Williams, ed., *Minutes Made by s.v., from Stage to Stage, on a Tour to Fort Pitt* (unpublished), Part II from Carlisle to Pittsburgh, 159.

39. McCauley, 1.

40. Letter "Governor Morris in Philadelphia to Sir Thomas Robinson, April 9, 1755," in *Pennsylvania Archives*, First Series, 2:284.

41. Balch, 37–38.

42. Letter "James Burd to Governor Morris, April 27, 1755," in *Minutes of the Provincial Council of Pennsylvania*, vol. 6, 436.

43. Balch, 40.

44. Letter, "Governor Morris to Thomas Penn, May 15, 1755," *Pennsylvania Archives*, First Series, 2:311.

45. Letter, "Richard Peters from Shippensburg to Governor Morris, May 17 and 18, 1755," *Pennsylvania Archives*, First Series, 2:313–315.

46. "Minutes of the Meeting near Sugar Cabins, Auckquick, Tuesday, May 20, 1755", *Pennsylvania Archives*, First Series, 2:320–321.

47. Horace Kephart, ed., *Captives Among the Indians: First-hand Narratives of Indian Wars* . . . (New York: Outing Publishing Company, 1915); and Rupp, 75–76.

48. Letter "Governor Morris in Philadelphia to General Baddock, June 3, 1755," in *Pennsylvania Archives*, Fourth Series, 2:393–394. Also see *Minutes of the Provincial Council of Pennsylvania*, vol. 6, 407.

49. Letter "Governor Morris, June 4, 1755," in *Pennsylvania Archives*, Fourth Series, 2:395–396.

50. Letter "William Allison and William Maxwell in the Conegochege to Richard Peters, June 12, 1755" in *Minutes of the Provincial Council of Pennsylvania*, vol. 6, 434.

51. Letter "Governor Morris to the Assembly," *Pennsylvania Archives*, Fourth Series, 2:401.

52. Letter "Governor DeLancey from New York to Morris, June 13, 1755," *Pennsylvania Archives*, First Series, 2:359–360. Letter "Edward Shippen from Lancaster to Governor Morris, June 13, 1755," in *Pennsylvania Archives*, First Series, 2:358–359; and Hunter, "First Line of Defense, 1755–56," 231.

53. *Pennsylvania Archives*, First Series, 2:359, 364, 372.

54. Letter "Charles Swaine's assessment from Shippensburg, June 14, 1755," in *Pennsylvania Archives*, First Series, 2:360–361.

55. Cyrus Cort, *Fort McDowell: Monument Dedicatory Service* (Union Bridge, Maryland: 1916), 15.

56. Bates, 216.

57. Bates, 216.

58. Rupp, Israel Daniel, *The History and Topography of Dauphin, Cumberland, Franklin, Bedford, Adams, and Perry Counties [Pennsylvania* (Lancaster, Pennsylvania: Gilbert Hills, Proprietor and Publisher, 1846.), 74–75.

59. Letter, "Edward Braddock to Governor Robert Hunter Morris at Carlisle, June 30, 1755," in *Minutes of the Provincial Council of Pennsylvania,* 6:475–476.

60. Letter "Governor Morris in Philadelphia to Sir Thomas Robinson, July 3, 1755," in *Pennsylvania Archives,* First Series, 2:365.

61. Letter "Governor Morris to General Braddock, July 3, 1755," *Pennsylvania Archives,* First Series, 2:372–3.

62. Etter, 11.

63. McCauley, 18.

64. The Rev. Dr. Cyrus Cort mentioned his great-grandfather, Andrew Byerly of Lancaster, going to bake bread for General Braddock's army at Fort Cumberland in Cyrus Cort, *Fort McDowell Monument Dedicatory Service* (Union Bridge, Maryland, 1917), 17–18.

65. Jay Gilfillan Weiser, *The Frontier Forts in the Cumberland and Juniata Valleys* (Clarence M. Busch State Printer of Pennsylvania, 1896), 545–549; and Etter, 14.

66. Bates, 163–164.

CHAPTER FIVE

1. Bates, Samuel Penniman, Fraise, Jacob, and Beers, Warner, *History of Franklin County, Pennsylvania, Containing a History of the County, its Townships* (Chicago: Warner, Beers and Company, 1887), 90.

2. Lee McCardell, *Ill-Starred General: Braddock of the Coldstream Guards* (Pittsburg: University of Pittsburgh Press, 1986 edition), 204–205, 268.

3. William A. Hunter, "First Line of Defense, 1755–56," 231; Hunter, *Forts on the Pennsylvania Frontier, 1753–1758,* 4–5; and see Archer Butler Hulbert, *Historic Highways of America, Volume V: The Old Glade (Forbes's) Road* (Cleveland, Ohio: The Arthur H. Clark Company, 1903).

4. Letter "Governor Morris to Governor Sharpe, July 20, 1755," *Pennsylvania Archives,* First Series, 2:382–383.

5. *Colonial Records* 6, 500, 516–517, as per Hunter, 232.

6. Land Records of Allegheny County, Maryland, Liber D, fol. 225 (p. 33–34) as per Jacob Fraise Richard, and Thomas Henry, *History of Beaver County, Pennsylvania: Including its Early Settlement . . . , Volume 1* (Pittsburgh: University of Pittsburgh, 1999 digital version of the 1888 edition), 561.

7. Cyrus Cort, *Fort McDowell Monument Dedicatory Service* (Union Bridge, Maryland, 1917), 15.

8. Letter "Governor Morris to General Shirley, July 30, 1755," in *Pennsylvania Archives,* Fourth Series, 2:442–444.

9. Letter "Governor Morris to the Justices and Sheriff of Cumberland County, July 30, 1755," *Pennsylvania Archives,* Fourth Series, 2:445.

Notes

10. Letter "Governor Morris to Colonel Dunbar, July 31, 1755," in *Pennsylvania Archives*, Fourth Series, 2:447.

11. Rupp, Israel Daniel, *The History and Topography of Dauphin, Cumberland, Franklin, Bedford, Adams, and Perry Counties [Pennsylvania* (Lancaster, Pennsylvania: Gilbert Hills, Proprietor and Publisher, 1846.), 77.

12. Letter "Petition of Defence from Cumberland, 1755," in *Pennsylvania Archives*, First Series, 2:385–386.

13. Eugene Etter, *History of Lemasters, Pennsylvania: Local History in and around Lemasters, Southern Franklin County on the Occasion of Their Centennial Celebration* (Chambersburg, Pennsylvania: Robson & Kaye, Inc., Printers, 1972), 8.

14. Penn Manuscripts, Indian Affairs III, p. 28 and *Pennsylvania Archives*, Eighth Series, 5:43–57, as per Hunter, *Forts on the Pennsylvania Frontier, 1753–1758*, 425.

15. Etter, 9.

16. "Officers of the Provincial Service, 1755," *Pennsylvania Archives,* Second Series, 2:517–537.

17. Rupp, 84.

18. Letter "Inhabitants of Lurgan Township to the governor, August 1, 1755," as per Rupp, 77–78.

19. Provincial Records. N. 340 as per Rupp, 79.

20. Rupp, 81.

21. Letter "John Harris from Paxton to Governor Morris, October 28, 1755," as per Rupp, 82.

22. Letter "Conrad Weiser from Heidelberg to Governor Morris, July 21, 1755," as per Rupp, 83.

23. Letter "John Harris from Paxton to Edward Shippen, Esq., Oct 29, 1755," as per Rupp, 88.

24. Sidney Nill, *Our Conococheague Settlement, 1732–1782* (Chambersburg: Franklin County Chapter of the Daughters of the American Revolution, 1971 edition), 4–6.

25. *Pennsylvania Archives*, Second Series, 2:695; and Hunter, *Forts on the Pennsylvania Frontier, 1753–1758*, 426.

26. Rupp, 76.

27. *Pennsylvania Archives*, First Series, 2:385–386, 392; and Hunter, "First Line of Defense, 1755–56," 232.

28. *Pennsylvania Gazette,* November 13, 1755, as per Bates, 163; and Letter "John Armstrong from Carlisle to Governor Morris, November 2, 1775," in Rupp, 92–95.

29. Archibald Loudon, *A Selection of Some of the Most Interesting Narratives, or the Outrages Committed by the Indians in their Wars with the White People: also, an account of their Manners, Customs, Traditions, Religious Sentiments, Mode of Warfare, Military Tactics, Discipline and Encampments, Treatment of Prisoners & c,* vol. 1 (Harrisburg: Harrisburg Publishing Co., 1811), 195.

30. Letter "Adam Hoops from Cannogogig/Conococheague to Governor Morris, November 3, 1755," in *Pennsylvania Archives*, First Series, 2:462–463.

31. Letter "Governor Morris to the Assembly November 3, 1755," in *Pennsylvania Archives*, Fourth Series, 2:516.

32. Letter "Adam Hoops from the Canegogig/Conococheague to Governor Morris, November 6, 1755," in *Pennsylvania Archives*, First Series, 2:474–475.

33. Letter "John Potter from Conococheague to Richard Peters, November 2, 1755," Provinical Record n, 262–3 as per Rupp, 91.

34. Bates, 162.

35. Letter "Adam Hoops from Conococheague to Governor Morris, November 3, 1755," in Rupp, 93.

36. Letter "John Armstrong from Carlisle to Richard Peters, November 2, 1755," in Rupp, 393.

37. Letter "John Armstrong from Carlisle to Governor Morris, November 2, 1755," as per Rupp, 92.

38. Bates, 164–5; and I. H. McCauley, *Historical Sketch of Franklin County, Pennsylvania* (Chambersburg: D. F. Pursel, 1878), 67.

39. William H. Egle, *An Illustrated History of the Commonwealth of Pennsylvania . . .* (Harrisburg: DeWitt C. Goodrich & Co, 1876), 91; and Bates, 161.

40. John McDowell, L.L.D. (February 11, 1751–December 22, 1820), son of William McDowell, Jr., attended King's Latin school until it was destroyed in 1763. King later arranged for his entrance into the College of Philadelphia in 1768. He graduated in 1771 and tutored and enlisted in Captain Samuel Patton's Company July 28, 1777 during the Revolutionary War. In 1782 he moved to Cambridge, Maryland, and studied law while teaching. He entered the Dorchester County Bar and earned an honorary Doctor of Laws. He became the first Principal of St. John's College in Annapolis, Maryland, corresponding with George Washington, and then the third Provost of the University of Pennsylvania and Professor of Natural Philosophy. Also see Virginia Shannon Fendrick, *American Revolutionary Soldiers of Franklin County Pennsylvania* (Chambersburg: Daughters of the American Revolution, 1944), 174; and "Penn Biographies: John McDowell (1751–1820)" on www.archives.upenn.edu/people/1700s/ Mcdowell_john.html.

41. Letter "Benjamin Franklin at Philadelphia to James Reed, Esq., November 2, 1755," Benjamin Franklin, William Temple Franklin and William Duane, *Memoirs of Benjamin Franklin, Volume 1* (Philadelphia: M'Carty and Davis, 1834), 14, 17–18.

42. Benjamin Franklin, William Temple Franklin, and William Duane, *Memoirs of Benjamin Franklin* (Philadelphia: M'Carty and Davis, 1834, 58–59.

43. Letter "John Elder from Paxton to Mr. Peters, Esq., November 9, 1755," as per Rupp, 95.

44. Hunter, *Forts on the Pennsylvania Frontier, 1753–1758*, 178, 237–238.

45. Bates, 163.

46. Rupp, 95–96.

47. *Pennsylvania Gazette*, February 12, 1756, as per Rupp, 9–10.

48. Letter "Governor Morris to the Assembly, March 3, 1756," in *Pennsylvania Archives*, Fourth Series, 2:585.

49. Letter "Governor Morris from Philadelphia to Governor Dinwiddie of Virginia, February 1, 1756," in *Pennsylvania Archives*, First Series, 2:560–562.

50. Nathan McDowell and Catherine Maxwell McDowell's daughter Mary would later marry John Holliday.

51. These 1756 Regiments are listed in *Pennsylvania Archives*, First Series, 3:89 and following.

52. "Deposition March 30, 1756," in Penn Manuscripts, Indian Affairs III.77 and *Pennsylvania Gazette* April 1, 1756, as per William A. Hunter, *Forts on the Pennsylvania Frontier, 1753–1758* (Harrisburg, Pennsylvania: The Pennsylvania Historical and Museum Commission, 1960), 426; and Rupp, 98–99.

53. Letter "William Trent at Carlisle to Richard Peters, Sunday February 12, 1756," in *Pennsylvania Archives*, First Series, 2:575.

54. Rupp, 99–100.

55. Bates, 616–617.

56. The story of John McDowell's hat is recorded in Cyrus Cort, Ed., *Fort McDowell Monument Dedicatory Serves* (Union Bridge, Maryland: Pilot Print, 1917), 12.

57. Thomas Creigh, *History of the Presbyterian Church of Upper West Conococheague: Now Mercersburg, Franklin County, Pennsylvania* (Chambersburg: Repository Printer, 1877), CPSIA reproduction 2016, 12. Creigh also repeats the hat story but he attributed it to William McDowell. Two later versions, including the dedication of the monument with McDowell heirs present, state it was John.

58. Bates, 91.

59. Letter "Governor Morris to Sir William Johnson," *Pennsylvania Archives*, Fourth Series, 2:601.

60. Letter from "John Craig, March 30, 1756," Penn Manuscripts, Indian Affairs III, 77, as per Hunter, 426.

61. See "About St. John's College" www.sjc.edu/about/history and "Penn Biographies: John McDowell (1751–1820) www.archives.upen.edu/people/1700s/Mcdowell-john.html. The *McDowell/Maynadier Correspondence Archives*, History Collection, Series 1, Box 2, Folder 1–9 at Greenfield Library, St. John's College, Annapolis, Maryland, gives more insight into this man as does the *John McDowell, LL.D. letters* in the Special Collections of Hornbake Library, University of Maryland.

62. Eugene Etter's grandfather was in the block house in the 1840 period. At that time it served as a butcher shop as per Eugene Etter, ed., with Mary M. Etter and Janet W. Ray, *History of Lemasters, Pennsylvania: Centennial Celebration: June 22–25, 1972*, (Chambersburg, Pennsylvania: Robson & Kaye, Inc., printers, 1972), 13.

63. "A List of the Officers in the Province Pay, with the Dates of Their Commissions, 1756," *Pennsylvania Archives*, Second Series, 2:511–512.

64. Hunter, 427.

65. "Shippen Family Papers," V, 33, as per Hunter, 427–428.

66. Woman's Club of Mercersburg, "Old Mercersburg, Pennsylvania," (1913 first printing in the *Journal of American History*, this edition printed Raleigh, North Carolina: Lulu Enterprises, Inc., 2012), 24.

67. Joseph Michael McDowell, and Mary Creigh McDowell, "The McDowell Family History: Scotland to Franklin County, PA, 1680–2011," unpublished paper dated 2001. Mary also mentions John McDowell as an early member of the Franklin County Bar. *Pennsylvania Archives*, Fifth Series, 3:200–206. Mercer graduated from the School of Medicine of Marshall College in Scotland.

68. Letter "Governor Morris in Philadelphia to Captain Steel, March 25, 1756," in *Pennsylvania Archives*, ser. 1, vol. 2, 601; and Frederic A. Godcharles, "Fort at McDowell's Mill," *Public Opinion* (originally published 1924 reprinted Friday June 18, 1976), 58.

69. Rupp, 101–104.

70. J. Pritts, *Incidents of Border Life* (Lancaster, Pennsylvania: G. Hills, 1841), 123–124.

71. Bates, 169.

72. See Webpage: Jim Wilks, Sidelinghill.pbworks.com/w/page/9500697/Battle%20 Narrative, 2009.

73. Bates, 169; and Rupp, 104.

74. Letter "Steel from Peters Township to Governor Morris, April 11, 1756, and April 17, 1756" as per Rupp, 105; and Woman's Club of Mercersburg, 8–9.

75. Letter from "Captain Burd to Governor Morris, April 19, 1756," in Rupp, 393–394.

76. Bates, 170; and Hunter, 431.

77. Hunter, V.

78. The third generation of McDowell children married the children of the Davies and Maxwells as well as Presbyterian clergy.

79. Archer Butler Hulbert, *Historic Highways of America, Volume V: The Old Glade (Forbes's) Road* (Cleveland, Ohio: The Arthur H. Clark Company, 1903), 57.

80. Hunter, 195; and Letter "Peters to the Proprietors, February 23, 1756," in the Gratz Collections, Peters Lutter Book; and letter "Morris orders to Captain John Potter, Mar 25, 1756," *Pennsylvania Archives*, First Series, 2:602.

81. Bates, 91–91.

82. Hunter, 431.

83. Letter from "Commissary Young at Carlisle, July 22, 1756," as per Rupp, 394–395.

84. The McCullough father's name is listed as Casper by Glen L. Cump, "A Disquisition Portraying the History Relative to the Enoch Brown Incident" on www.greencastlemuseum.org/Local_History/enoch.htm.

85. Votes of the Assembly, iv, 504, as per Rupp, 119.

86. Letter from the "Inhabitants of Cumberland County to the Governor, read in council August 21, 1756," as per Rupp, 120.

87. Letter from "Commissary Young at Carlisle, July 22, 1756," as per Rupp, 394–395; and Cort, Cyrus, *Memorial of Enoch Brown and Eleven Scholars who were Massacred in Antrim Township, Franklin County, Pa. by the Indians During the Pontiac War, July 26, 1764* (Lancaster, Pennsylvania: Steiman Hensel, printers, 1886, 2009 printing), 2. Also see J. Pritts, *Incidents of Border life*, 87–114.

J. Pritts, 87; and Cort, *Fort McDowell*, 15–16.

88. Letter "Hance Hamilton to Col John Armstrong at Carlisle, August 19, 1756," in Rupp, 115.

89. Letter from "John Armstrong at Carlisle to the Governor, August 20, 1756," in Provincial Record P., 10–12, as per Rupp, 116–118. Also in Provincial Record, P12 Printed CR, VII, 233, as per Hunter, 433; and Colonial Records, 231; and as per Etter, 11.

90. Archibald Loudon, *A Selection of Some of the Most Interesting Narratives, or the Outrages Committed by the Indians in their Wars*, Vol. 1 (Harrisburg: Harrisburg Publishing Co., 1811), 195.

91. Loudon, 195; and Bates, 170.

92. Letter from "Thomas Barton at Reading Township to the Governor, August 21, 1756," as per Rupp, 123.

93. Rupp, 110.

94. Pritts, 72, 124.

95. Bates, 93.

96. Letter "Colonel John Armstrong, Expedition to Kittaning, from Fort Littleton, September 14, 1756," in *Pennsylvania Archives*, First Series, 2:767–775.

97. I. H. McCauley, *Historical Sketch of Franklin County, Pennsylvania* (Chambersburg: D. F. Pursel, 1878), 67–68.

98. Hunter, 428–430. Letter "Morris to Steel and Burd et all," *Pennsylvania Archives*, ser. 1, vol. 2, 601–602, as per Hunter, 369.

99. Provincial Record P., 20, as per Rupp, 122.

100. Letter "James Young to Harris's Ferry, October 17, 1756," in *Pennsylvania Archives*, First Series, 3:12.

101. Frederic A. Godcharles, "Fort at McDowell's Mill," *Public Opinion* (originally published 1924 reprinted Friday June 18, 1976), 58. Also see Hunter, 434, and Cort, *Fort McDowell*, 17.

102. *Pennsylvania Archives*, Second Series, 2:459–460.

103. Letter "Colonel John Armstrong in Carlisle to Governor William Denny, November 8, 1756," *Pennsylvania Archives*, First Series, 3:40.

104. Letter "Colonel John Armstrong in Carlisle to Governor William Denny, November 11, 1756," in *Pennsylvania Archives*, First Series, 3:48–49.

105. Letter "Colonel John Armstrong in Carlisle to Governor Denny, November 12, 1756," *Pennsylvania Archives*, First Series, 3:51.

106. Letter "Col. John Armstrong to Governor Denny November 15, 1756," in *Pennsylvania Archives*, First Series, 3:55.
107. Letter "Colonel John Armstrong at Fort Morris to Governor Denny, November 21, 1756," *Pennsylvania Archives*, First Series, 3:25.
108. *Pennsylvania Archives*, First Series, 3:144–145.
109. Letter "Colonel John Armstrong at Carlisle to Governor Denny, November 30, 1756," in *Pennsylvania Archives*, First Series, 2:78.
110. Letter "Colonel John Armstrong to Governor Denny November 19, 1756," in *Pennsylvania Archives*, Second Series, 3:58.
111. Letter "Colonel John Armstrong to Governor Denny, December 22, 1756," in *Pennsylvania Archives*, First Series, 3:83.

CHAPTER SIX

1. Letter from "Captain Schmitt at McDowell's Mill Fort to Weiser, March 21, 1751," as per William A. Hunter, *Forts on the Pennsylvania Frontier, 1753–1758* (Harrisburg, Pennsylvania: The Pennsylvania Historical and Museum Commission, 1960), 371.
2. The regimental list of 1st Battalion in *Pennsylvania Archives*, First Series, 3:88.
3. Hunter, 433–434.
4. Archibald Loudon, *A Selection of Some of the Most Interesting Narratives, or the Outrages Committed by the Indians in their Wars . . .* , vol. 1 (Harrisburg: Harrisburg Publishing Co., 1811), 195; and *The Pennsylvania Gazette*, April 7, 1757, as per Israel Daniel Rupp, *The History and Topography of Dauphin, Cumberland, Franklin, Bedford, Adams, and Perry Counties [Pennsylvania* (Lancaster, Pennsylvania: Gilbert Hills, Proprietor and Publisher, 1846.), 128.
5. Rupp, 128.
6. Hunter, 208.
7. Seilhamer, Goerge O., Esq., "Early School Girls of the Conococheague," *Papers Read before the Society* (Chambersburg: The Kittochtinny Historical Society, March 1905–February 1908), 72–80.
8. Rupp, 129.
9. Letter from "John Armstrong at Carlisle to the Governor, July 11, 1757," as per Rupp, 133–134.
10. Ibid.
11. Letter "Colonel John Armstrong in Carlisle to Governor Denny, July 25, 1757" in *Pennsylvania Archives*, First Series, 3:239–244.
12. Rupp, 130.
13. *Pennsylvania Gazette*, September 1, 1757, as per Rupp, 131.
14. Rupp, 131–132.
15. Rupp, 130.
16. Rupp, 133.
17. Bates, 93, 94.

18. Loudon, 47.

19. Cyrus Cort, *Fort McDowell: Monument Dedication Service* (Union Bridge, Maryland: Monument Dedication Service, 1916), 10.

20. *Pennsylvania Archives*, Fifth Series, 1:130–131. The ensign rank in the army was abolished in 1815 but is still in the navy. The ensign as a junior officer carried the colors (flag), assisted the Captain and Lieutenant and had their authority when they were not present.

21. Burton K. Kummerow, Christine H. O'Toole, and R. Scott Stepheson, *Pennsylvania's Forbes Trail: Gateways and Getaways along the Legendary Route from Philadelphia to Pittsburg* (New York: Taylor Trade Publishing, 2008), French and Indian War Commemoration, 46.

22. Kummerow, 45.

23. Kummerow, 73.

24. Samuel Vaughan, *Samuel Vaughan's Diary, 1787–1796* (Washington, D.C.: Manuscript Division, only copy) or see Edward G. Williams, ed., *Minutes Made by s.v., from Stage to Stage, on a Tour to Fort Pitt, Part II from Carlisle to Pittsburgh,* 159, available on Open Journal Systems: journals.psu.edu/wph/article/download/1884/1732. Samuel Vaughan, a man of commerce traveled to Fort Pitt shortly after the Revolutionary War making notes about the roads, farms and other features on his journey.

25. Kummerow, 147.

26. Archer Butler Hulbert, *Historic Highways of America, Volume V: The Old Glade (Forbes's) Road* (Cleveland, Ohio: The Arthur H. Clark Company, 1903), 10.

27. Virginia Shannon Fendrick, *American Revolutionary Soldiers of Franklin County Pennsylvania* (Chambersburg: Daughters of the American Revolution, 1944), 175.

CHAPTER SEVEN

1. J. Pritts, *Incidents of Border Life* (Lancaster, Pennsylvania: G. Hills, 1841), 60–61. Later Smith accepted an ensign's commission in the regular army under King George in the Pennsylvania Line.

2. Ibid., 61.

3. Rupp, Israel Daniel, *The History and Topography of Dauphin, Cumberland, Franklin, Bedford, Adams, and Perry Counties* [*Pennsylvania* (Lancaster, Pennsylvania: Gilbert Hills, Proprietor and Publisher, 1846.), 136.

4. Rupp, 158.

5. Rupp, 159–160.

6. Unpublished Letter "Nathan McDowell in Lancaster County to brother James McDowell near Fort Loudon, April 6, 1761," as per Joseph Michael McDowell, and Mary Creigh McDowell, "The McDowell Family History: Scotland to Franklin County, PA, 1680–2011," unpublished paper dated 2001.

7. Bates, Samuel Penniman, Fraise, Jacob, and Beers, Warner, *History of Franklin County, Pennsylvania, Containing a History of the County, its Townships* (Chicago:

Warner, Beers and Company, 1887), 216; and Woman's Club of Mercersburg, "Old Mercersburg, Pennsylvania," *The Journal of American History*, 1913 (reprint Saltville, Virginia, Jeffrey C. Weaver, 2005), 13.

8. Bates, 97.

9. Bates, 171–172.

10. Cyrus Cort, *Fort McDowell: Monument Dedication Service* (Union Bridge, Maryland: Monument Dedication Service, 1916), 19.

11. Elizabeth A. Fenn, "Biological Warfare in Eighteenth-Century North America: Beyond Jeffery Amherst," www. politicsandthelifeschiences.org/Biosecurity. course.folder/readings/fenn.html.

12. Bates, 94.

13. Rupp, 138; and James G. Leyburn, *The Scotch-Irish: A Social History* (Chapel Hill: The University of North Carolina Press, 1962), 229–230.

14. Letter "Col. Henry Bouquet from Carlisle to Governor James Hamilton, July 2, 1763," in Sylvester K. Stevens, and Donald H. Kent editors, *The Papers of Col. Henry Bouquet*, Series 21649, Part I: Northwestern Pennsylvania Historical Series, Frontier Forts and Trails Survey (Harrisburg: Pennsylvania Historical Commission, 1942), 186–189.

15. Cyrus Cort, 10.

16. Letter from "Henry Bouquet at Carlisle to Governor Hamilton, July 3, 1763," as per Rupp, 145. Also see Votes of the Assembly, October 21, 1765, vol. 5, 285, and Provincial Records S, 379. Letter "Colonel Henry Bouquet from Fort Loudon to Governor James Hamilton, July 19, 1763," in Stevens, Sylvester K and Kent, Donald H. editors, *The Papers of Col. Henry Bouquet*, Series 21649, Part I: Northwestern Pennsylvania Historical Series, Frontier Forts and Trails Survey (Harrisburg: Pennsylvania Historical Commission, 1942), 237.

17. Rupp, 147.

18. Edward G. Williams, *The Orderly Book of Colonel Henry Bouquet's Expedition against the Ohio Indians, 1764* (Pittsburgh, Mayer Press, 1960), 7.

19. Rupp, 401.

20. Letter from "Carlisle (unnamed) dated July 12, 1763," published in the *Pennsylvania Gazette* in Rupp, 139.

21. Rupp, 139–141.

22. Rupp, 141–142.

23. Votes of the Assembly, vol. 5, 264, September 17, 1763.

24. Bates, 515; and Etter, Eugene, *History of Lemasters, Pennsylvania: Local History in and around Lemasters, Southern Franklin County on the Occasion of Their Centennial Celebration* (Chambersburg, Pennsylvania: Robson & Kaye, Inc., Printers, 1972), 9.

25. Letter from "Jonas Seely, Esq. at Reading, September 11, 1763", as per Rupp, 143.

26. Ibid.

27. Rupp, 144.

28. Rupp, 145.
29. Pritts, 61.
30. Ibid, 63.
31. *Colonial Records: Minutes of the Provincial Council of Pennsylvania from the Organization to the Termination of the Proprietary Government Vol. 9 (October 15, 1762–October 17, 1771)*, (Harrisburg: Theodore Fenn & Company printer, 1852), 62.
32. Ibid, 63.
33. Russell Bourne, *Gods of War, Gods of Peace: How the Meeting of Native and Colonial Religions Shaped Early America* (New York: Harcourt, Inc., 2002), 251.
34. Rupp, 165–167.
35. *Colonial Records: Minutes of the Provincial Council of Pennsylvania from the Organization to the Termination of the Proprietary Government Vol. 9 (October 15, 1762–October 17, 1771)*, (Harrisburg: Theodore Fenn & Company printer, 1852), 103–104.
36. Bates, 97.
37. Rupp, 171–172.
38. Letter "Colonel John Armstrong at Carlisle to Governor, December 14, 1763," in *Pennsylvania Archives*, First Series, 4:146–147.
39. Rupp, 427.
40. Letter "Colonel John Armstrong at Carlisle to Governor Penn, June 6, 1764" in *Pennsylvania Archives*, First Series, 4:175–176.
41. See Louis M. Waddell, ed., *The Papers of Henry Bouquet, Vol. VI: Selected Documents, November 1761–July 1765; with a Catalogue of Bouquet Papers from November 1761 to June 1767* (Harrisburg: Pennsylvania Historical and Museum Commission, 1994), 505; and Gary T. Hawbaker, *Fort Loudon on the Frontier* (Hershey, Pennsylvania, 1976), 20–30.
42. Etter, 12.
43. Glen L. Cump, Secretary of the Enoch Brown Park Association in an address dated August 1, 1992 and titled "A Disquisition Portraying the History Relative to the Enoch Brown Incident" on www.greencastlemuseum.org/Local_History/enoch.htm.
44. See Glen L. Cump; Rupp, 150–151; and Bates, 172–173, 296–303. Enoch, in the Bible, did not see death but was taken by God (Genesis 5:24). Also see McCauley, 65, 230; George O. Seilhamer, Esq., "Early School Girls of the Conococheague," *Papers Read Before the Kittochtinny Historical Society from March 1905, to February 1908* (Chambersburg, Pennsylvania: The Kittochtinny Historical Society, 1908), 73; and David Dixon, *Never Come to Peace Again: Pontiac's Uprising and the Fate of the British Empire in North America* (Norman, Oklahoma: University of Oklahoma Press, 2005), 223–224.

Andrew Brown Rankin, Esq. wrote a letter about his participation in exhuming the mass grave which is recorded in Rupp, 150–151. He was Justice of the Peace in Antrim and Greencastle and his maternal grandfather, Ann Brown Rankin's father, was cousin to Enoch Brown. Ann was born in Ulster, Northern Ireland and settled in Mercersburg, Pennsylvania, when she was a child. Enoch may have also been related to George Brown, miller. Andrew Rankin's son, Andrew, Jr., Esq., would later marry Elizabeth McDowell, a descendant of Justice William McDowell. These Rankins, Browns and McDowells are ancestors of the author.

45. Some reports list them as two old Indians and one young one.
46. Rupp, 148–149.
47. David Dixon in his book mentions him being shot in the chest, 223.
48. Some state one Indian.
49. McCauley, I. H., *Historical Sketch of Franklin County, Pennsylvania* (Chambersburg: D. F. Pursel, 1878), 230–231.
50. Bates, 172–174. Richard Bard, Esq. was taken captive by the Indians on April 13, 1758. He also mentions the Enoch Brown Incident in Pritts, *Incidents of Border Life*, 122; also see McCauley, 232.
51. Cyrus Cort, *Memorial of Enoch Brown and Eleven Scholars who were Massacred in Antrim Township, Franklin County, Pa. by the Indians During the Pontiac War, July 26, 1764* (Lancaster, Pennsylvania: Seiman Hensel, Printers, 1886), 3–12. The bodies were found on August 4, 1843, and re-buried with a monument over them in what is now Enoch Brown State Park. School children and teachers contributed a dime each for the memorial.
52. Cyrus Cort, 2. John McCullough was captive at the camp when the scalps of the teacher and children were presented by the raiding party. He testified that Night Walker and other elders denounced the act and called them cowards.
53. Bates, 172.
54. Bates, 421–424, and McCauley, 65.
55. Bates, 561.
56. Bates, 561.
57. Letter "Duke of Halifax at St. James's to Governor Penn, August 11, 1764," in *Pennsylvania Archives*, First Series, 4:202.
58. Letter "Duke of Halifax at St. James's to Governor Penn, August 11, 1764," *Pennsylvania Archives*, First Series, 4:202–203.
59. Letter from "Henry Bouquet to Governor Penn, August 22, 1764," in Rupp, 152.
60. Rupp, 402–403.

CHAPTER EIGHT

1. Dan Guzy, *The Black Boys Uprising of 1765: Traders, Troops & "Rioters" during Pontiac's War* (Mercersburg: The Conococheaque Institute, 2014), 48–60.
2. *Colonial Records*, 269.
3. "Justice William McDowell's Receipt for Guns Captured, 1765," in *Pennsylvania Archives*, First Series, 4:245.
4. "Obligation Jona. Smith, & C. 1765" in *Pennsylvania Archives*, First Series, 4:246.
5. Letter "Lieutenant Charles Grant to Colonel John Reid, 1765," *Pennsylvania Archives*, First Series, 4:246–247.

Notes

6. "Passes used by William and James Smith, 1765," in *Pennsylvania Archives*, First Series, 4:219–220.

7. Letter "Sir William Johnson at Johnson Hall to Governor Penn, April 12, 1765," in *Pennsylvania Archives*, First Series, 4:215–216.

8. *Pennsylvania Archives*, Fourth Series, 3:310–315.

9. Bates, 99.

10. Bates, 100.

11. McCauley, 144.

12. Woman's Club of Mercersburg, 15–16.

13. The church would later construct a simple building in Mercersburg in 1794.

14. Fendrick, Virginia Shannon, *American Revolutionary Soldiers of Franklin County Pennsylvania* (Chambersburg: Daughters of the American Revolution, 1944), 174.

15. Pritts, 66.

16. McCauley, 64.

17. Pritts, 64.

CHAPTER NINE

1. Samuel Penniman Bates, Jacob Fraise, and Warner Beers, *History of Franklin County, Pennsylvania, Containing a History of the County, its Townships.*, 100–101.

2. Stillé, Charles J., *Major-General Anthony Wayne and the Pennsylvania Line in the Continental Army* (Philadelphia: J. B. Lippincott Company, 1893), 13.

3. Bates, 176; and I. H. McCauley, *Historical Sketch of Franklin County, Pennsylvania* (Chambersburg: D. F. Pursel, 1878), 22.

4. A "Letter from Carlisle dated May 6th, 1775," in the *American Archives*, 2:516, as per McCauley, 22; and Bates, 179.

5. McCauley, I. H., *Historical Sketch of Franklin County, Pennsylvania* (Chambersburg: D. F. Pursel, 1878), 23–24.

6. Eugene Etter, *History of Lemasters Pennsylvania: Local History in and Around Lemasters, Southern Franklin County on the Occasion of their Centennial Celebration* (Chambersburg: Robson & Kaye, Inc., 1972), 15.

7. Alfred Nevin, *Men of Mark of Cumberland Valley, PA: 1776–1876* (Philadelphia: Fulton Publishing Company, 1876), 45–46; and in Etter, 16.

8. A Letter "Col. Irvine at Carlisle to John Hancock, President of Congress, on March 22, 1776," in the *Pennsylvania Archives*, Second Series, 10:167.

9. Stillé, 28.

10. Stillé, 53.

11. Stillé, 43.

12. Captain Grier's Company is listed in the *Pennsylvania Archives*, Second Series, 10:172–177. The privates in this company included William Anguis, Patrick Barnes, George Baker, Ebenezer Bacheldor, James Barry, Robert Beard, John Brian, Archibald Campbell, John Clemmonds, Adam Conn, George Conner, Charles Conway, George Cooper, Cornelius Corrigan, David Davis, Thomas Dulany, John Dorcel Deis,

Charles Dougherty, John Dougherty, Alexander Esson, John Falkner, John Frick, Robert Forsyth, Joseph Geddes, Peter Grant, Charles Guscager, Charles Gyfinger, James Harkins, Edward Hickenbottom, Isaac Hodge, Thomas Hoy, Archibald Jackson, Robert Johnston, William Johnston, George Kelly, Thomas Kelly, James Leeson, William Mason, Jacob Mathews, John McCall, William McCoy, John McDaniel, Samuel McGowan, Henry McKissack, Michael McMeehan, James McMullan, Lawrence Mealy, Michael Murphy, Patrick O'Loan, Peter O'Neil, John Pearcy, James Price, William Quigley, Murtough Redmond, James Robinson, Patrick Roney, Joseph Russell, Patrick Scullion, Peter Sehregh, Archibald Shaw, Francis Standley, Philip Shive, Michael Schultz, Peter Seidle, John Schneider, Edward Spencer, James Stevenson, Baltzer Swank, George Swartz, Peter Swartz, John Taylor, Jacob Trees, Joseph Wade, Adam Weaverlling, Edward Welch, Isaac White, William Wilkinson, Joseph Wilson, George Worley, and Matthias Wright.

    13. Bates, 179.

    14. *Pennsylvania Archives*, Second Series, 10:414.

    15. Justice McDowell's son William, Jr., recorded in his Lieutenant's book mandatory training of doctors in his unit led by trained physicians during the southern campaign. William McDowell, "Journal of Lieut. William McDowell of the First Penn'A Regiment, in the Southern Campaign, 1781–1782," *Pennsylvania Archives*, Second Series, 15:295–340.

    16. George Washington ordered the inoculation of his troops in February of 1777 as per the Jamestown-Yorktown Foundation, *Colonial Medicine* (Williamsburg, Virginia: 1992), 7–8.

    17. William McDowell, 295–340.

    18. See Captain John Steele, http://pasocietyofthecincinati.org/Names/JohnSteele,html. The Society of the Cincinati was formed in Philadelphia on October 4, 1783 with President Major-General St. Clair, Vice President Brigadier-General Wayne, Treasurer Brigadier-General Irvine, Vice Treasurer Colonel Johnston, and Secretary Lieutenant-Colonel Harmer. John Steel was an original member as was William McDowell. President George Washington was an honorary President. Cincinati was a Roman general who saved the Roman Empire.

    19. Letter of the "Council of Safety, Philadelphia to County Committees, January 13, 1777," in *Pennsylvania Archives*, First Series, 5:176.

    20. J. Pritts, *Incidents of Border Life* (Lancaster, Pennsylvania: G. Hills, 1841), 72.

    21. Woman's Club of Mercersburg, "Old Mercersburg, Pennsylvania", *The Journal of American History*, 1913 (reprint Saltville, Virginia, Jeffrey C. Weaver, 2005), 13–14.

    22. McCauley, 36.

    23. Stillé, 249.

    24. Ibid., 22.

    25. Letter "Major-General John Armstrong at Carlisle to President Warton, April 13, 1778" in *Pennsylvania Archives*, First Series, 6:412–414; and "April 2, 1778,

complaint to Major-General Armstrong from concerned members of Peter's Township, April 2, 1778," in *Pennsylvania Archives*, Second Series, 3:150.

26. Letter "Alexander McDowell to Vice President Bryan, June 1, 1778" in *Pennsylvania Archives*, First Series, 6:572.

27. Israel Daniel Rupp, *The History and Topography of Dauphin, Cumberland, Franklin, Bedford, Adams, and Perry Counties* [*Pennsylvania* (Lancaster, Pennsylvania: Gilbert Hills, Proprietor and Publisher, 1846.), 152–153.

28. Rupp, 155.

29. Letter "General Wayne to the Board of War, Camp at Mount Prospect, June 3, 1777", in Stillé, 64–65.

30. Letter "General Armstrong to President Wharton August 28, 29, 1777," in *Pennsylvania Archives*, First Series, 5:558, 563–4; "Council to General Armstrong February 6, 1778," in *Pennsylvania Archives*, series 1, vol. 6, 238; and "The Council to General Anthony Wayne December 12, 1777," in *Pennsylvania Archives*, First Series, 6:86–87.

31. William McDowell, 324.

32. Bates, 180.

33. Stillé, 130.

34. *Pennsylvania Archives*, First Series, 6:372.

35. Letter "Colonel James Potter from Penns Valley to Major-General Armstrong at Carlise, May 17, 1778" and "Samuel Hunter from Fort Augusta to John Hambright, Esq., Member of the Supreme Executive Council in Lancaster, May 31, 1778," in *Pennsylvania Archives*, First Series, 6:86–90. Also see Arthur Buchanan at Kishacoquilles to Lieutenant John Carothers of Cumberland County, *Pennsylvania Archives*, First Series, 6:487.

36. Letter "General Armstrong at Carlise to Congress, 1778," *Pennsylvania Archives*, First Series, 6:599.

37. Stillé, 158.

38. Stillé, 165.

39. Letter "John Armstrong at Carlisle to President Reed, November 27, 1779," *Pennsylvania Archives*, First Series, 7:31–32.

40. Letter "Abraham Smith at Cumberland County to Joseph Reid, Esq., August 7, 1780," as per Rupp, 155–156.

41. Bates, 174.

42. Pritts, J., *Incidents of Border Life* (Lancaster, Pennsylvania: G. Hills, 1841). 260–261.

43. *Pennsylvania Archives*, Second Series, 3:333, 356.

44. "Overview of Pennsylvania History" on www.portal.state.pa.us/portal/server.pt/community/overview_of_pennsylvania_history/4281/1681–1776.

45. *Pennsylvania Archives*, Third Series, 20:216, 351, 477, 634; and Thomas Creigh, *History of the Presbyterian Church of Upper West Conococheague: Now Mercersburg, Franklin County, Pennsylvania* (Chambersburg: Repository Printer, 1877),

CPSIA reproduction 2016, 85. Also see Magdelena Radovic-Moreno, *Mercersburg's "Little Africa:" Free African American Communities of Franklin County and the Underground Railroad* posted 2015 on franklincountypa.gov/index.php?section=archives_blog/littleafrica for a better understanding of the African American community in Franklin County.

    46. Virginia Shannon Fendrick, *American Revolutionary Soldiers of Franklin County Pennsylvania* (Chambersburg: Daughters of the American Revolution, 1944), 175.

    47. Eugene Etter, *History of Lemasters, Pennsylvania: Local History in and around Lemasters, Southern Franklin County on the Occasion of Their Centennial Celebration* (Chambersburg, Pennsylvania: Robson & Kaye, Inc., Printers, 1972), 17; and John Appel's *Light of Parnell* (Philadelphia: The Heidelburg Press, 1916), 18, 49, 56.

    48. Magdelena Radovic-Moreno webpage.
    49. McDowell, 295–340.
    50. Stillé, 244.
    51. McDowell, 298–302.
    52. Ibid., 303–305.
    53. *Pennsylvania Archives*, First Series, 9:355–356.
    54. Stillé, 286–287.
    55. Stillé, 296–297.
    56. Letter "General Wayne to General Irvine, Waynesborough, 18 May 1784" in Stillé, 296–297.
    57. The McDowell family is listed in the Peters Township Taxables of 1781.
    58. Bates, 193, 200.

CHAPTER TEN

    1. Virginia Shannon Fendrick, *American Revolutionary Soldiers of Franklin County, Pennsylvania* (Chambersburg: Daughters of the American Revolution, 1944), 173; Pennsylvania Genealogy Trails: "History of Venango County, PA" transcribed by Nancy Piper on www.genealogytrails.com/penn/ venango/history/index.html; and Donald H. Kent and Merle H. Deardorff, "John Adlum on the Allegheny: Memoirs for the Year 1794, Part I" in *The Pennsylvania Magazine of History and Biography*, July 1960, 265 and following.

    2. *Pennsylvania Archives*, First Series, 10:217–218.
    3. *Pennsylvania Archives*, First Series, 10:325–326.
    4. Charles J. Stillé, *Major-General Anthony Wayne and the Pennsylvania Line in the Continental Army* (Philadelphia: J. B. Lippincott Company, 1893), 320–321.
    5. Stillé, 338.
    6. Bates, Samuel Penniman, Fraise, Jacob, and Beers, Warner, *History of Franklin County, Pennsylvania, Containing a History of the County, its Townships* . . . (Chicago: Warner, Beers and Company, 1887), 216; and Woman's Club of Mercersburg, "Old Mercersburg, Pennsylvania," *The Journal of American History*, 1913 (reprint Saltville, Virginia, Jeffrey C. Weaver, 2005), 112.

Notes

7. *Pennsylvania Archives*, Second Series, 3:220, 221, 294.

8. Bates, 403.

9. *Pennsylvania Archives*, Fourth Series, 4:288–310; and Bates, 191.

10. Eugene Etter, *History of Lemasters, Pennsylvania: Local History in and around Lemasters, Southern Franklin County on the Occasion of Their Centennial Celebration* (Chambersburg, Pennsylvania: Robson & Kaye, Inc., Printers, 1972), 13–14.

11. "Flood Damages Property on West Conococheague," *The Centinel*, November 21, 1810.

12. *Pennsylvania Archives*, Second Series, 12:48, 49, 223, 404; and Bates, 236, 244.

13. Woman's Club of Mercersburg, "Old Mercersburg, Pennsylvania", *The Journal of American History*, 1913 (reprint Saltville, Virginia, Jeffrey C. Weaver, 2005), 15.

14. Etter, 13.

15. Israel Daniel Rupp, *The History and Topography of Dauphin, Cumberland, Franklin, Bedford, Adams, and Perry Counties [Pennsylvania]* (Lancaster, Pennsylvania: Gilbert Hills, Proprietor and Publisher, 1846.), 483.

16. Etter, 13.

17. Oliver Evans, *Young Mill-Wright and Miller's Guide* (Philidelphia: Printed by the author, 1795) wrote a book which was filled with great detail of work on the function of gravity on hydraulics. It shows the evolution in scientific thinking about mill work and gives time saving solutions.

18. Harry Foreman, *History of Little Cove of Franklin County Pennsylvania* (Chambersburg: Kerr Printing Company, 1967).

19. Fulling involved pounding woolen cloth to mat the fibers together.

20. Etter, 14; and Rupp, 483. Little was known about the place of worship in Markes as per I. H. McCauley, *Historical Sketch of Franklin County, Pennsylvania* (Chambersburg: D. F. Pursel, 1878), 141.

21. J. Fraise Richard, *History of Franklin County, Pennsylvania* (1887), 573.

22. Jay Gilfillan Weiser, *The Frontier Forts in the Cumberland and Juniata Valleys*, Volume I (State of Pennsylvania, Clarence M. Busch Publisher, 1896), 545–549. Though the fort was not present during the Mexican War (1846–1848), the mill was and Franklin County men enlisted in the wake of the annexation of Texas in 1845. Thirteen years later the militia respond to Lincoln's call for troops following the fall of Fort Sumter in 1861. Descendants of the original Ulster-Scots and Germans in Franklin County served as Union officers and enlisted men. The county suffered three Confederate raids: J.E.B. Steward Raid of October 19, 1862; General Robert E. Lee invasion of July 1864; and McCausland's Invasion with the burning of Chambersburg in 1864. It was the only northern town to be destroyed during the Civil War.

23. Etter, 13–14. Also see Frederic A. Godcharles, "Fort at McDowell's Mill," *Public Opinion* (originally published 1924 and reprinted Friday June 18, 1976), 56–58. Also see John W. Thompson, *Historic Views of Old Mercersburg: the Jewel box of Franklin County* (Mercersburg Printing, 2000), 204–207.

24. The location of the markers is at the intersection of Lemar Road and Mercersburg Road in Markes, Peters Township, Franklin County, Pennsylvania. For details on the installation service for the 1916 stone marker, see Cyrus Cort, *Fort McDowell: Monument Dedicatory Service* (Union Bridge, Maryland: 1916).

APPENDIX A

1. This incomplete genealogy attempts to follow the pioneer William McDowell's children and grandchildren. Providing a correct genealogy for this family is complex because there are many lists with conflicting information. This is not authoritative but gives the reader a general sense of how the family was related to others in the Cumberland Valley and how they were tied to Pennsylvania History. This genealogy is based largely on ones provided by Joseph Michael McDowell and written by Mary Creigh McDowell, "The McDowell Family History: Scotland to Franklin County, PA, 1680–2011," unpublished paper dated 2001; *Biographical Annals of Franklin County, Pennsylvania: Containing Genealogical Records of Representative Families, Including Many of the Early Settlers, and Biographical Sketches of Prominent Citizens* (Chicago, The Genealogical Publishing Company, 1905), 80–91; Virginia Shannon Fendrick, *American Revolutionary Soldiers of Franklin County Pennsylvania* (Chambersburg: Daughters of the American Revolution, 1944), 173–175; Sidney Nill, *Our Conococheague Settlement 1732–1782* (Chambersburg: Franklin county Chapter of the Daughters of the American Revolution, 1971 reprint); Cyrus Cort, *Fort McDowell: Monument Dedicatory Service* (Union Bridge, Maryland: 1916); George O. Seilhamer, Esq., "Early School Girls of the Conococheague," in *Papers Read Before the Society from March 1905 to February 1908* Volume 5 (Chambersburg: The Kittochtinny Historical Society), 72–80; *Marriages West Conococheague Presbyterian Church, 1769–1812*; and the grave stones at Spring Grove Cemetery, Lemasters, Pennsylvania. Also see abstracted records by Mrs. H. Virginia Gress Smith of the Upper West Conococheague Presbyterian Church Records, Mercersburg, Pennsylvania, deaths (recorded in 1985 from original documents) on www.fendrick library.org/Deaths%20part%20 1%201770.pdf.

Some references list pioneer William's birth in 1680 but most point to 1682 and his grave lists that date.

Bibliography

Albert, George Dallas, *Report of the Commission to Locate the Site of the Frontier Forts of Pennsylvania, Volume 2* (Clarence M. Buch, State Printer of Pennsylvania, 1896).

Appel, John, *The Light of Parnell* (Philadelphia: The Heidelberg Press, 1916).

Balch, Thomas, ed., *Letters and Papers Relating Chiefly to the Provincial History of Pennsylvania, with some Notices of the Writers* (Philadelphia: Crissy and Markley, Printers, 1855).

Bates, Samuel Penniman, Jacob Fraise, and Warner Beers, *History of Franklin County, Pennsylvania, Containing a History of the County, its Townships, Towns, Villages, Schools, Churches, Industries, Etc; Portraits of Early Settlers and Prominent Men; Biographies; History of Pennsylvania, Statistical and Miscellaneous Matter, etc.* (Chicago: Warner, Beers and Company, 1887).

Bourne, Russell, *Gods of War, Gods of Peace: How the Meeting of Native and Colonial Religions Shaped Early America* (New York: Harcourt, Inc., 2002).

Bricker, Jr., Calvin E., "Notes on the Early History Along the Conococheague Creek in Antrim Township, Franklin County, Pennsylvania," March 25, 1998 (unpublished paper).

Buckalew, John M., *The Frontier Forts within the North and West Branches of the Susquehanna River, Pennsylvania: A Report of the State Commission Appointed to Mark the Forts Erected Against the Indians Prior to 1783* (Wyoming Historical and Genealogical Society, 1895).

Butler, Jon, *Religion in Colonial America* (New York: Oxford University Press, 2000).

Chernow, Ron *Washington: a Life*, (New York: The Penguin Press, 2010).

Colonial Records: Minutes of the Provincial Council of Pennsylvania, from the Organization to the Termination of the Proprietary Government, Vol. 6

(February 7, 1735–6 to October 15, 1745) and *Vol. 9 (October 15, 1762–October 17, 1771)* (Harrisburg: Theodore Fenn & Company Printer, 1851 and 1852).

Cort, Cyrus, *Fort McDowell: Monument Dedicatory Service* (Union Bridge, Maryland: 1916).

———. *Memorial of Enoch Brown and Eleven Scholars who were Massacred in Antrim Township, Franklin County, Pa. by the Indians During the Pontiac War, July 26, 1764* (Lancaster, Pennsylvania: Steiman Hensel, printers, 1886, 2009 printing).

Cort, Cyrus, and William Smith, *Bouquet and the Ohio Indian War: Two Accounts of the Campaigns of 1763–1764, "Bouquet's Campaigns" by Cyrus Cort (1883) and William Smith's The History of Bouquet's Expeditions (1765)*, (Leonaur, Ohio: Ohio Historical Society, 2008).

Creigh, Thomas, *History of the Presbyterian Church of Upper West Conococheague: Now Mercersburg, Franklin County, Pennsylvania* (Chambersburg: Repository Printer, 1877), CPSIA reproduction 2016.

Dixon, David, *Never Come to Peace Again: Pontiac's Uprising and the Fate of the British Empire in North America* (Norman, Oklahoma: University of Oklahoma Press, 2005).

Dowd, Gregory Evans, *The Indians of New Jersey* (New Jersey Historical Commission Department of State: Trenton, New Jersey, 2001).

Ellis, Franklin and Samuel Evans, *History of Lancaster County, Pennsylvania with Biographical Sketches of Many of the Prominent Men* (Philadelphia: Everts and Peck, 1883).

Engle, William H., *An Illustrated History of the Commonwealth of Pennsylvania, Civil, Political and Military, from its Earliest Settlement to the Present Time* (Harrisburg, DeWitt C. Goodrich & Co., 1876).

Etter, Eugene, *History of Lemasters, Pennsylvania: Local History in and around Lemasters, Southern Franklin County on the Occasion of Their Centennial Celebration* (Chambersburg, Pennsylvania: Robson & Kaye, Inc., Printers, 1972).

Evans, Oliver, *Young Mill-Wright and Miller's Guide* (Philadelphia: Self-Publish, 1795).

Fendrick, Virginia Shannon, *American Revolutionary Soldiers of Franklin County Pennsylvania* (Chambersburg: Daughters of the American Revolution, 1944).

Bibliography

Fenstermacher, Shirley B. and Margaret L. McDonnell, *Franklin A Frontier Country* (Mercersburg, Pennsylvania: Mercersburg Printing Company, 1975).

Fletcher, Charlotte, "John McDowell, Federalist: President of St. John's College," *The St. John's Review*, Volume XL, Number two (1990–91).

Foreman, Harry, *History of Little Cove of Franklin County Pennsylvania* (Chambersburg: Kerr Printing Company, 1967).

Franklin, Benjamin, William Temple Franklin, and William Duane, *Memoirs of Benjamin Franklin, Volume 1* (Philadelphia: M'Carty and Davis, 1834).

Garrard, L. H., *Chambersburg in the Colony and in the Revolution* (Philadelphia: J.B. Lippincott and Company, 1856)

Godcharles, Frederic A., "Fort at McDowell's Mill" *Public Opinion* (originally published 1924 reprinted Friday June 18, 1976) p. 56–58.

Goldsborough, Charlotte, *John McDowell, Federalist: President of St. John's College* (Maryland Historical Society, 1989).

Gordon, Thomas Francis, *The History of Pennsylvania: From its Discovery by Europeans, to the Declaration of Independence in 1776* (Philadelphia: Jesper Harding, Printer, 1829).

Guzy, Dan, *The Black Boys Uprising of 1765: Traders, Troops & "Rioters" during Pontiac's War* (Mercersburg, Pennsylvania: The Conocoheague Institute, 2014). H

Hamilton, Edward P., *The French and Indian Wars: The Story of Battles and Forts in the Wilderness* (Garden City, New York: Doubleday and Company, Inc., 1962).

Hawbaker, Gary T., Fort Loudon on the Frontier (Hershey, Pennsylvania, 1976).

Hocker, Kris, "The Problem with Owning Land as a German in Colonial Pennsylvania," November 3, 2013 on www.krishocker.com/the-problem-with-owi=ning-land-as-a-german-in-colonial-pennsylvania/.

Hulbert, Archer Butler, *Historic Highways of America, Volume V: The Old Glade (Forbes's) Road* (Cleveland, Ohio: The Arthur H. Clark Company, 1903).

Hunter, William A., "First Line of Defense, 1755–56," *Pennsylvania History*, Volume 22, Number 3, July 1955.

———. *Forts on the Pennsylvania Frontier, 1753–1758* (Harrisburg, Pennsylvania: The Pennsylvania Historical and Museum Commission, 1960).

Jamestown-Yorktown Foundation, *Colonial Medicine* (Williamsburg, Virginia: 1992).

Kent, Donald H. and Merle H. Deardorff, "John Adlum on the Allegheny: Memoirs for the Year 1794: Part I," in *The Pennsylvania Magazine of History and Biography*, July 1960; "Part II," October 1960.

———. "John Adlum on the Allegheny: Memoirs for the Year 1794, Part I" in *The Pennsylvania Magazine of History and Biography*, July 1960, pp. 265 and following.

Kephart, Horace, ed., *Captives Among the Indians: First-hand Narratives of Indian Wars, Customs, Tortures, and Habits of Life in Colonial Times-James Smith and Francesco Giuseppe Bressani and Mary White Rowlandson and Massy Harbison* (New York: Outing Publishing Company, 1915).

Keyser, Naaman Henry, "Old Historic Germantown: an Address with Illustrations Presented at the Fourteenth Annual Meeting of the Pennsylvania-German Society (Lancaster, Pennsylvania, 1906).

Knapp, Samuel L., *Memoirs of General Lafayette; with an Account of his Present Visit to this Country and a Description of His Tour Through the United States; and a Detail of the Arrangements for the Celebration of the 17th June, and Laying the Corner Stone of the Bunker Hill Monument; with a Correct Likeness* (Boston: E. G. House Publisher, 1825).

Kniffen, Fred and Henry Glassie, "Building in Wood in the Eastern United States: a Time-Place Perspective," *Geological Review*, pp. 40–66.

Kummerow, Burton K., Christine H. O'Toole, and R, Scott Stepheson, *Pennsylvania's Forbes Trail: Gateways and Getaways along the Legendary Route from Philadelphia to Pittsburg* (New York: Taylor Trade Publishing, 2008).

Leepson, Marc, *Lafayette: Lessons in Leadership from the Idealist General*, (New York: Macmillan, 2011).

Leyburn, James G., *The Scotch-Irish: a Social History* (Chapel Hill: The University of North Carolina Press, 1962).

Loudon, Archibald, *Loudon's Indian Narratives*, Two Volumes (Carlisle, Pennsylvania: Press of Archibald Loudon, 1808, using the 2007 edition printed in Lewisburg, Pennsylvania by Wenna Woods Publishing).

———. *A Selection of Some of the Most Interesting Narratives, or the Outrages Committed by the Indians in their Wars with the White People: also, an account of their Manners, Customs, Traditions, Religious Sentiments, Mode of*

Warfare, Military Tactics, Discipline and Encampments, Treatment of Prisoners & c, Vol. 1 (Harrisburg: Harrisburg Publishing Co., 1811).

McCardell, Lee, *Ill-Starred General: Braddock of the Coldstream Guards* (Pittsburg: University of Pittsburgh Press, 1986 edition).

McCauley, I. H., *Historical Sketch of Franklin County, Pennsylvania* (Chambersburg: D. F. Pursel, 1878).

McCrum, Robert, William Cran, and Robert MacNeil, *The Story of the English* (New York: Viking Penguin Inc., 1986).

McDowell, Joseph Michael, and Mary Creigh McDowell, "The McDowell Family History: Scotland to Franklin County, PA, 1680–2011," unpublished paper dated 2001.

McDowell, William, "Journal of Lieut. William McDowell of the First Penn'A Regiment, In The Southern Campaign, 1781–1782," *Pennsylvania Archives*, Series 2, XV, pp. 295–340.

McDowell/Maynadier Correspondence Archives, History Collection, Series 1, Box 2, Folder 1–9 at Greenfield Library, St. John's College, Annapolis, Maryland and *John McDowell, LL.D. letters* in the Special Collections of Hornbake Library, University of Maryland.

Myer, James P., "French and Indian War: Brigadier General John Forbes Expedition," *Military History Magazine*, December 2001. Posted on www.historynet.com/french-and-indian-war.

Nevin, Alfred, *Men of Mark of Cumberland Valley, PA: 1776–1876* (Philadelphia: Fulton Publishing Company, 1876)

Nill, Sidney, *Our Conococheague Settlement, 1732–1782* (Chambersburg: Franklin County Chapter of the Daughters of the American Revolution, 1971 edition).

Nixon, Lily Lee and John W. Oliver, *James Burd: Frontier Defender, 1726–1793* (Philadelphia: University of Pennsylvania Press, 1941).

Orr, John G., Esq., "The Three Mountain Road," *Papers, Read Before the Kittochtinny Historical Society from March 1905, to February 1908* (Chambersburg, Pennsylvania: The Kittochtinny Historical Society, 1908).

Patterson, George, *A History of the Cumberland Valley in Pennsylvania* (Harrisburg: Susquehanna History Association, 1930).

Parkman, Francis, *The Conspiracy of Pontiac and the Indian War After the Conquest of Canada, Volume I* (Boston: Harvard University Press, 1851).

Pennsylvania Archives, Hazard, Samuel editor Series I, Vols. 1–7 and 10 (Philadelphia: State Printer, 1852–1853 1855); Linn, John B. and Egle,

William H., editor, Series 2, Vols. 2–3, 10 and 15 (Harrisburg, State Printer, 1896); William H. Egle, editor, Series 4, Vols. 1–3, and 5 (Harrisburg; State Printer, 1900).

Pennsylvania Gazette, February 12 and April 1, 1756, and April 7, 1757.

Pennsylvania Historical Museum Commission, *Report of the Commission to Locate the Site of the Frontier Forts of Pennsylvania* (Harrisburg, Pennsylvania, 1896).

Pritts, J., *Incidents of Border Life* (Lancaster, Pennsylvania: G. Hills, 1841).

Richard, Jacob Fraise and Thomas Henry, *History of Beaver County, Pennsylvania: Including its Early Settlement; Its Erection into a Separate County; Its Subsequent Growth and Development; Sketches of Its Boroughs, Villages and Townships . . . Biographies of Many of Its Representative Citizens, Statistics, etc., Volume 1* (Pittsburgh: University of Pittsburgh, 1999 digital version of the 1888 edition).

Roberts, James A., *New York in the Revolution as Colony and State* (Albnany: Brandow, 1898).

Rupp, Israel Daniel, *The History and Topography of Dauphin, Cumberland, Franklin, Bedford, Adams, and Perry Counties [Pennsylvania]: Containing a Brief History of the First Settlers, Notices of the Leading Events, Incidents and Interesting Facts, Both General and Local, In the History of These Counties, General & Statistical Descriptions of all the Principal Boroughs, Towns, Villages, & c., with an Appendix: Embellished with Several Engravings* (Lancaster, Pennsylvania: Gilbert Hills, Proprietor and Publisher, 1846.).

Seilhamer, George O., Esq., "Early School Girls of the Conococheague," *Papers Read Before the Kittochtinny Historical Society from March 1905, to February 1908* (Chambersburg, Pennsylvania: The Kittochtinny Historical Society, 1908).

———. "Old Mother Cumberland," *The Pennsylvania Magazine of History and Biography*, Volume 24, No. 1 (1900), pp. 17–47.

Shoemaker, Mary Craig, *Five Typical Scotch Irish Families of the Cumberland Valley* (New York: 1922).

Stevens, Sylvester K and Donald H. Kent, eds., *The Papers of Col. Henry Bouquet*, Series 21649, Part I: Northwestern Pennsylvania Historical Series, Frontier Forts and Trails Survey (Harrisburg: Pennsylvania Historical Commission, 1942).

Stillé, Charles J., *Major-General Anthony Wayne and the Pennsylvania Line in the Continental Army* (Philadelphia: J. B. Lippincott Company, 1893).

Bibliography

Smyth, Albert Henry, ed., *The Writings of Benjamin Franklin, Vol. III* (London: The Macmillan Company, 1905).

Thompson, John W., *Historic Views of Old Mercersburg: the Jewel box of Franklin County* (Mercersburg Printing, 2000), pp. 204–207.

Vaughan, Samuel, *Samuel Vaughan's Diary, 1787–1796* (Washington, D.C.: Manuscript Division, only copy). or see Edward G. Williams, ed., *Minutes Made by s.v., from Stage to Stage, on a Tour to Fort Pitt, Part II from Carlisle to Pittsburgh*, (March 1961), p. 159 available on Open Journal Systems: journals.psu.edu/wph/article/download/1884/1732.

Waddell, Louis M., ed., *The Papers of Henry Bouquet, Vol. VI: Selected Documents, November 1761–July 1765; with a Catalogue of Bouquet Papers from November 1761 to June 1767* (Harrisburg: Pennsylvania Historical and Museum Commission, 1994).

Weaver, William W., "The Pennsylvania German House: European Antecedents and New World Forms," *Winterthur Portfolio* 21(4):243–64, 1986.

Weiser, Jay Gilfillan, *The Frontier Forts in the Cumberland and Juniata Valleys*, Volume I (State of Pennsylvania, Clarence M. Busch Publisher, 1896).

Welsh, Peter C., "The Brandywine Mills: A Chronicle of an Industry, 1762–1816" in *Delaware History*, Vol. 7, 1956.

Weslager, C.A., "Log Houses in Pennsylvania During the Seventeenth Century," *Pennsylvania History*, January 1955 Vol XXII, No 1.

Williams, Edward G., ed., *The Orderly Book of Colonel Henry Bouquet' Expedition Against the Ohio Indians, 1764* (Pittsburg, Pennsylvania: Mayer Press, 1960).

———. *Minutes Made by s.v., from Stage to Stage, on a Tour to Fort Pitt* (unpublished).

Woman's Club of Mercersburg, "Old Mercersburg, Pennsylvania", *The Journal of American History*, 1913 (reprint Saltville, Virginia, Jeffrey C. Weaver, 2005).

Ziegler, J.L., *An Authentic History of Donegal Presbyterian Church: Located in East Donegal Township, Lancaster County, Pa.*, (Philadelphia: F. McManus, Jr., and Company Printers and Publishers, 1902).

Letters:

Correspondence John McDowell and Colonel Henry Maynadier, 1905–1816, St. John's College, Greenfield Library, Annapolis Archives (History Collection, Series 1, Box 2, Folders 1–9).

Unpublished letter from Nathan McDowell in Lancaster County to James McDowell near Fort Loudon, April 6, 1761, recorded by McDowell, Joseph Michael, and McDowell, Mary Creigh, "The McDowell Family History: Scotland to Franklin County, PA, 1680–2011," unpublished paper dated 2001.

Websites:
Chester County Deed Book, 1730s on www.pa-chestercounty.civicplus.com
The Conococheague Institute, 12995 Bain Road, Mercersburg, PA, 17236, at http://cimlg.org/.
Cump, Glen L., "A Disquisition Portraying the History Relative to the Enoch Brown Incident," Enoch Brown Park Association, August 1, 1992 at www.greencastlemuseum.org/Local_History/enoch.htm.
Elizabeth A. Fenn, "Biological Warfare in Eighteenth-Century North America: Beyond Jeffery Amherst," www. politicsandthelifeschiences.org/ Biosecurity.course.folder/ readings/fenn.html.
"Donegal, Pennsylvania History" on www.doak.ws/donegal.htm for more information on the settlement. www.donegalpresbyterianchurch.org.
"Donegal, Pennsylvania History" on www.doak.ws/donegal.htm.
Hocker, Krisr, "The Problem with Owning Land as a German in Co-lonial Pennsylvania," November 3, 2013 on www.krishocker.com/the-problem-with-owi=ning-land-as-a-german-in-colonial-pennsylvania/.
"Native American Tribes of Pennsylvania," www.native-languages.org/ pennsylvania.htm.
"Native Languages of the Americas: Lenape (Unami, Delaware, Lenni Lenape)," www.native-languages.org/lenape.htm.
"Native Languages of the Americas: Munsee Delaware (Minsi, Muncey, Minisink)," www.native-languages.org/munsee.htm.
Pennsylvania Genealogy Trails: "History of Venango County, PA" transcribed by Nancy Piper on www.genealogytrails.com/penn/venango/history/index.html.
"Susquehannock Indian Languages (Conestoga)," www.native-languages.org/ Susquehannock.htm.
"Native Languages of the Americas: Shawnee (Shawano, Savannah, Sewanee)," www.native-languages.org/Shawnee.htm.
"The Delaware Nation," www.delawarenation.com/Home/tabid/37/DefauH.aspx.

Bibliography

"Penn Biographies: John McDowell (1751–1820)" on www.archives.upenn.edu/ people/1700s/Mcdowell_john.html and "About St. John's College," www.sjc.edu/about/history

Piper, Nancy (transcriber), "History of Venango County, PA," *Pennsylvania Genealogy* on www.genealogytrails.com/penn/venango/history/index.html.

Radovic-Moreno, Magdelena, *Mercersburg's "Little Africa:" Free African American Communities of Franklin County and the Underground Railroad* posted 2015 on franklincountypa.gov/index.php?section=archives_blog/littleafrica.

Smith, Mrs. H. Virginia Gress of the Upper West Conococheague Presbyterian Church Records, Mercersburg, Pennsylvania, deaths (recorded in 1985 from original documents) on www.fendrick library.org/Deaths%20 part%201%201770.pdf.

Wilks, Jim, Sidelinghill.pbworks.com/w/page/9500697/Battle%20 Narrative, 2009.

Edward G. Williams, ed., *Minutes Made by s.v., from Stage to Stage, on a Tour to Fort Pitt* (unpublished), Part II from Carlisle to Pittsburgh.

Index

Abercrombie, Maj.-Gen. James, 151
Act (British Parlamentary)
   Declaratory/American Colonies Act (1766), 195
   Intolerable, 197–198
   Navigation (1660), 10
   Quartering, 195–197
   Quebec Act (1774), 197
   Tea (1773), 73; (1777–1778), 196–167, 232
   Stamp, 189–190
   Staple (1663), 191
   Townsend (1767), 195–196
   Toleration (1689), 8
   Uniformity (1662), 8
   Union, 11
   Woolens (1699), 10
Adams, John, 199
Alisson, Robert, 186
Allison, William (Justice), 101
American Indians, 13, 16–18, 28, 30, 37, 53–54, 56, 63, 109, 172–173
   Algonquian league with French, 18, 66–68
   biological weapons against, 151 165, 167, 174
   Caughnewaga, 82
   Cherokee, 147, 152–154
   Conestoga, 25
   Delaware/Lenni Lenape, 16–17, 37, 39, 63–64, 157, 169; Lenape language, 37
   Five Nations Confederacy/Iroquois Indians, 16, 64
   Indian lands in Pennsylvania, 29
   Indian Removal Act, 1830 237, 273
   Moravians, 24, 44, 176
   Mingo, 169
   Ohio tribes, 16
   Shawnee, 44, 64, 157, 167, 169
   Six Nations Confederacy/Iroquois, 16–17, 25, 29–30, 39, 44–46, 70
   Wyandot, 169
   Walking Purchase, 17–18
American Wars
   French and Indian War, 59–158
   Pontiac's Rebellion, 159–184
   Revolutionary War, 195–233
   War of 1812, 241–242
Anglo-Spanish War (1739–1748)/Jenkin's Ear, 52
Anne (Queen of England), 10–11
Antrim Township, Pennsylvania, 61
Armstrong, George, 116, 133
Armstrong, John, ix, 68, 102, 109, 111, 116, 132, 134–135, 138, 141–142, 146, 152, 155, 163, 176–177, 204, 214, 216, 220
Armstrong, Joseph, 97, 133
Arnold, Gen. Benedict, 203, 228
Associators, military, 1747–1748, 54, 56
   Provincial officers 1755, 98–100

Baltimore, Lord. *See* Cecilius Calvert
Bard, Isaac, 263
Bard. Rocjard, 82
Barr, Thomas, 117–118
Battle of Brandywine, Pennsylvania (Revolutionary War), 217
Battle of Breed's/Bunker Hill, Massachusetts (Revolutionary War), 197–199
Battle of Bushy Run, Pennsylvania (Pontiac Rebellion), 169
Battle of Camden, South Carolina (Revolutionary War), 228
Battle of Flat Bush, 205, 208
Battle of Fort Washington, New York (Revolutionary War), 210

INDEX

Battle of Germantown, Pennsylvania (Revolutionary War), 217–218
Battle of Jumonville Glen, Pennsylvania (French and Indian War), 66–67
Battle of Kekionga, Ohio country (Indian Wars), 235–236
Battle of Lexington and Concord, Massachusetts (Revolutionary War), 198–199
Battle of Quebec, Canada (Revolutionary War), 202–203
Battle of Monmouth, New Jersey (Revolutionary War), 221–222
Battle of Paoli 217Battle of Princeton, New Jersey (Revolutionary War), 210
Battle of the Clouds, Pennsylvania (Revolutionary War), 217–218
Battle of the Monongahela, Pennsylvania (French and Indian War), 91–96
Battle of three rivers (Revolutionary War), 203
Battle of Trenton, New Jersey (Revolutionary War), 211
Battle of White Plains, New York (Revolutionary War), 209
Battle of Yorktown, Virginia (Revolutionary War), 230
Bedford (Raystown/Ray's Town), Pennsylvania, ix, 167
Black, Rev. John, 41
Black's Town, Pennsylvania. See Mercersburg
Black Boys, x, 185–194
Blunston License, 39–40
Boston, Massachusetts
  Breed's Hill, 198–199
  Massacre, 196, 199–200
  Occupation, 196–198
  Port Bill, 197–198
  Tea Act, 196
Bouquet, General Henry, 151, 154–155, 163, 167–169, 178, 183–185
Bouquet's plan to prevent regional starvation, 168
Braddock, Major-General Edward, ix, 71–72, 75–81, 85, 86, 91–92
Bradstreet, Col., 183
Bridgeport, Pennsylvania. See Markes

British Monarchs, a list of those covered in this book, 4, 268–269
British troops: Regiment of Foot, British 44th, 72
48th, 72
42nd Royal Scottish Highlander/Black Watch, ix, 152, 167–168,
77th Royal Scottish Highlanders/ Montgomery's. Regiment of Foot: British-Continental, 156, 167; 1st Battalion of Royal Americans, 168; 360 Highlanders, 167
Broadhead, Col. Daniel, 205
Brown, Enoch; school and massacre; memorial park. See Enoch Brown massacre/incident
Brownson, Dr. Richard, 52, 204, 251
Bull, Col. John, 202
Burns, Patrick, 104
Burd/Bird, James, 86, 96, 101, 108, 129, 138

Cabin (Pennsylvanian colonial style), 24, 41
Callender, Capt. Robert, 116, 160, 178, 185
Callender, Joseph, 133
Calvert, Cecilius (Lord Baltimore), 7, 14–15, 46–47
Campbell, Maj.-Gen. John/Earl of Loudoun, 130-131
Campble/Campbell, Joseph, 70
Campbell, Thomas, 206, 262, 210
Canada Campaigne (Revolutionary War), 202
Céloron, Pierre Joseph (de Blainville), 58, 65
Chambers, Benjamin, 101, 201, 240
Chambers, Gen. James, 201, 205, 208, 217
Chambers, Robert, 101
Charles I (King of England), 5–7, 269
Charles II (King of England), 8, 269
Charles III (King of England), 269
Clinton, Sir Henry, 228
colonial dress, 41–42
colonial mills, 243–245
Conococheague Creek, 30–
  west branch, 31
  east branch, 30, 33
  Conococheague Settlement, 32–33
Conococheague Institute, xiv
Constitution, United States, 235

Cornplanter, Chief, 234–235
Cortwallis, Lord Charles, 230
Covenanters, 6
Cox, John, 116
Cox, Richard, 116
Craig, John, 116, 119
Croghan, George, 70–71, 75, 124, 185, 187
Cromwell, Oliver, 6, 8
Culbertson, Alexander, 100–101, 127–128
Culbertson, Samuel, 204, 206, 241
Cumberland Valley, North, 28–35

Davidson, Elias, 51–52, 251, 186, 202
Davidson, Elizabeth, 259
Davidson, Hugh, 52, 252
Davidson, Mary Craig, 259
De Hass, John Philip, 204
Declaration of Independence, 199, 208
Denny, William (Governor of Pennsylvania), 270
Dickey, Capt. Robert, 206
Dinwiddie, Robert (Governor of Virginia), 65, 115
Doctor John (Delaware Indian), 160–161
Donated Lands (to Revolutionary War soldiers), 214–235
Donegal Settlement, Pennsylvania, xv, 21–25
Donegal Presbyterian Church (Old), 22
Donegal Synod, 22
Dunbar, Col. Thomas, 72, 93, 95–96
Dunlap, Mary Jo, 264
Dunmore, Lord, 196
Duqesne, Michel-Ange (de Menneville), 64, 66

Enoch Brown Massacre/incident, 179–182
Erie Triangle, 237
Erwin, Mary, 263

Findlay, James, 265
Findlay, John, 101, 263
Findlay, William, 263
Flag of the United States of America, 216
Forbes, Gen. John, ix–x, 151–157
Forbes Road. *See* roads
Fort Bedford. *See* Bedford
Fort Bull, 90

Fort Carlisle, 103, 167
Fort Chambers, 103, 139
Fort Cumberland, 86
Fort Davis/Davie (Phillip), 68–103
Fort David (David), 117–118
Fort Detroit, 167
Fort Duquesne/Du Quesne, ix, 66, 91, 92, 93, 156
Fort Edward, 90
Fort Frederic, 90
Fort Granville, 115, 129
Fort Henry, 115
Fort Hunter, 150
Fort LaRay, 167
Fort Le Boeuf, 64, 97, 163, 167
Fort Ligonier, 169
Fort Littleton, 128
Fort Loudon/Loudoun, ix, 136, 143
Fort Louisbourg, Nova Scotia, 157
Fort Machault, 64
Fort McCord (William), 102, 127, 137
Fort McDowell. *See* McDowell Mill Fort
Fort McIntosh, 238
Fort Maxwell (William), 148, 168
Fort Miamis, 167
Fort Michilimackinac, 167
Fort Necessity, ix, 67–68
Fort Niagara, 45, 90, 167
Fort Onaethtanon, 167
Fort Oswego, 90
Fort Pitt/Pittsburg, 157, 166–167, 169, 185
Fort Pomfret Castle, 115
Fort Presqu'Isle, 64, 163, 167, 183
Fort Prince George, 66–68
Fort St. Joseph, 167
Fort Sandusky, 167
Fort Shirley, 115, 129, 134
Fort Ticonderoga (Carillon), 90, 203
Fort Venango, 163, 167
Fort Waddle, 102
Fort Wayne, 236
Fort William Henry, 90
Fort Williams, 90
Franklin, Benjamin, 78–79, 112–113, 130, 199, 235
French and Indian War/Nine Years War, ix, 67–158

INDEX

French land encroachments in the Penn colony, 44–45

Galissoniere, Marquis de la, 57–58
Gage, Gen. Thomas, 185, 187, 197
George I (King of England), 11, 25–26
George II (King of England), 25, 26, 163
George III (King of England), 27, 163, 174
German Pennsylvania settlers, 19, 26–27, 43–44
Gist, Christopher, 63, 65
Gordon, Patrick (Governor of Pennsylvania), 25, 46, 270–271
Glorious Revolution, 8
Grant, Lieut. Charles, 186–189
Grant, Major James, 156, 186–189
Great Cove/Big Cove, Pennsylvania, 106
Great Meadows, Pennsylvania, 66–67

Halkett, Sir Peter, 72
Hamilton, James (Governor of Pennsylvania), 57, 68, 270–271, 160
Hamilton, Hance, 106, 116, 128, 133, 138
Hamilton, Thomas, 153
Hancock, John, 202
Harris, Samuel, 41
Edward Hand, 204–205
Harmar, Josiah, 235–237
   Campaign against the Indians, xi, 235–237
Harris, John, 86, 101
   Harris' Ferry, 86
Hogg, Captain, 86
Holland Land Company, 234–235
Holliday, Elizabeth McDowell. *See* McDowell
Holliday, Lieut. James, 116, 253, 217
Holliday, John, 260
Hoops, Adam, 101, 104–106
Humpton, Capt. Richard, 204, 206
Huston, William, 206, 212

Indian John (Conestoga Indian), 175
Irish migration, 19, 25, 26
Irish revolt, 1641, 6
Ironcutter/Eisenhauser, 191–192
Irvine, William, 201–204, 207
Irwin, Archibald, 161–162, 265
Irwin, Elizabeth "Betsy", 262

Irwin, Jane, 265
Irwin, James, 265
Irwin, James, 266
Irwin, Jean McDowell Irwin. *See* McDowell
Irwin, John, 101, 265
Irwin, Margaret, 265
Irwin, Mary, 265
Irwin, Nancy, 265
Irwin, Nancy Jean, 260

Jacobs, Captain, (see Tewea), 97, 104, 127–128, 137
James I (King of England), 5
James II (King of England), 8
Jefferson, Thomas, 199
John, Indian (Conestoga Indian), 160
Johnson, Maj. John, 262, 174
Johnson, Sir William, 119
Johnston, George, 267
Johnston, Lt.-Col. James, 205
Johnston, John, 266
Johnston, Lt.-Col. John, 266
Johnston, Jane, 267
Johnston, Mary, 267
Johnston, Rebecca, 267
Johnston, Samuel, 267
Johnston, Thomas, 205, 267

Keith, Sir William (Governor of Pennsylvania), 21, 270–271, 194
King, George, 52, 252
King, Rev. John, 52, 252
   Latin School, 161
   See also Upper West Concocochegue Presbyterian Church, 193, 200, 204
Kittanning (Indian village), 97, 116, 127, 132–137
Kittatinny Mountains, 28

Lafayette, Marquis de, 229
Langlade, Charles, 64
Le Cavelier, Toussaint, 44
Legion of the United States (Post-Revolutionary War army), 236
Livingston, Robert, 199
Logan, James, 25-26, 46–47
Louis XIV, King of France, 8–9

Lovett, John N., xvi, 49

McClellan, David, 104
McCoy, Capt. Robert, 206
McCullough, John, 82
McDowell, Agnes Craig (wife miller John), 37, 51, 250
McDowell, Agnes (daughter miller John), 51, 251
McDowell, Alexander (son of Justice William), 206, 212–215, 235, 257
McDowell, Dr. Andrew (son of Justice William), 208, 258
McDowell, Annabelle (daughter of James), 205, 262
McDowell, Annabelle (daughter of pioneer), 266, 208
McDowell, Catherine (daughter of John) 51, 252
McDowell, Catherine Maxwell (wife of Nathan, son of pioneer), 260
McDowell, Elizabeth (daughter of John), 51, 252
McDowell, Elizabeth (daughter pioneer), 37, 253
McDowell, Lt. James (son of James), 262
McDowell, James (son of Justice William), 255
McDowell, James (Constable/Sub-Lieutenant, son of pioneer), 161, 206
McDowell, James (Son of Nathan), 260
McDowell, James II (son of James), 241, 242
McDowell, Jane "Jannet", 263
McDowell, Judge James (Son of pioneer), 38, 261, 193–194
McDowell, Jean (daughter of James), 265
McDowell, Jean B. (daughter of pioneer), 38, 208
McDowell, John (miller/surgeon, son of pioneer)
   birth, 4, 250
   Death, 238–240
   miller, 37
   French and Indian War, 125–126
   Pontiac War, 168
   Revolutionary War Surgeon, x, 195–233, 202–204, 206–208, 231
   US Infantry Surgeon, 235–237

McDowell, John LL.D. (son of Justice William), 206, 255, 214
McDowell, John (son of Nathan), 260
McDowell, Margaret (daughter of James), 264
McDowell, Margaret (daughter of John), 51, 252
McDowell, Margaret (daughter of pioneer), 38, 266
McDowell, Margaret (daughter of Justice William), 259
McDowell, Mary "Polly" (daughter of Justice William), 255
McDowell, Mary (daughter of John), 51, 251
McDowell, Mary (daughter of James), 206, 210, 262
McDowell, Mary (daughter of Nathan), 260
McDowell, Mary Irvine (wife of pioneer), 37, 111–112, 249
McDowell, Mary Maxwell (wife of Justice William), 60, 253
McDowell, Nancy "Agnes" (daughter of Justice William), 259
McDowell, Nathan (son of pioneer), 38, 260
McDowell, Nathan (son of Justice William), xi, 161, 206, 212, 214, 236, 256
McDowell, Nathan (son of Nathan), 260
McDowell, Dr. Maxwell (son of Nathan), 260
McDowell, Patrick (son of Justice William), 259
McDowell, Robert (son of James), 206, 262
McDowell, Sarah, 263
McDowell, Sarah (daughter of pioneer), 38, 208, 266
McDowell, Susan (daughter of Nathan), 260
McDowell, Susan/Susanna (daughter of pioneer), 38, 267
McDowell, Thomas (son of pioneer), 38, 204, 206, 212, 234, 261
McDowell, Thomas (son of Justice William), 206, 259
McDowell, William (pioneer), 4, 157-158, 249–250
McDowell, William (Justice, son of pioneer), xi, 37, 106, 111–112, 253, 188–190, 234
McDowell, William (Captain, son of Justice William), 254, 116, 133, 201, 205, 217, 228–236

INDEX

Journal of the Southern Campaign of the Revolutionary War, 228–230
McDowell, William Smith (son of James), 263
McDowell, William (son of Nathan), 260
McDowell Genealogy, partial, 249–267
McDowell's Mill Fort
  mill construction, 47–51, 68–70
  French and Indian War, 82–83, 87–89, 90–91, 98, 102, 117–118 119–122, 150
  Pontiac Rebellion, 162, 178–178, 182
  Revolutionary War, 211–212, 220
  razed, 243–248
  stone marker, 1–3
  historical marker, 2–3
McKinney, Isabel, 257
McLanahan, Mary, 256
McLene, 263
McPherson, Nancy "Agnes", 258
Magaw, Dr. William, 206, 255
Markes, Pennsylvania (also called McDowell's Mill and Bridgeport), ix, 47, 242–247
Maris, Mathias, 259
Martin, Dr. John, 255
Mary II, (Queen of England), 8
Mason and Dixon Line, 163–164, 227
Maxwell, Catherine, 260
Maxwell, Mary, 37
Maxwell, Justice William, 38, 60, 98, 187
medicine (Revolutionary War), 207, 218
Mercer, Hugh, 116, 125, 129, 133, 138, 157, 207
Mercersburg, Pennsylvania (Black's Town/Smith's Town), 47, 59–60
Mercersburg, Lemasters and Markes Electric Company, 245
Middlebrook Encampment (Revolutionary War), 216
Mifflin, Gen. Thomas, 204
mills, colonial, 49–50
  miller's toll/wage, 5
Montour, Andrew, 75
Morris, Robert (Governor of Pennsylvania), 68, 77–81, 84, 93–95, 111, 115, 129, 270–271
mountains
  Appalachian, 13–14, 28
  Blue Ridge, 28
  Kittatinny, 28
  North, 28
  Parnell, 28, 33–35
  South, 28
  Tuscarora, 28
musket and rifle repair, 38–39

New France/Canada, 44–46, 59, 64–65
New Side, 42–43
Nine Years War, 9. *See also* French and Indian War
Northern Campaign (Revolutionary War), 202 ff

Officers of Associated Regiments of Lancaster Co., 1747–1748
  Officers Commissioned, (1755), 99–100; (1756), 122–124
Ohio Company, 15, 57, 63, 65, 74
Old Red Church, Greencastle, PA, 42
Old Side/Old Lights, 42

Palmer, Anthony (Governor of Pennsylvania), 270
Patterson, James, 117, 138
Patton, Capt. James, 204, 212
Patton, Matthew, 142
Patton, Capt. Samuel, 206
Pawlings Tavern, 185
Paxton Boys, 175–176
Penn, John (son of founder), 25
Penn, Richard (son of founder), 25
Penn, Thomas (son of founder), 25
Penn, Sir William (father of the founder), 12
Penn, William (founder of colony), 12, 21
Penn's Woods (Pennsylvania), 12–21
Pennsylvania Boundary Conflicts (Maryland) (Virginia) (Connecticut), 14–16, 47, 163, 192, 196, 230. *See also* French land encroachments
Pennsylvania Governors, 270–271
Pennsylvania Historical and Museum Commission, xiii, 3
Peters, Richard, 57, 81, 107–108, 116, 160, 203
Peters Township, Pennsylvania, 28, 61

/ 311 /

Philadelphia Campaign, 216–217. *See also* Revolutionary War
Piper, Margaret, 265
Piper, Margaret (married William Smith), 266
Piper, Capt. William, 208, 266
Pisquetomen (American Indian), 97, 156
Plan for Defense of the Frontier, 1754, ix, 68–70, 100
Pontiac Rebellion/War, x, 164–184
Post, Christian Frederick, 156
Potter, James, 116, 148
Potter, Sheriff John, 86, 101, 106–108, 116, 133, 142
Proclamation Line, 174
Presbyterian meeting houses in Franklin County, Pennsylvania, 42–43

Quincy, Josiah, 199

Ramsey, Mary, 265
Rankin, Elizabeth Robinson McDowell, 246–247
Ray's Town, Pennsylvania. *See* Bedford
Revolutionary War, x, 195–233
Reynolds, Mr. (husband of Susan McDowell), 38, 267
rivers
    Delaware, 12–14, 16
    Ohio and Allegheny, 44, 63, 132, 235
    Kiskiminetas, 44
    Mississippi, 14
    Susquehanna, 16, 47
    Youghiogheny, 50
roads
    Harris Ferry/Great, 34–35, 43
    Braddock's, ix, 74, 76–77
    Burd's, ix, 79–86, 96, 134, 154
    Forbes', 151–152, 154
Rochambeau, Jean-Baptiste Donatien de Vimeur, Comte de, 230

Sasoona, Delaware King, 97
Scottish Highlanders, 4–6
Scottish Lowlanders, 4–7
Scottish settlers in America, 19, 25–27
Seven Year's War, 53. *See also* French and Indian War

St. Clair, Sir John, 72, 75, 153
Siege of Boston, x, 196–202
Siege of Charlestown, South Carolina (Revolutionary War), 228
Shaheas/Sheehays (American Indian Chief), 175
Sherman, Roger, 199
Shingas (American Indian Chief), 97, 104, 127–128, 137
Shippen, Edward, 84–86, 101, 108
Shirley, William (Governor of Massachusetts), 67, 90, 93–95
Slavery, 225–228
    Abolition of Slavery (1780), 227
    Little Africa, 227
    Underground Railroad, 227–228
Smith, James, 38, 81–82, 159–160, 161, 186, 194, 205
Smith, Jean "Jane", 38, 161
Smith, Justice William, 38, 81, 161, 266, 186
Smith, William, Jr., 212
Smith's Town, 59, 185–186
Smallpox as biological warfare, 166–167
Smith, Abraham, 202, 208, 224
Smith, Elizabeth Irwin (daughter of Archibald and Jean McDowell Irwin), 265
Smith, James, 60, 172, 187, 212
Smith, Jean "Jane/Janet", 261
Smith, Robert, 265
Smith, William (Justice), 60, 101, 187
Smith's Town, Pennsylvania. *See* Mercersburg
Snider, Conrad, 206, 208
Soc, Bill (Conestoga Indian), 175
Society of Cincinnati, 231–232
Southern Campaign, 228–231
Spear, Joseph, 187
Spring Grove/Waddels/Etters Cemetery, Franklin County, Pennsylvania, xi, 73–74
Stanwix, Gen. John, 157
Steel/Steele, Rev.-Capt. John, 73–74, 97–98, 126, 128–129, 138, 162, 208, 211
Stump, Frederick, 191–192
Suffolk Resolve, 198

Tamagua (American Indian), 97, 138
Teedyuscung (American Indian), 151, 155

INDEX

Tewea. *See* "Captain Jacobs"
Thomas, George (Governor of Pennsylvania), 52–53, 57
Thompson, Gen. William, 203
Tonoloways Sesttlement (Conoloways), Pennsylvania, 104–105
Treaty, *Jay's*, 237
Treaty of Aix-la-Chapelle, 1748, 56
Treaty of Alliance, 1778, 221
Treaty of Easton
　1756, 138
　1758, 156–157
Treaty of Paris
　1763, 166
　1777–1778, 232
　1783, 232
Trent, William, 116
Tuscarora Mountains, 28

Ulster Plantation,
　Northern Ireland, 4–11
　Ulster-Scot, xi, 5–11, 39, 272
United Stated Infantry, 236
Upper West Conococheage Presbyterian Church/White Church, Franklin County, Pennsylvania, 73, 98, 172

Valley Forge encampment, Pennsylvania, 217–220
Van Campen, Moses, 224
Van Lear, Elizabeth, 254
Van Lear, Matthew, 265
Van Lear, Mary, 265
Von Steuben, Baron Friedrich Wilhelm, 220, 230

War of Spanish Succession, 10, 52
Washington, George
　young officer, 53, 6–67, 93, 97
　general, 199–200, 208, 210–11, 216, 223–224, 230–232, 238–240
　President, 237–240
Wayne, Maj.-Gen. Anthony, x, 203–204, 212–214, 217, 222, 231–232
Weiser, Conrad, 64, 70, 86, 100, 116, 144
Whiskey Insurrection, 237–240
William III (King of England), 8, 10
Wolfe, James, 151
Wrights Ferry/Wrightsville, Pennsylvania, 111–112

About the Author

Pamela A. Bakker is a lover of history. She is a published author of books, articles, and historical poetry. She has also written curriculums, short stories and music. Her books include: *Eyes on the Sporting Scene, 1870–1930: Will and June Rankin, New York's Sportswriting Brothers* (McFarland Publishers, 2013); *The 104th Field Artillery Regiment of the New York National Guard, 1916–1919* (McFarland Publishers, 2014); and *McDowell's Mill Fort in Markes, Pennsylvania, 1953–1840: French and Indian War to the establishment of a new nation* (Sunbury Press, Inc., 2020)

Some of her articles include: "The Rankin Brothers: Will and June," *Nineteenth Century Notes*, 19th Century Committee of the Society for American Baseball Research, summer 2013, 1–3; "Franklin County, Pennsylvania Abolitionist, Andrew Nerva Rankin, Esq." in Schiwek, Beate A., Ed., *Franklin County Historical Society-Kittochtinny Journal*, Vol. XXIII, the 150th Anniversary Civil War Issue (Chambersburg: Heritage Books, 2011); and "Mike Moynahan (1856–April 19, 1899), hard-hitting shortstop," in *The 1883 Philadelphia Athletics* (Society for American Baseball Research, 2020).

Made in the USA
Middletown, DE
31 October 2022

13854088R00196